THE GOOD SAMARITAN
AND THE LAW

JAMES M. RATCLIFFE is Assistant Dean of The
University of Chicago Law School

THE
GOOD SAMARITAN
AND THE LAW

———◆———

EDITED BY
JAMES M. RATCLIFFE

ANCHOR BOOKS
DOUBLEDAY & COMPANY, INC.,
GARDEN CITY, NEW YORK
1966

The Anchor Books edition
is the first publication of
The Good Samaritan and the Law.

Anchor Books edition: 1966

LIBRARY OF CONGRESS CATALOG CARD NUMBER 66–21014

ACKNOWLEDGMENTS

The essays by Messrs. Gregory, Tunc, Morris, Waller, Barth, Freedman, Gusfield, Goldstein, Zeisel, Fingarette, and Honoré were originally prepared as papers for the conference on "The Good Samaritan and the Bad," held at the University of Chicago on April 9, 1965. James Barr Ames' "Law and Morals" is from an address delivered at the seventy-fifth anniversary of the Cincinnati Law School. It was published in 22 *Harvard Law Review* 92 (1908), with the permission of the University of Cincinnati Record. "Rewards for the Rescue of Human Life?" by John P. Dawson first appeared in *XXth Century Comparative and Conflicts Law,* published in 1961 by A. W. Sijthoff's Vitgeversmaatschappij, N.V., Leyden, the Netherlands. This is the first publication of Aleksander W. Rudzinski's "The Duty to Rescue: A Comparative Analysis."

"The Duty to Act: A Proposed Rule" by Wallace M. Rudolph was originally published in 44 *Nebraska Law Review* (1965). Warren P. Miller and Michael A. Zimmerman drafted "The Good Samaritan Act of 1966: A Proposal" for Professor Allison Dunham's seminar in Law Revision at The University of Chicago Law School in the autumn of 1965.

CONTENTS

INTRODUCTION

. . . ."A certain man went down from Jerusalem to Jericho, and fell among thieves, which stripped him of his raiment, and wounded him, and departed, leaving him half dead.

And by chance there came down a certain priest that way; and when he saw him, he passed by on the other side.

And likewise a Levite, when he was at the place, came and looked on him, and passed by on the other side.

But a certain Samaritan, as he journeyed, came where he was; and when he saw him he had compassion on him.

And went to him, and bound up his wounds, pouring in oil and wine, and set him on his own beast, and brought him to an inn, and took care of him.

And on the morrow, when he departed, he took out two pence, and gave them to the host, and said unto him, 'Take care of him; and whatsoever thou spendest more, when I come again, I will repay thee.'

Which now of these, thinkest thou, was neighbour unto him that fell among the thieves?

And he said, 'He that shewed mercy on him.' Then said Jesus unto him, 'Go, and do thou likewise.' " (Luke 10:30–37)

An engaging custom of times past required that an author or editor who was about to inflict yet another book upon a harried public should offer some justification for his action.

The so-called "Good Samaritan" problem is being brought to our attention with increasing frequency and force. In the case of Kitty Genovese, for example, thirty-eight people watched or listened for an extended period of time while a young woman was being murdered immediately outside their apartment building. No one intervened; no one even called the police. Occurrences of this kind have called sharply into question the current state of the law, and have stimulated a renewed examination of the moral obligations owed to fellow citizens in peril.

In recognition of the importance of the questions involved, the Law School of The University of Chicago last year sponsored a "Conference on the Good Samaritan and the Bad—The Law and Morality of Volunteering in Situations of Peril, or of Failing to Do So." The conference was first suggested to the school by the Sentry Insurance Companies of Stevens Point, Wisconsin, and was made possible by the companies' sympathetic interest and support. The conference was planned and carried out by a faculty committee composed of Stanley A. Kaplan, chairman, Walter J. Blum, Harry Kalven, Jr., and James M. Ratcliffe. Most of the chapters of this book were prepared as contributions to that conference.

The problems involved are neither small in number nor easy of solution. Is a citizen required, and should he be required, to lend assistance to another who is in danger of severe personal injury or substantial loss of property? Should it make any difference if the potential loss stems from the commission of a crime, or from accident, Act of God, or other causes? Must the passer-by intervene only when he can do so at no peril to himself? Only when the peril to himself is less than the harm which the victim will suffer? Only when a police officer or other public official asks his help? Always, and at whatever cost?

The cloud of secondary questions which accompanies those above is immediately apparent. Suppose the Good Samaritan suffers physical injury as a result of his intervention. Must he be content with his reward in heaven, or should he be compensated, and if so, by whom? The person committing the crime, if he has the means—the person causing the accident, if he has the means—the victim who

benefited by the intervention—the state, if all other pockets
are empty?

Before appropriate solutions can be provided for such
problems, it is necessary to consider four groups of questions more basic in nature.

First, how do people really behave in Good Samaritan
situations, why do they behave as they do, and has their
behavior changed significantly in the past generation or
two?

The papers which follow, as much through what they
do not say as through what they do, reveal the paucity of
our knowledge of these problems with startling clarity. It
has become customary to assure ourselves that cases like
the Genovese incident, or the New York subway stabbings,
grow out of a society increasingly urbanized, increasingly
rootless, increasingly, shatteringly, anonymous. We are as-
sured that in the rural or small-town centered society of a
century ago or even a generation ago, such occurrences
were virtually unknown. It is possible, however, that we
have merely become more sensitive to such problems.
There may well have been numerous instances at the turn
of the century in which the Levites passed by on the other
side without drawing a modicum of the attention such
omissions cause today. Indeed, it might be argued that the
very publicity now attendant upon such events stands as
evidence that they are becoming less common. In a society
of killers, murder would pass without comment.

In addressing himself to these problems, Dr. Freedman
describes the insights his discipline has to offer, carefully
emphasizing their tentative nature. Professor Gusfield sets
forth some possible social causes and suggests that the
capacity of the law to offer solutions is sharply limited.
The view of the expert journalist, as presented by Mr.
Barth, is helpful in considering why cases of callousness
and apathy are, if not more frequent, at least more apparent
than heretofore. Professor Goldstein is concerned with the
low state of citizen cooperation with the police, and
with measures to encourage improvement in this area.

Even if we do not know very much about how people act, and less about why, we should be able, by examining the current state of the law, to discover how society believes they should act. Dean Ames' classic essay sets the more recent papers in perspective by providing a sense of the continuity and evolution of the law. Professor Gregory supplies the necessary solid base for any subsequent discussion by setting forth the applicable rules of law in common law jurisdictions, principally the United States. It is not a great overstatement to suggest that the supreme command of this mighty repository of Anglo-American thought and experience is: "Mind your own business!" This considered judgment of the past concludes that, in the absence of any of a number of special relationships which Professor Gregory spells out, the law does not recognize a legal obligation to render assistance and, indeed, warns the volunteer that he undertakes to provide such assistance at his peril. Professor Waller focuses upon the English and Australian experience, and describes a tendency to depart from the traditional common law rules.

The continental countries of the civil law tradition see things differently. Professor Tunc points out that French law creates an affirmative obligation to render assistance; so, it would appear, does the law of Germany and Switzerland, as described by Professor Dawson. Some commentators have stressed the irony of the fact that among the first countries to recognize the duty to succor were Nazi Germany and Vichy France. Dr. Rudzinski demonstrates that the question has been of long-standing concern in European countries of widely varying ideologies.

Any analysis which suggests that the law and the morality applicable to a given group of problems are separate, unrelated considerations demeans the law and diminishes the operational importance of morality. Nevertheless, since most problems worthy of serious attention are too complex to be seen in all their aspects by a single discipline, it is sometimes useful to call for expert appraisal from a different point of view. Professor Fingarette and Mr.

Honoré contribute professional philosophical analyses of the moral considerations involved, which is to say that they are concerned with how people ought to behave.

Finally, Professor Zeisel tells us how the people themselves feel they ought to act. In so doing, he also suggests means of acquiring more reliable information as to both opinion and behavior in this area.

Thus far we have been concerned with the nature and causes of actual behavior in a "Good Samaritan" situation, with the rules governing such behavior as set forth in the law, with the moral considerations which should affect such behavior, and with the views of the population generally as to the kinds of behavior which should be expected. It is appropriate now to turn our attention to questions of public policy regarding possible change in the law in this area. Three basic approaches suggest themselves. The first possibility is to alter the law to provide both safeguards and rewards for those who act to aid a fellow citizen in peril. Such provisions might be confined to situations in which assistance is offered at the request of a police officer or other public official. This is the approach of the statute recently enacted in California. Or, such safeguards might be extended to the case of one who volunteers help in a highway accident, or an armed robbery, or in a variety of similar situations, where no official request has been made. The Miller-Zimmerman model statute is here in point, as are some of the suggestions of Professor Morris. The nature of these safeguards and rewards must then be considered. They might be confined to protecting the intervenor from liability for damage which he himself caused by his intervention. They might extend to compensating him, in part or in whole, for damage which he suffered as a result of his intervention. They might, finally, include positive incentives as encouragement to intervention, such as the rewards sometimes offered for the apprehension of criminals. None of these approaches is without cost, social cost going far beyond the modest financial burden which would result. In the criminal area especially, grave

difficulties arise. Are we to encourage the ordinary citizen
to take direct action in the prevention of crime or the apprehension of criminals, after centuries of social development clearly pointing toward the elimination of vigilante
action and the concentration of the responsibility for keeping the peace in the hands of public officials? Recently, a
householder who discovered someone in the act of stealing his car shot and killed the thief. We find it hard to require that the car owner simply call the police and otherwise stand idly by and allow the theft to take place, yet
surely every state legislature in the country would regard
the death penalty for auto theft as a barbarous punishment. Even in non-criminal areas, the traditional common
law aversion to the officious intermeddler may have much
to recommend it. Often he only makes things worse.

The alternative means of inducing citizens to behave like
Good Samaritans is to punish those who act like priests or
Levites. Dr. Rudzinski is willing to do so. The manifold
problems resulting from such legislation are obvious.
Should we require aid only to police and other public officials, or to private citizens as well? In requiring aid, should
all adult citizens be held to the same standard, or should a
variety of considerations such as age, health, special skills,
even intelligence, be applied? Professor Rudolph's careful
and detailed analysis is very helpful in this area. Furthermore, many will find it morally distasteful for the state
to say to its citizens, "You will be your brother's keeper—
or else!"

Protection from the consequences of an action, reward
for undertaking it, and penalty for failure to act are not
mutually exclusive policies. It may be that all should be
adopted. Finally, it is quite possible that this is one of the
many problem areas in which the wisest possible course of
action is to take no action at all.

Basically, the issues here involved go beyond the narrow problem of the existence and nature of an obligation
to assist a fellow citizen in peril. They constitute only one
facet of a larger question, the appropriate role of individual

action in a society increasingly committed to the minimizing of personal responsibility and the enlargement of the sphere of agencies of the state and other mass organizations.

JAMES M. RATCLIFFE

Chicago
February 1966

THE GOOD SAMARITAN
AND THE LAW

Law and Morals

JAMES BARR AMES*

Primitive law regards the word and the act of the individual; it searches not his heart. "The thought of man shall not be tried," said Chief Justice Brian, one of the best of the medieval lawyers, "for the devil himself knoweth not the thought of man."[1]

As a consequence, early law is formal and unmoral. Are these adjectives properly to be applied to the English common law at any time within the period covered by the reports of litigated cases? To answer this question let us consider, first, the rule of liability for damage caused to one person by the act of another. Not quite six hundred years ago an action of trespass was brought in the King's Bench for a battery. The jury found that the plaintiff was beaten, but that this was because of his assailing the defendant who had acted purely in self-defense, and that the action was brought out of malice. It was nevertheless adjudged that the plaintiff should recover his damages according to the jury's verdict, and that the defendant should go to prison. The defendant had committed the act of battery; therefore he must make reparation. He was not permitted to justify his act as done in protecting himself from the attack of the plaintiff. That attack rendered the plaintiff liable to a cross action, but did not take away his own action.

The case we have just considered was an action for compensation for a tort. Suppose, however, that the defendant,

* Professor (from 1877) and Dean (from 1895), Harvard University Law School, until his death in 1910.
[1] Y. B. 7 Ed. IV, f. 2, pl. 2.

instead of merely injuring his assailant, had killed him in self-defense, using no unnecessary force. Did the early English law so completely ignore the moral quality of the act of killing in self-defense as to make it a crime? Strictly speaking, yes. An official reporter of the time of Edward III[2] and Lord Coke[3] were doubtless in error in stating that prior to 1267 a man "was hanged in such a case just as if he had acted feloniously." But such killing was not justifiable homicide. The party indicted was not entitled to an acquittal by the jury. He was sent back to prison, and must trust to the king's mercy for a pardon. Furthermore, although he obtained the pardon, he forfeited his goods for the crime. But the moral sense of the community could not tolerate indefinitely the idea that a blameless self-defender was a criminal, or that he should have to make compensation to his culpable assailant. By 1400 self-defense had become a bar to an action for a battery. Pardons for killing in self-defense became a matter of course; ultimately the jury was allowed to give a verdict of not guilty in such cases, and the practice of forfeiting the goods of the defendant died out.

Let us test the rule of liability by another class of cases. One person may have injured another without fault on either side, by a pure accident. The case against the actor in such a case is obviously stronger than against one who inflicts damage in self-defense. Accordingly we are prepared for this language of the Statute of Gloucester, 6 Ed. I, c. 9, 1278: "If one kills another in defending himself, or by misadventure, he shall be held liable, but the judge shall inform the king, and the king will pardon him, if he pleases."[4] *A fortiori* the actor was bound to make compensation to the victim of the accident. The criminal liability disappeared comparatively early, as in the case of killing in self-defense. But the doctrine of civil liability for accidental damage caused by a morally innocent actor

---

[2] Y. B. 21 Ed. III, f. 17, pl. 22.
[3] Coke, Second Inst., 148.
[4] See also Y. B. 2 Hen. IV, f. 18, pl. 6, per Thirning, C. J.

was very persistent. It was stated forcibly by an eminent judge in 1681 as follows: "In all civil acts the law doth not so much regard the intent of the actor, as the loss and damage of the party suffering. If a man shoot at butts and hurt a man unawares an action lies. . . . If a man assault me and I lift up my staff to defend myself and in lifting it up hit another, an action lies by that person, and yet I did a lawful thing. And the reason is because he that is damaged ought to be recompensed. But otherwise it is in criminal cases, for there *'Actus non facit reum, nisi mens sit rea.'* "[5] As pointed out by Sir Frederick Pollock, in his treatise on torts,[6] a similar opinion was expressed subsequently by Blackstone, Erskine, Mr. Justice Grose, and as late as 1868 by Lord Cranworth. Erskine's statement goes very far: "If a man rising in his sleep walks into a china shop and breaks everything about him, his being asleep is a complete answer to an *indictment* for trespass, but he must answer in an *action* for everything he has broken." There were, however, from time to time certain intimations from the judges that in the absence of negligence, an unintentional injury to another would not render the actor liable, and finally in 1891 a case was brought in the Queen's Bench[7] which required the court to decide whether the old rule of strict liability was still in force or must give way to a rule of liability based upon moral culpability. The defendant, one of a hunting party, fired at a pheasant. The shot, glancing from the bough of an oak tree, penetrated the eye of the plaintiff, destroying his sight. The jury found that the defendant had not acted negligently, and the court decided that the defendant was not liable. The same result was reached in Massachusetts forty years earlier,[8] and this precedent has been followed in other states.

So that today we may say that the old law has been

[5] Lambert v. Bessey, T. Ray. 421.
[6] 8 ed., 142.
[7] Stanley v. Powell, [1891] 1 Q. B. 86.
[8] Brown v. Kendall, 6 Cush. (Mass.) 292.

radically transformed. The early law asked simply, "Did the defendant do the physical act which damaged the plaintiff?" The law of today, except in certain cases based upon public policy, asks the further question, "Was the act blameworthy?" The ethical standard of reasonable conduct has replaced the unmoral standard of acting at one's peril. Nor is the modern ethical doctrine applied even now to all cases logically within its scope. Under this doctrine a lunatic unable to appreciate the nature or consequences of his act ought not to be responsible for the damage he has inflicted upon another. The lunatic homicide ceased to forfeit his goods or to require the king's pardon centuries ago. But there is no English decision that a lunatic need not make reparation to one injured by his act. There is, to be sure, no English decision to the contrary; but there are several *dicta* against the lunatic, and an unreasoning respect for these *dicta* has led to several regrettable decisions in this country and in the British colonies. These decisions must be regarded as survivals of the ancient rule that where a loss must be borne by one of two innocent persons, it shall be borne by him who acted. Inasmuch as nearly all the English writers upon torts, and many of the American writers also, express the opinion that the lunatic, not being culpable, should not be held responsible, it is not unreasonable to anticipate that the English courts and the American courts, not already committed to the contrary doctrine, will sooner or later apply to the lunatic the ethical principle of no liability without fault. The continental law upon this point is instructive. By the early French and German law the lunatic was liable as in England for damage that he caused to another. In France today the lunatic is absolutely exempt from liability. The new German Code has a general provision to the same effect, but this code, resembling in this respect the law of Switzerland and Portugal, makes this qualification of the rule of non-liability. If compensation cannot be obtained from the person in charge of the lunatic, the court may order the lunatic to pay such compensation as seems equitable under the circumstances, having regard especially to the relative pecuniary situation of the parties, and so that the lunatic shall not in any event be deprived of the means of maintaining himself in accordance with his station in life, or of complying with his legal duties as to the maintenance of others. This compulsory contribution by the rich lunatic to his poor victim with freedom from liability in other cases may well prove to give the best practical results.

We have seen how in the law of crimes and torts the ethical quality of the defendant's act has become the measure of his liability instead of the mere physical act regardless of the motive or fault of the actor. The history of the law of contracts exhibits a similar transformation in the legal significance of the written or spoken word. By the early law, in the absence of the formal word, there was no liability, however repugnant to justice the result might be. On the other hand, if the formal word was given, then the giver was bound, however unrighteous, by reason of the circumstances under which he gave it, it might be to hold him to his promise. The persistence of this unmoral doctrine in the English law is most surprising. As late as 1606 the plaintiff brought an action alleging that the defendant, a goldsmith, sold him a stone affirming it to be a bezoar stone, whereas it was not such a stone. The court gave judgment against the plaintiff on the ground "that the bare affirmation that it was a bezoar stone, without warranting it to be so, is no cause of action."[9] The buyer reasonably supposed that he was getting a valuable jewel for his hundred pounds, but he must pocket his loss, since the goldsmith did not use the magic words "I warrant" or "I undertake." Today, of course, the sale of a chattel as being of a particular description implies a warranty or undertaking to that effect. But the notion of implying a promise from the conduct of the party was altogether foreign to the mental operations of the medieval lawyer. For this reason the buyer took the risk of the seller's not being the owner of the property sold unless the seller expressly warranted the title. In the case of goods, the mere selling as

[9] Chandler v. Lopus, Dy., 75a, n. 23; Cro. Jac. 4.

owner is today a warranty of title, but the rules of real
property not being readily changed the archaic law still
survives in the case of conveyances of land, the grantee
being without remedy if there is no covenant of title in
the deed. The inability to imply a promise from the conduct of the parties explains this remark of Chief Justice
Brian: "If I bring cloth to a tailor to have a cloak made, if
the price is not ascertained beforehand that I shall pay for
the work, he shall not have an action against me."[10]
Similarly in the reign of Elizabeth a gentleman of quality
put up at an inn with his servants and horses. But no price
was agreed upon for his accommodations. The gentleman
declining to pay, the innkeeper could obtain no relief at
law.[11] Neither the customer nor the guest had made an
express promise to pay. The law could not continue in this
state. It was shocking to the moral sense of the community
that a man should not pay for what was given him upon
the mutual understanding that it should be paid for. Accordingly the judges at length realized and declared that
the act of employing a workman, ordering goods, or
putting up at an inn meant, without more, an undertaking
to make reasonable compensation.

There is a certain analogy between the ethical development of the law and that of the individual. As early law is
formal and unmoral, so the child or youth is wont to be
technical at the expense of fairness. This was brought
home to me once by an experience with one of my sons,
then about twelve years old. I asked him one day about
his plans for the afternoon, and he told me he was to play
tennis with his friend John. In the evening, when asked if
he had had a good afternoon with John, he said, "Oh, I
haven't been with him. I thought I would rather play with
Willie." "But didn't John expect you?" "Yes, I suppose
he did." "Was it quite right, after you had led him to expect you, to disappoint him?" "Oh, but I didn't promise

---

[10] Y. B. 12 Edw. IV, f. 9, pl. 22.
[11] Young v. Ashburnham, 3 Leon. 161.

him that I would come." Remembering Chief Justice Brian, I was lenient with the boy.

The significance of the written word in the early law is illustrated by the rule that one who claimed the benefit of a promise under seal must produce it in court. The promise under seal was regarded not as evidence of the contract, but as the contract itself. Accordingly, the loss or destruction of the instrument would logically mean the loss of all the promisee's rights against the promisor. And such was the law: "When the action is upon a specialty, if the specialty is lost the whole action is lost," is the language of a Year Book judge.[12] The injustice of allowing the obligor to profit at the expense of the obligee by the mere accident of the loss of the obligation is obvious. But this ethical consideration was irrelevant in a court of common law. It did finally prevail in Chancery, but not until the seventeenth century.[13] A century later the common law judges, by judicial legislation and against the judgment of Lord Eldon, allowed the obligee to recover upon secondary evidence of a lost specialty.

The formal and unmoral attitude of the common law in dealing with contracts under seal appears most conspicuously in the treatment of defenses based upon the conduct of the obligee. As the obligee, as we have seen, who could not produce the specialty, was powerless at common law against the obligor, who unconscionably refused to fulfill his promise, so the obligor who had formally executed the instrument was at common law helpless against an obligee who had the specialty, no matter how reprehensible his conduct in seeking to enforce it. In 1835, in an English case, the defendant's defense to an action upon a bond, that it had been obtained from him by fraudulent representations, was not allowed, Lord Abinger saying: "You may perhaps be relieved in equity, but in a court of law it has always been my opinion that such a defense is unavailing when once it is shown that the party

[12] Y. B. 24 Ed. III, f. 24, pl. 1.
[13] See 9 Harv. L. Rev. 50, n. 1.

knew perfectly well the nature of the deed which he was executing."[14]

Similarly, in an action upon a specialty, it was no defense at common law that the consideration for it had failed.[15] Nor that it was given for an illegal or immoral purpose, if this did not appear upon the face of the instrument.[16] How completely ethical considerations were ignored by the common law judges in dealing with formal contracts is shown by the numerous cases deciding that a covenantor who had paid the full amount due on the covenant, but without taking a release or securing the destruction or cancellation of the instrument, must, nevertheless, pay a second time if the obligee was unconscionable enough to bring an action.[17] In the eye of the common law in all these cases the defendant had given the specialty to the plaintiff intending it to be his: the plaintiff still had it; therefore, let him recover the fruit of his property. In all these cases, however, equity sooner or later gave relief. Equity recognized his common law property right in the specialty, but, because of his unconscionable acquisition or retention of it, commanded him, under pain of imprisonment, to abstain from the exercise of his common law right. Finally, by legislation in England and in nearly all our states, defendants were allowed to plead at common law, as equitable defenses, facts which would have entitled them to a permanent, unconditional injunction in equity. It is to be observed, however, that there is no federal legislation to this effect, so that it is still true that in the federal courts fraud cannot be pleaded in bar of a common law action upon a specialty, the only remedy of the defendant being a bill in equity for an injunction to restrain the action.[18]

The illustrations, thus far considered, of the unmoral

---

[14] Mason v. Ditchbourne, 1 M. & Rob. 460.
[15] See 9 Harv. L. Rev. 52.
[16] *Ibid.*
[17] See 9 Harv. L. Rev. 54.
[18] *Ibid.* 51.

character of the early common law exhibit that law in its worst aspect, as an instrument of injustice, as permitting unmeritorious or even culpable plaintiffs to use the machinery of the court as a means of collecting money from blameless defendants.

Let us turn from the sins of commission to some of the sins of omission in the common law, and consider how these defects in the law were cured.

The early common law, as might be supposed, gave fairly adequate remedies for the infringement of the rights of personal safety or personal liberty, and also for the violation of the rights to or in tangible property. But for injuries to one's reputation or damage to one's general welfare or pecuniary condition the relief was of the slightest. Suppose, for example, a person circulated a false story that a tradesman cheated by giving false measure, or that a servant had stolen from his master, in consequence of which the tradesman lost his customers or the servant his place. The common law prior to 1500 gave no redress against the slanderer.[19] If a buyer was induced by the fraudulent representations of the seller to give a large price for a worthless chattel, he could for centuries maintain no action for damages against his deceiver.[20] Not until near the end of the seventeenth century could an innocent man who had been tried and acquitted upon an indictment for murder or other crime obtain compensation for the ignominy and damage to which he had been subjected, although it was clear that the defendant had instigated the criminal prosecution malevolently, and knowing that the plaintiff was innocent.[21] Prior to the reign of Henry VII there was no action for the breach of a promise not under seal, although given for a consideration.[22] Sooner or later the law was changed and the courts allowed an action for damages in all these cases. These in-

---

[19] Y. B. 17 Ed. IV, f. 3, pl. 2; Y. B. 27 Hen. VIII, f. 14, pl. 4.
[20] See 2 Harv. L. Rev. 9.
[21] Savile v. Roberts, 1 Ld. Ray. 374.
[22] 2 Harv. L. Rev. 13.

novations were not, however, the result of successive statutes passed to satisfy the popular demand for reform at the time. On the contrary, they were all the product of a few lines in a statute enacted near the end of the thirteenth century, providing that "Whensoever from thenceforth a writ shall be found in the Chancery, and in a like case falling under the same right and requiring a like remedy, no precedent of a writ can be produced, the clerks in Chancery shall agree in forming a new one; lest it happen for the future that the court of our lord the king be deficient in doing justice to the suitors."[23] This beneficent statute of Edward I, the origin of all our actions of trespass on the case, has been the great reforming agency in supplying the defects of the common law. Upon this statute is based our whole law of actions for defamation, for malicious prosecution and for deceit, as well as the whole law of assumpsit, which came practically to be the remedy for all modern contracts except contracts under seal. Of the great number of applications of the Statute of Westminster, these actions on the case for defamation, deceit, malicious prosecution, and breach of promise, together with the action for nuisances, are the ones which, more than all others, have contributed to the beneficent expansion of the common law. Even after these great innovations there were many grievous defects in the common law scheme of remedies for damage inflicted upon one person by the reprehensible act of another. Until the time of Lord Holt, one who had suffered from the unauthorized misconduct of a servant acting within the scope of his employment could obtain no compensation from the master.[24] The earliest suggestions of relief against the unauthorized printing by a stranger of the unpublished work of an author are in the second quarter of the eighteenth century.[25] Prior to 1745, no husband whose wife had been induced to leave him by the wrongful persuasion of another had ever re-

---

[23] St. Westminster 2, 13 Ed. I, c. 24.

[24] Boson v. Sanford, 2 Salk. 440.

[25] Webb v. Rose, 3 Sw. 674; 1 Ames Cases in Eq. Jur., 659.

covered compensation from the disturber of the marriage relation.[26] Not until twenty years after the establishment of this school would an action lie against one who wantonly or selfishly induced a person under contract with the plaintiff to break the contract.[27] As recently as 1874 the English court decided for the first time that one who untruthfully disparaged the goods of a tradesman must make compensation for the resulting damage.[28] In all these cases the remedy when finally introduced by the court was in the form of the action on the case, sanctioned by the Statute of Edward I.

Is this statute, now more than six hundred years old, still a living force for the betterment of the common law in England and the United States? There can be but one answer to that question. This statute is a perennial fountain of justice to be drawn upon so long as, in a given jurisdiction, instances may be pointed out in which the common law courts have failed to give a remedy for damage inflicted upon one person by the reprehensible act of another, and the continued absence of a remedy would shock the moral sense of the community.

But with everything done that could be done by this statute, our law as a whole would have been a very imperfect instrument of justice if the system of common law remedies had not been supplemented by the system of equitable remedies. Blackstone has asserted that the common law judges by a liberal interpretation of the Statute of Westminster by means of the action on the case might have done the work of a court of equity. Such an opinion betrays a singular failure to appreciate the fundamental difference between law and equity, namely, that the law acts *in rem,* while equity acts *in personam.* The difference between the judgment at law and the decree in equity goes to the root of the whole matter. The law regards chiefly the right of the plaintiff, and gives judgment that he recover

---

[26] Winsmore v. Greenbank, Willes, 577.
[27] Lumley v. Gye, 2 E. & B. 216.
[28] Western Co. v. Lawes Co., L. R., 9 Ex. 218.

the land, debt, or damages, because they are his. Equity lays the stress upon the duty of the defendant, and decrees that he do or refrain from doing a certain thing because he ought to act or forbear. It is because of this emphasis upon the defendant's duty that equity is so much more ethical than law. The difference between the two in this respect appears even in cases of concurrent jurisdiction. The moral standard of the man who commits no breach of contract or tort, or, having committed the one or the other, does his best to restore the *status quo,* is obviously higher than that of the man who breaks his contract or commits a tort and then refuses to do more than make compensation for his wrong. It is this higher standard of morality that equity enforces wherever the legal remedy of pecuniary compensation would be inadequate, by commanding the defendant by injunction to refrain from the commission of a tort or breach of contract, or by compelling him, after the commission of the one or the other, by means of a mandatory injunction, or a decree for specific performance, so called, to make specific reparation for his wrong.

The ethical character of equitable relief is, of course, most pronounced in cases in which equity gives not merely a better remedy than the law gives, but the only remedy.

The great bulk of the exclusive jurisdiction of equity falls under two heads, Bills for Restitution and Bills for Specific Performance. The object of bills for restitution is to compel the surrender by the defendant of property wrongfully obtained from the plaintiff, or of property properly acquired but improperly retained because of some misconduct after its acquisition. Bills for restitution are very ancient. In the fourteenth and fifteenth centuries there were bills for the reconveyance of property acquired by fraud or mistake or retained by a defendant after failing to give the stipulated equivalent for the property.[29] Somewhat later we find bills to restrain the enforcement and compel the surrender of specialty contracts obtained fraud-

[29] 21 Harv. L. Rev. 262.

ulently, illegally, or by mistake, or retained after payment or in spite of failure of consideration.[30] Early in the seventeenth century Lord Ellesmere, in his famous controversy with Lord Coke, established the right to restrain the enforcement of a common law judgment obtained by fraud.[31] In this same century mortgagees were compelled to surrender the mortgaged property notwithstanding the default of the mortgagor and in disregard of the express agreement of the parties, upon payment of the mortgage debt and interest,[32] and to prevent a similar hardship, holders of penal bonds were compelled to give them up without exacting the penalty.[33] In the eighteenth century, without proof of any fraudulent misrepresentation, decrees for reconveyance were made upon the ground of undue influence, growing out of the relations of the parties, as in the case of conveyances by client to attorney, ward to guardian, child to parent and the like. And in the last century grantees, who had acquired property by innocent misrepresentation, were obliged to restore it to their grantors.[34] The relief in these cases consists in undoing the original transaction and restoring the *status quo,* a result, of course, not anticipated by either party at the outset. In other words, equity treated the defendant as holding the property upon a constructive trust for the plaintiff.

On the other hand, bills against express trustees form the staple of the exercise of the exclusive jurisdiction of equity by way of specific performance. Equity began to enforce the performance of uses and trusts soon after 1400.[35]

In giving relief by decrees for restitution against constructive trustees, or by decrees for specific performances

---

[30] 9 *Ibid.* 51, 52, 54–55.
[31] Wilson, Life of James I, 94, 95; 2 Campbell, Lives of Lord Chancellors, 241.
[32] 1 Spence, Eq. Jur., 602–3.
[33] *Ibid.* 629.
[34] Redgrave v. Hurd, 20 Ch. D. 1.
[35] 21 Harv. L. Rev. 265.

against express trustees, equity has acted upon the highly moral principle that no one should, by the wrongful acquisition or retention of a title, unjustly enrich himself at the expense of another.

In the cases thus far considered, this doctrine of unjust enrichment was enforced against the original grantee of the property and because of his misconduct in the relation between him and the grantor. But it is a long-established principle that anyone who acquires property from another who, as he knows, holds it subject to a trust or other equity, and also anyone who, without such knowledge, acquires property so held, if he gives no value for it, may be compelled himself to perform the trust or other equitable obligation. It is true there is no direct relation between the equitable claimant and the buyer with notice or the donee without notice. But if the one could knowingly acquire, or the other knowingly keep, the property free from the trust or other equity, he would be profiting unconscionably at the expense of the *cestui que trust,* or other equitable claimant. These applications of the doctrine of unjust enrichment are good illustrations of the highly moral quality of equity jurisdiction. They are almost unknown to the Roman law, and are but imperfectly recognized in modern continental law.

There is another doctrine of equity which has only a limited operation in countries whose law is based on the Roman law, the doctrine that no one shall make a profit from the violation of an equitable duty, even though he is ready to make full compensation to him whose equitable right he has infringed. A trustee, for example, of land worth $5,000 in breach of trust conveys it to a purchaser for value without notice of the trust, receiving in exchange fifty shares of corporate stock. The shares appreciate and become worth $10,000, while the land depreciates to $3,000. The delinquent trustee may be compelled to surrender the shares to the *cestui que trust,* although the latter thereby gets $7,000 more than he would have had if there had been no breach of trust. If the shares had depreciated and the land appreciated, the *cestui que trust* would be entitled to the increased value of the land. It is a wholesome principle that whatever the misconducting trustee wins he wins for his beneficiary, and whatever he loses he loses for himself.

The equitable rules which prohibit a fiduciary, while in the performance of his fiduciary duty, from competing in any way with the interest of his beneficiary, and permit dealings between them only upon clear evidence of the good faith of the fiduciary, and of a complete disclosure of all his knowledge as to the matters entrusted to him, and in fact the whole law of equity as to fiduciaries, enforce a moral standard considerably in advance of that of the average businessman. Enough has been said to make plain that much as our law owes to the action on the case for its ethical quality, it is to the principles of the court of equity, acting upon the conscience of the defendants and compelling them by decrees of restitution and specific performance to do what in justice and right they ought to do, that we must look to justify our belief that the English and American systems of law, however imperfect, are further on the road to perfection than those of other countries.

In considering the possibility of further improvements of the law, we must recognize at the outset that there are some permanent limitations upon the enforcement in the courts of duties whose performance is required in the forum of morals.

On grounds of public policy there are and always will be, on the one hand, many cases in which persons damaged may recover compensation from others whose conduct was morally blameless, and, on the other hand, many cases in which persons damaged cannot obtain compensation even from those whose conduct was morally most reprehensible.

Instances of unsuccessful actions against persons free from fault readily suggest themselves. The master, who has used all possible care in the selection of his servants, is liable for damage by them when acting within the scope of their employment, although they carelessly or even willfully disregard his instructions. The business is carried on

for the master's benefit, and it is thought to be expedient
that he, rather than a stranger, should take the risk of the
servant's misconduct. One keeps fierce, wild animals at his
peril, and also domestic animals, after knowledge that
they are dangerous. By legislation, indeed, in several states,
one who keeps a dog must make three-fold compensation,
in one state ten-fold compensation, for damage done by
the dog, without proof of the keeper's knowledge of its
vicious quality. The sheep farmers must be encouraged,
even if some innocent persons have to pay dearly for the
luxury of keeping a dog. A Massachusetts bank was entered by burglars who carried off and put into circulation
a large quantity of bank notes which had been printed but
never issued by the bank. The bank had to pay these notes.
The bank must safeguard the notes it prints at its peril, to
prevent the possibility of a widespreading mischief to the
general public.

The results in these cases are much less disturbing to
one's sense of fairness than in those in which the innocent
victims of the unrighteous are allowed no redress. For example, a will is found after a man's death giving all his
property to his brother. In the same box with the will is a
letter, not referred to in the will, addressed to the brother,
telling him that he is to hold the property in trust for their
sister. The brother insists upon keeping the property for
himself. The court is powerless to help the defrauded
sister. The rule that the intention of the testator must be
found exclusively in the duly-witnessed document, in view
of the danger of perjury and forgery, is the best security
for giving effect to the true will of the generality of testa-
tors. The defenses of infancy, statute of frauds, statute of
limitations, or that a promise was gratuitous are only too
often dishonorable defenses, but their abolition would
probably increase rather than diminish injustice. An English judge said from the bench: "You are a harpy, preying
on the vitals of the poor." The words were false and spoken
for the sole purpose of injuring the person addressed. The
latter could maintain no action against the judge. It is believed to be for the public interest that no judge should

be called to account in a civil action for words spoken while on the bench.

The law is utilitarian. It exists for the realization of the reasonable needs of the community. If the interest of an individual runs counter to this chief object of the law, it must be sacrificed. That is why, in the cases just considered and others that will occur to you, the innocent suffer and the wicked go unpunished.

But unless exempted from liability by considerations of enlightened public policy, I can see no reason why he who has by his act willfully caused damage to another should not in all cases make either specific reparation or pecuniary compensation to his victim.

Has this principle become a part of our law? Let us consider a few concrete cases. A man kills his daughter in order to inherit her real estate. Under the statute the land descends to him as her heir. May he keep it? It seems clear that equity should compel him to surrender the property. As it is impossible to make specific reparation to the deceased, he should be treated as a constructive trustee for those who represent her, that is, her heirs, the murderer being counted out in determining who are the heirs. But in several states the murderer is allowed to keep the fruits of his crime.[36]

A handsome, modest young lady is photographed without her consent and her likeness is reproduced and sent broadcast through the land as part of an advertising label with the legend, "The Flower of the Family," placed upon thousands of barrels of flour. Here, too, the courts are divided as to whether she should have relief. It being well settled and properly settled that the recipient of a letter commits a tort if he publishes it without the consent of the writer, there should be little difficulty in preventing the greater invasion of privacy in using the portrait of a modest girl as an advertising medium. Suppose, again, that

---

[36] 36 Am. L. Reg. and Rev. 225; Wellner v. Eckstein, 117 N. W. 830 (Minn., 1908. Two judges dissenting). In New York the rule is the other way.

the owner of land sinks a well, not in order to get water for himself, but solely for the purpose of draining his neighbor's spring, or that he erects an abnormally high fence on his own land, but near the boundary, not for any advantage of his own, but merely to darken his neighbor's windows or to obstruct his view. Is the landowner responsible to his neighbor for the damage arising from such malevolent conduct? In thirteen of our states he must make compensation for malevolently draining the neighbor's spring. In two other states the opposite has been decided. In four states one who erects a spite fence must pay for the damage to the neighbor. In six others he incurs no liability. Six states have passed special statutes giving an action for building such a fence. In Germany and France and in other continental countries an action is allowed against the landowner in both cases.

The principle I have suggested would allow relief in all of these cases, and its adoption by the courts is fairly justified by the rules of equity and the Statute of Edward I. This principle is very neatly expressed in the new German Code: "Any act done willfully by means of which damage is done to another in a manner *contra bonos mores* is an unlawful act."

To put quite a different case, should statutes be passed giving compensation by the state to an innocent man for an unmerited conviction and punishment? The state, it is true, has merely done its duty in carrying through the prosecution. But the prosecution was made for the benefit of the community, and is it not just that the community rather than an innocent member of it should pay for its mistakes? By recent legislation Germany has provided compensation for the innocent sufferer in such cases.

In these cases in which it is suggested that the person damaged ought to recover compensation, the damage was caused by the willful act of the party to be charged. It remains to consider whether the law should ever go so far as to give compensation or to inflict punishment for damage which would not have happened but for the willful inaction of another. I exclude cases in which, by reason of some relation between the parties like that of father and child, nurse and invalid, master and servant and others, there is a recognized legal duty to act. In the case supposed the only relation between the parties is that both are human beings. As I am walking over a bridge a man falls into the water. He cannot swim and calls for help. I am strong and a good swimmer, or, if you please, there is a rope on the bridge, and I might easily throw him an end and pull him ashore. I neither jump in nor throw him the rope, but see him drown. Or, again, I see a child on the railroad track too young to appreciate the danger of the approaching train. I might easily save the child, but do nothing, and the child, though it lives, loses both legs. Am I guilty of a crime, and must I make compensation to the widow and children of the man drowned and to the wounded child? Macaulay, in commenting upon his Indian Criminal Code, puts the case of a surgeon refusing to go from Calcutta to Meerut to perform an operation, although it should be absolutely certain that this surgeon was the only person in India who could perform it, and that, if it were not performed, the person who required it would die.

We may suppose again that the situation of imminent danger of death was created by the act, but the innocent act, of the person who refuses to prevent the death. The man, for example, whose eye was penetrated by the glancing shot of the careful pheasant hunter, stunned by the shot, fell face downward into a shallow pool by which he was standing. The hunter might easily save him, but lets him drown.

In the first three illustrations, however revolting the conduct of the man who declined to interfere, he was in no way responsible for the perilous situation, he did not increase the peril, he took away nothing from the person in jeopardy, he simply failed to confer a benefit upon a stranger. As the law stands today there would be no legal liability, either civilly or criminally, in any of these cases. The law does not compel active benevolence between man and man. It is left to one's conscience whether he shall be the good Samaritan or not.

But ought the law to remain in this condition? Of course any statutory duty to be benevolent would have to be exceptional. The practical difficulty in such legislation would be in drawing the line. But that difficulty has continually to be faced in the law. We should all be better satisfied if the man who refuses to throw a rope to a drowning man or to save a helpless child on the railroad track could be punished and be made to compensate the widow of the man drowned and the wounded child. We should not think it advisable to penalize the surgeon who refused to make the journey. These illustrations suggest a possible working rule. One who fails to interfere to save another from impending death or great bodily harm, when he might do so with little or no inconvenience to himself, and the death or great bodily harm follows as a consequence of his inaction, shall be punished criminally and shall make compensation to the party injured or to his widow and children in case of death. The case of the drowning of the man shot by the hunter differs from the others in that the hunter, although he acted innocently, did bring about the dangerous situation. Here, too, the lawyer who should try to charge the hunter would lead a forlorn hope. But it seems to me that he could make out a strong case against the hunter on common law grounds. By the early law, as we have seen, he would have been liable simply because he shot the other. In modern times the courts have admitted as an affirmative defense the fact that he was not negligent. May not the same courts refuse to allow the defense, if the defendant did not use reasonable means to prevent a calamity after creating the threatening situation? Be that as it may, it is hard to see why such a rule should not be declared by statute, if not by the courts.

It is obvious that the spirit of reform which during the last six hundred years has been bringing our system of law more and more into harmony with moral principles has not yet achieved its perfect work. It is worth-while to realize the great ethical advance of the English law in the past, if only as an encouragement to effort for future improvement. In this work of the future there is an admirable field for the law professor. The professor has, while the judge and the practicing lawyer have not, the time for systematic and comprehensive study and for becoming familiar with the decisions and legislation of other countries. This systematic study and the knowledge of what is going on in other countries are indispensable if we would make our system of law the best possible instrument of justice. The training of students must always be the chief object of the law school, but this work should be supplemented by solid contributions of their professors to the improvement of the law.

The Good Samaritan and the Bad:
The Anglo-American Law

CHARLES O. GREGORY*

What is the Anglo-American law in this area? As I understand our common law, it could be summed up by the
moral of a James Thurber fable: "Stay where you are,
you're sitting pretty."[1] Our common law has always refused
to transmute moral duties into legal duties.[2] As the New
Hampshire court said in 1897:[3] "With purely moral
obligations the law does not deal. For example, the priest
and the Levite who passed by on the other side were not,
it is supposed, liable at law for the continued suffering of
the man who fell among thieves, which they might and
morally ought to have prevented or relieved." That court
then supposes a man standing near a two-year-old babe
on a railroad track, a train approaching in the distance.
With no danger to himself he could lift the child from the
track. Or take the case of a man who sees a baby tod-
dling to the brink of a deep well. He could easily stop the
child. As the New Hampshire court observed: "If he does
not, he may, perhaps, justly be styled a ruthless savage
and a moral monster; but he is not liable in damages for the
child's injury, or indictable under the statute for its death."

I suppose that if our moral monster had a movie camera

Professor of Law, University of Virginia.

[1] Thurber, *Fables for Our Time* (1943) p. 3.

[2] Ames, *Law and Morals,* 22 *Harv. L. Rev.* 97 (1908) [*Supra;*
pp. 1–21]; Bohlen, *The Moral Duty to Aid Others as a Basis
of Tort Liability,* 56 *U. of Pa. L. Rev.* 217 (1908); Prosser,
Law of Torts (3d ed. 1964) 336; Minor, *Moral Obligation as a
Basis of Liability,* 9 *Va. L. Rev.* 420 (1923).

[3] Buch v. Amory Manufacturing Co., 69 N.H. 257, 44 Atl.
809 (1897).

and took pictures of these incidents, he would be considered even more loathsome. Yet I also suppose that he still would not be liable for what befell the child or be subject to punishment.[4]

Of course, these are extreme cases and are not likely to happen. But it is remarkable that we can be so confident in stating what the law *would* be in these cases. For it is clear at common law that nobody has to lift a finger—let alone spend a dime and dial a phone number or actually render aid—to help a stranger in peril or distress. I say "stranger" because there are relationships which require people to help others or avert danger toward them.[5] A father, mother, or husband must render aid to a child or spouse in peril or distress—even where the aid in question, medication or getting a doctor, is against the parent's religion. Consider the Australian couple sitting on the edge of a deep swimming pool, quarreling bitterly as they were alone.[6] In a pique the wife, who could not swim, jumped into the water, obviously making a bid for attention. Her husband sat there and watched her flounder until she drowned. Apparently he told of this, since he was duly convicted for criminal homicide. The court said that since they were married, the husband was under a legal duty to render aid. The clear implication was that if they were *not* married, he would be under no such duty. This makes you

---

[4] See authorities cited *supra* note 2. In addition see text and authorities cited in 2 Harper & James, *The Law of Torts* (1956) § 18.6, pp. 1044 *et seq.*

[5] Harper & James, *op. cit. supra* note 4 at pp. 1048 *et seq.*

[6] See Rex v. Russell, 1933 *Victoria Law Rep.* 59 (1932, Victoria Supreme Court). The facts of this case were somewhat different from the situation set forth by my statement in the text. For instance, the defendant's two small children also were drowned at the same time; and his wife no doubt intended to drown herself and the two children. Moreover, the whole situation was somewhat complicated by a bigamous marriage of the defendant, although the woman who drowned was his true wife. But the *Russell* case certainly supports the statement in the text.

wonder what would have happened if they had been merely engaged, or were lovers. Or suppose their marriage was shown to depend on an invalid Mexican divorce!

The master of a ship must render assistance to a seaman who is ill or in peril.[7] Of course he would be under a similar obligation to a passenger; but that would go back to the contract of carriage. Such contract imposes a similar duty on all public carriers.[8] Others under a duty imposed by contract are the headmaster of a boys' school and the manager of a boys' camp—together with teachers and counselors—toward their charges. A baby-sitter is presumably under a like obligation, for what it is worth. But courts are reluctant to recognize a contractual duty of care in simple business visitor situations. If a woman shopper faints on the floor in a department store, the books seem to indicate that she may with impunity be left there by the store management, as long as she is not stepped on.[9] And I have no reason to suppose that her plight must even be reported. But if she is moved to the ladies' room, she has been taken

[7] Prosser, *op. cit. supra* note 2 at p. 337.

[8] *Ibid.* 2 Harper & James, *op. cit. supra* note 4, pp. 1048–50.

[9] While the old cases on principle seem to bear me out, both Prosser and Harper & James assert that a trend away from this position has already taken place. See Prosser, *op. cit. supra* note 2 at p. 337; and see 2 Harper & James, *op. cit. supra* note 4, at 1048–49. The implication in both these texts is that the law in the past has been about as I described it. Thus, in Zelenko v. Gimbel Bros., 158 Misc. 904, 287 N.Y. Supp. 134 (1935) Lauer, J. observed: "Plaintiff's intestate was taken ill in defendant's store. We will assume that defendant owed her no duty at all; that defendant could have let her be and die. . . .

"The plaintiff is wrong in thinking that the duty of a common carrier of passengers is the same as the duty of this defendant. The common carrier assumes its duty by its contract of carriage. This defendant assumed its duty *by meddling in matters with which legalistically it had no concern.*" (italics inserted) It appears that one of defendant's employees had removed plaintiff's deceased from the floor of the store to a ladies' rest room and left her there, where she died.

in charge and must then be given reasonable attention and care.[10]

There is another general type of case—seemingly indistinguishable—where some courts have come to recognize a duty to render aid. But even here in the early cases the courts consistently applied the old basic principle. Thus, a railroad engine, without negligence of its crew, cuts off the legs of a trespasser on the tracks. Ample authority upholds the railroads in refusing to render aid.[11] Of course they may not increase the danger by continuing to operate the vehicle without moving the victim aside. Consider what happened when something called a safety guard nonnegligently fell from the front of a trolley car onto a trespassing pedestrian drunkenly asleep on the right of way. This safety guard eventually crushed the life out of him. Had the car backed up, it would have relieved the deceased of this pressure. But the Alabama court said the trolley crew were no more required to remove this safety guard than a casual bystander would be.[12] The only danger of liability would be if the crew, in moving the victim, *did* something negligently that caused him harm. Under this view it would behoove the company—financially, at least—to leave things exactly as they were until the victim expired. And take the case of Ames's hunter.[13] He nonnegligently fired a bullet which ricocheted and knocked an-

[10] Zelenko v. Gimbel Bros., *op. cit. supra* note 9.

[11] Union Pacific R. R. v. Cappier, 66 Kan. 649, 72 Pac. 281 (1903). See generally 2 Harper & James *op. cit. supra* note 4, p. 1047 and Prosser, *op. cit. supra* note 2, p. 336.

[12] Turberville v. Mobile L. & R. Co., 221 Ala. 91, 127 So. 519 (1930).

[13] Ames, *op. cit. supra* note 2, at pp. 19–20. Of course, I like to think that Ames was correct in his conclusion that the hunter would have been liable for trespass at old common law. See Gregory, *Trespass to Negligence to Absolute Liability*, 37 *Va. L. Rev.* 359 (1951). But as to this see Roberts, *Negligence: Blackstone to Shaw to ? An Intellectual Escapade in a Tory Vein*, 50 *Corn. L. Quart.* 191 (1965), particularly pp. 204 *et seq.*

other unconscious, so that he fell with his face in a tiny pool of water and drowned. Fifty-seven years ago Ames conceded that a lawyer trying to make out a case against the hunter for not rolling the victim over "would lead a forlorn hope." But he declared that under the early common law of trespass he would have won.

Fortunately the law may be changing in this type of case. Consider this situation. Two of defendant's trucks, due to no fault of the drivers, became stalled on a narrow road, completely blocking the highway. Also, without fault, the men were unable to get the trucks started again. This was at the foot of a short hill, which obscured the view of approaching drivers. Moreover, the hill was somewhat icy. Plaintiff came driving along at a normal speed. By the time he saw the stalled trucks, he was unable to stop and crashed into them. Had one of defendant's truck drivers climbed the hill and posted a warning, this accident would not have happened. Since his plight was not due to negligence, defendant insisted that he had no duty to warn others, any more than he would have to warn of a tree that had fallen across the highway. Nobody but the police would have to report the fallen tree. And a casual pedestrian would not be required to warn others about the stalled trucks. But the South Carolina court said the truck drivers had to post a warning and held defendant liable.[14] Under our law this must have been because defendant's truck drivers *did* something to create the hazard. In effect the court said that if you're going to drive trucks on the highway—and if the truck's presence there *in any way* creates a danger—then because the trucker created the hazard, he must do something about protecting others. If you don't like this, don't take trucks onto the highway!

Now this seems childishly simple. Yet it represents a great advance over the law with respect to railroad engines innocently cutting off a trespasser's legs. Some courts might now actually declare that if you do innocently mow another down, you would have to stop and do something about it.[15] But I am not sure about this. I am not even sure that the truckers' case just discussed would be generally followed. Our law says that you do not have to volunteer to relieve others from dangers not due to your own fault; but if you *do* volunteer—if you engage in some activity that is followed by harm to such another—then a court may let a jury scrutinize what you did and call it actionable negligence—no matter how hard you tried.[16] Many people aware of this think it much wiser to do nothing at all. If you are not under a duty to "fease," then nonfeasance can never be held actionable. But if you do engage in feasance toward anybody, then under most circumstances you must "fease" carefully. Moral: Don't ever "fease" unless you have to![17]

On the basis of the foregoing, it is tempting to generalize as follows: if one acting in public innocently creates a dangerous condition, then he must take care to neutralize, avert, or warn of the danger; whereas if his conduct innocently causes the harm in the first place, he is not required to do anything—only to avoid conduct making it worse. Several states' statutes now require motorists in any way involved, however innocently, with causing harm to another on the highway to stop, give information, and render as-

[15] See Summers v. Dominguez, 29 Cal. App. 2d 308, 84 P. 2d 237 (1938). See also 2 Harper & James, *op. cit. supra* note 4, at 1047.

[16] See Prosser, *op. cit. supra* note 2, at 335–36. See also Coggs v. Bernard, 2 Ld. Raymond 909 (K.B. 1703) and Gill v. Middleton, 105 Mass. 477 (1870). See, generally, Gregory, *Gratuitous Undertakings and the Duty of Care*, 1 *De Paul Law Rev.* 30 (1951).

[17] This has reference to the distinction between misfeasance and nonfeasance—doing something wrong and not doing anything at all. As to this, see Prosser, *op. cit. supra* note 2 at 334; 2 Harper & James, *op. cit. supra* note 4 at 1044 *et seq.* See also Gregory, *op. cit. supra* note 16. Of course I do not want to be understood as advising people never to help others who are in danger or distress.

sistance.[18] Liability insurance companies encourage this by allowing the expenditure of substantial sums for ambulance and medical care, regardless of fault.[19]

What *should* people do when they see somebody in distress—sick, unconscious, or actually dying? Most people hurry away. They do not want to get involved. But if they do intercede—do take the hurt person in charge—they must do so carefully and see it through. "The very act of charity puts a noose around the neck of the kind-hearted person from which he can escape only by persuading a court and jury that he proceeded without reproach."[20] How far would courts push this idea, short of defendant's actually taking the hurt person in charge so that nobody else could help him? A motorist sees a hurt person beside the road and, without touching him, says he will fetch him aid. If he then drives off and forgets the whole matter, can he be held? Would it be different if he drove to a garage, rang a couple of doctors and the rescue squad, and then gave it up in impatience because the lines were busy? Has he entered upon performance so that not going further might

[18] Ark. Stats. of 1947 Ann., § 75-903; Calif. Vehicle Code, § 20003; Conn. Gen. Stats. Ann., § 14-224; Ga. Code Ann., § 68-1620; Idaho Code, § 49-1003; La. Rev. Stats., §§ 14-100 and 32-414; Miss. Code 1942 Ann., § 8163; N.J. Stats. Ann., Title 39 § 4-129; N.M. Stats. 1953 Ann., § 64-17-3; N.C. Gen. Stats. § 20-166; Purdon's Penn. Stats. Ann., § 75-1027; S.C. Code of Laws, § 46-323; Vernon's Tex. Penal Code, § 1150; W. Va. Code of 1961 Ann., § 1721 (317). For a complete annotation of cases arising under these statutes, see 80 ALR 2d 299 (1961).

[19] One standard automobile liability insurance policy reads, concerning medical payments: "With respect to such insurance as is afforded by this policy for bodily injury liability and for property damage liability the company shall: . . . pay expense incurred by the insured for such immediate medical and surgical relief to others as shall be imperative at the time of the accident; . . ." This, of course, is regardless of liability by the insured to such others.

[20] Gregory, *op. cit. supra* note 16, at p. 44.

make him liable? If the hurt person had in the meantime
told the next passer-by not to bother—that help was on its
way—wouldn't this be like promissory estoppel? Or suppose the defendant got the doctor or rescue squad on the
phone but negligently couldn't remember where the hurt
person was or how to direct others to find him. And so
on.[21] Theoretically the defendant has undertaken to help
and has bungled it, just as much as if he had taken the
victim in hand and really hurt him by starting a hemor-
rhage or breaking a bone.

To encourage doctors and others to render assistance to
people in distress, several states have passed so-called Good
Samaritan statutes.[22] These laws, in effect, confer on the
doctor immunity from liability for any suit that might be
brought against him. This seems to be an obvious step;
but some people believe that doctors should not be freed
of liability for negligence or gross negligence, even under

---

[21] These situations are discussed at length in Gregory, *op.
cit. supra* note 16, at pp. 44 *et seq.*

[22] There are about thirty-one or more of these statutes—too
many to cite here. They occur in Alaska, Arkansas, California,
Connecticut, Georgia, Maine, Maryland, Massachusetts, Michigan, Mississippi, Montana, Nebraska, Nevada, New Hampshire,
New Jersey, New Mexico, New York, North Dakota, Ohio,
Oklahoma, Pennsylvania, Rhode Island, South Carolina, South
Dakota, Tennessee, Texas, Utah, Virginia, Wisconsin, and Wyo-
ming. The statutes in all of these states are cited and discussed
and the whole problem of the Good Samaritan (and the bad)
is expertly analyzed in a long note in 64 *Col. L. Rev.* 1301
(1964). Some of these statutes are short and to the point, simply affording immunity from suit for doctors who help others in
emergencies. Others have all sorts of questionable angles and
approaches that may create as many problems as they purport
to abolish. All these are discussed in the *Columbia Law Review*
note just cited. See also an excellent critical note in 42 *Ore. L.
Rev.* 328 (1963). Other notes appear in 17 *U. of Fla. L. Rev.*
586 (1965); 43 *Marq. L. Rev.* 80 (1964); 15 *Mercer L. Rev.*
477 (1964); 32 *Tenn. L. Rev.* 287 (1965); 18 *Vand. L. Rev.*
323 (1964); 10 *Vill. L. Rev.* 130 (1964); and *Wis. L. Rev.*
494 (1964).

these circumstances.[23] Of course, what doctors really dislike is to be sued at all, which they can easily avoid by not volunteering their aid. I suppose the state could require doctors to render aid in emergencies as a condition to their being licensed to practice at all. No doubt they could back this up by a penal sanction or suspension of their license. But is there any practicable way of requiring people in general to render aid to somebody in distress? Some countries have imposed such requirements;[24] but this sort of thing fits uneasily into the framework of the common law. As Dr. Goodhart[25] has observed, the only people who will offer their services to others in distress do not have to be required to do so; and those who will not do it voluntarily pay no attention to official sanctions.

What fundamentally underlies the reluctance of most people to help others in distress? Probably the desire not to get involved, and the instinct to mind one's own business. The latter is sometimes carried to extremes. A Vermont farmer, taking his seat in the country store, finally

[23] See the discussions in the notes cited *supra* note 22, particularly those in 64 *Col. L. Rev.* 1301 (1964) and 42 *Ore. L. Rev.* 328 (1963).

[24] For instances of foreign law on this, see 64 *Col. L. Rev.* 1301, at 1317 (1964); 52 *Col. L. Rev.* 631, at 640, note 66 (1952) with a translation from the French Penal Code; Dutch Penal Code, Art. 450, translated in Gregory and Kalven, *Cases and Materials on Torts* (1959) 267; German Criminal Code, translated in 64 *Col. L. Rev.* 1301 (1964) at 1318 and in Dawson, *Rewards for the Rescue of Human Life?, infra,* pp. 63–89; Hazard, *Soviet Socialism and the Duty to Rescue,* appearing in *XXth Century Comparative and Conflicts Law* (1961) 160; Dawson, *The Altruistic Intermeddler,* 74 *Harv. L. Rev.* 817 and 1073, at 1101–6; Amendment to the Belgium Penal Code: *The Duty to Rescue Persons in Serious Danger,* 11 *Am. J. Comp. Law* 66 (1962). And see the discussion and citations in Rudolph, *The Duty to Act: A Proposed Rule,* 44 *Nebraska L. Rev.* 499, *infra,* at 243 *et seq.* (1965).

[25] Dr. Arthur L. Goodhart, editor of the *Law Quarterly Review* and noted authority on tort law, in an unpublished discussion.

observed: "I see Si Smith hung himself in his barn."
After a few moments he was asked: "Well, did you cut
him down?" The first farmer answered: "No, he hadn't
stopped twitching yet." Perhaps eventually people may
realize that we are a community—that as each helps another today, so tomorrow he or one of his family may likewise be helped by strangers. This suggests a sort of social
contract; but I agree with Dr. Goodhart that it is an obligation of manners or morals and may never have full legal
sanction.

In many of these cases the worst thing that can happen
to the helper is that he may be held civilly liable for ag-
gravation of the victim's harm or may have the nuisance
of defending an action for damages. But suppose the victim
is in a position of helpless peril from impending hazard,
where a rescuer would endanger his own life. Lots of people are scared to take a chance. There is, however, this
inducement: if they do, and get hurt, they may recover
damages from the third party endangering the rescued
person—if he was negligent![26] In this connection don't forget *Saylor v. Parsons*.[27] There defendant negligently endangered himself; and plaintiff who rescued him was badly
hurt. The Iowa court threw plaintiff's suit out, declaring
that defendant could not have been negligent to himself
since a man owes himself no duty of care. Happily a better analysis shows that defendant foreseeably invites
rescue even in such cases and thus owes a duty to and is
negligent toward his rescuer![28] Enabling rescuers to recover damage they suffer in rescuing people negligently
endangered is the least the legal system can do. Even those
who must let their property be used by others in dire emergencies can recover its value from them.

However, the victim may be endangered by circumstances not involving anybody's fault. This last year sev-

[26] Prosser, *op. cit. supra* note 2, at 316–17.
[27] 122 Iowa 697, 98 N.W. 500 (1904).
[28] See authorities cited in 2 Harper & James, *op. cit. supra*
note 4, § 16.12, note 1, p. 940.

eral people drowned in front of small crowds who just stood and looked. In such cases people fall in, they upset boats, get cramps in swimming, or squirm out of autos that have hurtled into rivers or lakes. Naturally most rescuers don't want to risk drowning themselves—or the water is very cold—or something! But why the apathy? They could at least tie their shirts together and make a rope or run to a phone and call the police or rescue squad. Perhaps some people are like me. Since my coronary I have been told not to catch or lift fainting people or jump in after drowning persons. But even a cardiac case can take steps to call *others* to come and help.[29]

Where rescue involves active, as against passive, danger, the Good Samaritan is apt to be *not* so good. This is where thugs attack others with rape, robbery, beatings, or even murder in mind. While the murder of Kitty Genovese remains the *cause célèbre*,[30] the papers have lately been full of similar things. Perhaps when thugs read what they can get away with, they are encouraged to attack people in public places in the presence of others. Why did the thirty-eight people in Kew Gardens, Queens, New York, behave as they did on the night of March 13, 1964? Because they were scared and did not want to get involved. Also, because they did not have faith in the police and did not want to stick their necks out. It seems perfectly incredible; but a year later they appear not to have changed and still don't see why they should have done anything.[31] Perhaps Margaret Mead is right. In the April

[29] This past year, in Galveston, Texas, a cardiac case did jump in to save a drowning girl when everybody else stood by apathetically. He suffered another heart attack—but the girl was saved. I have the clipping for this, but it is unidentified as to time and place.

[30] See Rosenthal, *Thirty-eight Witnesses* (1964), a hair-raising account of the public and protracted murder of Miss Catherine Genovese in Queens, New York, during the night of March 13–14, 1964.

[31] See anniversary story on the Kitty Genovese case in the *New York Times,* Friday, March 12, 1965, at pp. 33 and 37.

Redbook[32] she says that our obsession with privacy has resulted in mass anonymity in our large cities—a dulling of our senses which kills neighborliness and caring about what happens to others. It is the opposite of the small-town atmosphere where everybody knows—and cares. Even the intimate enclaves of the slums, as Jane Jacobs warns,[33] are giving way to the impersonality of great housing developments where nobody knows—or gives a damn. At least, now New York has one centralized police call that even I can remember—440-1234—which is a great step forward.

Look what a time the police had getting the three girls to come forward and testify about the murder of young Mormile.[34] He was the seventeen-year old stabbed on the subway while rescuing them, in the presence of ten other people. True, the girls finally testified when the police promised to keep their names secret. But since Arnold Schuster's underworld murder—after police publicity gave him credit for fingering Willie Sutton, public enemy number 1—most people would rather remain live cowards than be dead public servants.[35] Also in future cases rescuers may die like Mormile and not be as lucky as sailor James George in the Philadelphia subway,[36] although even he was badly beaten up while a group of men stood by, not trying to protect the young girl or to help the sailor rescue her. But I suppose hesitation to effect a rescue under these circumstances is natural when you might be killed or maimed.

---

[32] Mead, *Our Right to Privacy, Redbook*, April 1965, p. 15 *et seq.* See also Rudolph, *op. cit. supra* note 24, p. 243 *infra*.

[33] Jacobs, *The Death and Life of Great American Cities* (1961).

[34] See story in *New York Times* for Tuesday, March 16, 1965.

[35] Schuster v. City of New York, 5 N.Y. 2d 75, 154 N.E. 2d 534 (1958).

[36] See *New York Times,* Tuesday, March 9, 1965; and see also *Richmond* (Va.) *Times-Dispatch*, March 9, 1965, under front-page headline: " 'Samaritan' Beaten as Six Just Look On."

Also, I understand why people remain aloof when they think they might become the victims of retributory vengeance at the hands of unknown criminals. But it is too bad we cannot eradicate that quality which prevents people from taking the trouble to call the police or rescue squad. Perhaps we can create a cowards-carry-a-dime club—to make emergency phone calls. First, however, we must get people to believe that the police will take them seriously and respect their anonymity when they telephone. Possibly other inducements might persuade people to intervene when people are attacked. Why not consider public compensation for harm incurred while rescuing those endangered otherwise than by a negligent third person? England now has public compensation for the victims of muggers, rapists, and thugs.[37] Why not extend the idea to those hurt in *rescuing* the victims of muggers, rapists, and thugs?[38]

[37] This non-legislative program, which seems to have been set up administratively by the Home Office and is operated informally by a board, is described at length in 78 *Harv. L. Rev.* 1683 (1965). Also described in this note is a recent law to the same effect in New Zealand—Jan. 1, 1964, Public Act No. 134 (N.Z.). An editorial in the October 1, 1965, issue of the *Charlottesville* (Va.) *Daily Progress* describes a recent California statute of this type signed by Governor Brown in July 1965. Also described is a bill to create a federal Violent Crimes Compensation Commission introduced in Congress by Senator Yarborough of Texas. And a somewhat modest measure of this sort —House Bill 682—was approved by Governor Kerner of Illinois on August 11, 1965. For a fairly complete discussion of this matter of compensating the victims of crime see Worsnop, *Compensation for Victims of Crime,* Vol. II, No. 11 *Editorial Research Reports,* September 22, 1965, a largely historical account of what has been done and what is now being done in this area.

[38] After all, such Good Samaritans are also "victims" of such muggers, rapists, and thugs. So far as I know, only Illinois has taken concrete steps in this direction. There State Senator John J. Lanigan introduced Senate Bills 899 and 900 which would set up a fund for the benefit of rescuers of victims who

We should re-examine other aspects of how the law treats those who rescue others. There is not much law on the privilege to use force in the protection of others—but most of it has said in the past that there is no such privilege.[39] True, if a stranger attacks your wife or child, you may use force defending your relative as you would defending yourself. But suppose he attacks your mistress![40] If you leap to her defense—or anyone else's—you may be committing actionable battery. Thus a rescuer in such a case (1) may get beaten up while onlookers refuse to help him; (2) may be sued by the rescued person if he bungles it; and (3) now may be held liable in damages to the

---

are hurt in rescuing them. The awards would be limited to $500. See editorial captioned "Helping the Good Samaritan" in the Tuesday, June 15, 1965, issue of the *Chicago Daily News.* The first *New York Times* published after the newspaper strike was settled—that of Monday, October 11, 1965—carried on page 41 a heart-rending story of a young father, Arthur F. Collins, who attempted to prevent several women passengers from being molested on a New York subway by what appeared to be a drunken thug. In full view of his wife, who was holding their fifteen-months' old daughter, the unknown drunk turned on Collins, stabbed him to death through the heart, and then fled from the stopped subway train. The report of this incident relates that John J. Gilhooley, acting chairman of the Transit Authority, is now urging that financial compensation be given to the families of people disabled or killed aiding others.

[39] I have reference to the old common law rule that the privilege of using force to defend others was confined to protecting members of the actor's family, his servants, or (as with a common carrier) people toward whom he had some sort of special contractual obligation. See Frew v. Teagarden, 111 Kan. 107, 205 Pac. 1023 (1922). See generally Prosser, *op. cit. supra* note 2, at 114–15. However, Prosser thinks the law in this respect should change and actually is becoming more liberal. He quotes Salmond on *Torts,* 8th ed. 1934, p. 44, as follows: "Every man has the right of defending any man by reasonable force against unlawful force."

[40] See Morrison v. Commonwealth, 24 *Ky. L. Rep.* 2493, 74 S.W. 277 (1903).

thugs whose attack against others he is repelling. The least
the law could do here is to let the rescuer use such force
in protecting another against attack as *he* might use to
protect himself.

The problem of the Good Samaritan is really much
broader than just the question of helping people in physical
danger and distress. The whole problem of remaining silent is now an acute one everywhere. Recently I read a
letter to the editor in our local newspaper.[41] It excoriated
an unnamed storekeeper for inexcusably accusing a small
Negro child of intending to shoplift and threatening him
with jail. But the writer of the letter really seemed to
be flaying herself for not having lashed out at the storekeeper. She felt that she should have alleviated the child's
horrible embarrassment and the wound to his psyche. Indeed, she equated her failure with the betrayal of Kitty
Genovese by her neighbors. On the other hand, if she had
spoken up, she might have provoked even greater harm
to the child. How about hospital staffs and doctors who
fail to comply with the law in reporting babies and young
children seriously hurt by beatings—obviously inflicted by
their parents? The *New York Times* challenged this failure in its editorial: "Suffer Little Children."[42] Doctors and
hospitals probably fear law suits, economically harmful
publicity, or personal attacks for making such reports, although they are protected by statutory immunity. An
honor system, a university athletic program threatened by
bribes of professional gambling rings, an honest quiz program—all depend on somebody's having the courage to
speak out.

Remember Louis Brandeis. He didn't mind the attacks
of enemies or of prejudiced bigots in Boston when his

---

[41] This letter, editorially captioned "On Remaining Silent,"
appeared on the editorial page of the March 12, 1965, issue of
the *Charlottesville* (Va.) *Daily Progress*.

[42] This editorial appeared in the March 5, 1965, issue of the
New York Times. It was reprinted in the March 9, 1965, issue
of the *Charlottesville* (Va.) *Daily Progress*. The original editorial evoked a considerable number of letters to the editor.

confirmation to the Supreme Court hung in the balance. What he deplored was the failure of his friends to speak out and support him—"the unmanliness, the pussilanimity of those who believed that my efforts were commendable, but feared to speak out; feared because of either financial or social considerations or for the love of enjoyment or ease."[43] Yet there is no legal sanction to make people speak up; and there is no legal protection against the social consequences of doing so. Many believe that President Eisenhower should have destroyed McCarthy when the senator was trying to destroy General Marshall. At parties should we let someone give vent to racial and religious prejudice and bigotry without calling him on it? Lots of people are too cautious to speak up. Too bad we don't have a National Social Relations Board to protect those who take unpopular stands!

Suppose you are next in line at the ticket window and see the agent give the customer back ten dollars too much change. All you have to do is speak. But in doing so you may make a fool of the agent and a knave of the customer. I was in this position at a railway ticket office some months ago. The customer started away, counted his change—and then turned to the window and gave back the ten dollars. What if he had not done so? I doubt very much if I would have had the courage—or the gall—to intervene. Yet at the day's end the agent would have had to pay the ten dollars. To what extent is one his brother's keeper? Should you tell somebody his house may be on fire when you're not sure? or that his car is illegally parked? or his fly is open? Where do you draw the line?

I suppose there is much to be said for the old Anglo-American attitude of minding your own business—except that as the world changes, other peoples' business in more and more ways becomes yours. But I do not see how we can legislate charity, altruism, and courage—both physical

---

[43] Written by Brandeis to Judge Amidon in response to a letter congratulating him on his confirmation by the Senate. See Mason, *Brandeis: A Free Man's Life* (1946), pp. 505–6.

and moral. Some things we can do. We can widen the area of immunity of rescuers from tort liability—and even from criminal liability. We may even compensate them for harm they incur themselves. And we can punish people for failing to do something about situations with which their acts *causally* connect them, innocently or otherwise. We might even go so far as to punish moral monsters who refuse to prevent babies from crawling down wells or to intercede in similar cases. After all, we have Justice Ulysses Schwartz's assurance that "to deny relief because of lack of precedent is to freeze the common law as of a particular date."[44] He invokes Holmes to show that the judiciary should expand the law "to grant redress in a case without precedent for injuries resulting from conduct which universal opinion in a state of civilized society would unhesitatingly condemn as indecent and outrageous."[45] And he cites Cardozo as saying that in such cases "there is nothing for the court to do except to declare what fair and reasonable men, mindful of the habits of life of the community, and of the standards of justice and fair dealing prevalent among them, ought, in such circumstances, to do."[46] However, our moral monsters are going to insist that what happened did not "result" from any "conduct" of theirs. They fall back on the hopeless dichotomy of feasance and nonfeasance and all it implies in the law.[47]

But in the spirit of Holmes and Cardozo perhaps we can cut through these labels and treat egregiously dread-

[44] In Eick v. Perk Dog Food Co., 347 Ill. App. 293, at 303–4, 106 N.E. 2d 742, at 747 (1952), a right-to-privacy case.

[45] Justice Schwartz does not cite the source of the observation he attributed to Holmes.

[46] While this passage is not a quotation from Cardozo, Justice Schwartz, in making this statement, referred to Cardozo, *The Growth of the Law* (1934), pp. 19–20, and to his *The Nature of the Judicial Process* (1921), p. 142.

[47] See the discussions in the Prosser and Harper & James citations referred to above in note 17, *supra*.

ful behavior as conduct.[48] And if acting otherwise would
have averted the harm, we could declare that such behavior *did* result in the mischief complained of. Also, we
might read something like Section 483 of the New York
Penal Code as a sanction against our moral monster. That
provision makes a criminal of one who "wilfully causes
or *permits* the life or limb of any child to be injured or
imperilled."[49] Certainly in admiralty[50] they have not had
too much trouble in developing sanctions to compel rescues at sea; and as noted above,[51] some of the civil law
countries have legislated far more extensively.

But if we do this generally, we embark on a line-
drawing task that is delicate indeed. Who is to judge
what circumstances threaten danger to the rescuer—or when
an undertaking is not "onerous" to another? In abstract

[48] A splendid discussion of all the possibilities of introducing
effective sanctions or inducements in this field—from all points
of view—breaking it down as between professionals (e.g., doctors) and amateurs (e.g., all of us)—appears in Rudolph, *The
Duty to Act: A Proposed Rule* [*infra*, pp. 243–278]. That article
holds out about as much a hope for a workable rule as is practicable in our law.

[49] 39 McKinney's Cons. Laws N.Y. Ann. § 483.

[50] 46 U.S.C. Ann. § 728, reading: "The master or person in
charge of a vessel shall, so far as he can do so without serious
danger to his own vessel, crew, or passengers, render assistance
to every person who is found at sea in danger of being lost; and
if he fails to do so, he shall, upon conviction, be liable [for fine
and imprisonment]." See also Articles 11 and 12 of the International Salvage Treaty, 37 U.S. Stats. 1658, 1672, in connection
with which see Warhauser v. Lloyd Sabaudo S.A., 71 F. 2d 146
(C.C.A. 2, 1934), commented on in 12 *N.Y.U.L.Rev.* 301
(1934). A perusal of Judge Swan's opinion in the case just
cited indicates how cautious American courts will probably be
in taking advantage even of statutes to impose liability for harm
against the "Bad Samaritan." Indeed, the penal sanctions mentioned above are aimed at the master of the vessel and not at
his employer; and it seems likely that liability for damages will
also be restricted.

[51] See citations in note 24, *supra*.

terms we can weigh the interest to be rescued against the risk or inconvenience to be incurred—and come out with an answer. We could borrow Prosser's language from the *New Tort* and declare illegal only "extreme and outrageous" behavior.[52] Should the court then handle such matters, or a jury? I don't know. But I think I have said enough. Now I would like to close with the words of Chief Justice Holt in *Coggs v. Bernard*,[53] a landmark in this area: "I don't know whether I may have settled [the law], or may not rather have unsettled it. But however that happen, I have stirred these points, which wiser heads in time may settle."

[52] Or "extreme outrage." See Prosser, *op. cit. supra* note 2 at p. 52.

[53] Coggs v. Bernard, 2 Ld. Raymond 909 at 920 (K.B. 1703).

The Volunteer and the Good Samaritan

ANDRÉ TUNC*

In a Judeo-Christian civilization, the Good Samaritan, the man who takes care of others as he would of his brother, should be the permanent model of the citizen.

If this is true, it seems clear that we lack either Christian spirit or civilization, or perhaps both. It is enough to read the *New York Times* or *Le Monde* to find, from time to time, shocking examples of complete lack of attention to the distress of others. There is something rotten in a city where a killer may injure his victim, stop to hide when the latter screams—awakening many people who open their windows and listen to the appeals for help—may return to the victim and hit him again, retreat once more, and, after a while, finally achieve his murder without any of the witnesses having taken the trouble to call the police. There is something rotten in a city where a physician refuses to leave his home to render assistance to the victim of a traffic accident. Yet such behavior has recently been observed in the United States and in France and, in fact, can be found nearly everywhere.

Behavior of this kind should be of concern to the jurist. It is true that a change in men's hearts cannot be ordered by legislation. Law is even powerless to oblige all citizens to behave according to the requirements of ethics, even when there is unanimous agreement in the community on some of these requirements. However, it is the duty of the jurist to bring the law closer to the unequivocal requirements of ethics, when these requirements can be enforced without an unduly heavy process. Furthermore, re-

* Professor of Law, University of Paris.

cent developments in the United States have demonstrated the extraordinary sway of the law as a shaper of opinion. The law can help to awaken public opinion to the requirements of justice and even to the requirements of ethics.

This having been said in well-deserved tribute to Professor Rheinstein and Professor Kaplan, who organized the Chicago colloquium, and to the Sentry Insurance Company which supported it, further tribute should be paid to them for having had the idea of considering this matter with a comparative approach. The past has shown how fruitful it can be to consider foreign experiences. The value of the 1933 *Securities Act* and of the 1934 *Securities Exchange Act,* for instance, has now not only gained world-wide recognition but has also given an impetus to world-wide improvement of the law of corporations. Reciprocally, the study of continental experience with the law of the Good Samaritan may perhaps prompt similar legislation in the United States. The writer must, however, proffer his apologies for the narrow field of his report. He will discuss mainly French law, and only incidentally other continental laws.[1] Since the relationship of law to behavior must be studied, only teamwork would have permitted a larger field to be covered. On the other hand, French experience may be of particular value, for a number of reasons. It may be the one which, on the whole, gives the greatest encouragement to the Good Samaritan. Furthermore, a statute creating a duty to rescue has been law for twenty

[1] On German law, see Dawson, "Rewards for the Rescue of Human Life?" *infra,* pp. 63–89. On Soviet law, see Hazard, "Soviet Socialism and the Duty to Rescue" in *XXth Century Comparative and Conflicts Law. Legal Essays in Honor of Hessel E. Yntema,* 160 (1961). Presently, the Penal Code of the RSFSR makes it a crime to fail to rescue a person in danger (Article 127), a sick person (Article 128), or shipwrecked persons (Article 129). The Civil Code of the RSFSR provides for indemnities to the person who has acted in someone else's interest in a case of emergency (Article 449, Par. 2) and to the person who has spontaneously protected socialist property (Article 472).

years—a period which gives some range of experience and at the same time permits the statute's entire history to have been observed by a man in middle life.

Since a statute of 1941, amended in 1945, imposes upon citizens, under criminal sanction, the duty to rescue, it appears appropriate to consider this statutory duty in the first part of the report. The second part will be devoted to the civil consequences of a failure to rescue and of a rescue, as the case may be. The third part of the report will attempt to assess the impact of the law on social behavior in this field.

I THE DUTY TO RESCUE

Under the original provision of the French Penal Code, no criminal sanction was incurred by a person who failed to rescue somebody else. A mere omission could never be punished, even in shocking circumstances. A certain number of cases are well known. In one of them, the brother of an insane person allowed the latter to die for want of care and food. In another, a servant knew that the wife and the son of his master had tried to poison the latter and that they would try again, and yet he gave him no warning. In a third case, somebody's servants did nothing to prevent a killer from performing his crime. In all these cases the courts declared themselves powerless to impose any criminal sanction.[2]

Such decisions may have been dictated by principles of interpretation of penal law. They were hardly commendable. From a philosophical point of view, it does not appear possible to distinguish between the man who does something and the man who allows something to be done, when he can interfere. Such a distinction would disregard the liberty of man, his freedom of choice, his creative

[2] See Marcel Reynaud, *"L'Omission de Secours en Droit Pénal"* (1945); H. et L. Mazeaud et A. Tunc, *Traité Théorique et Pratique de la Responsabilité Civile Délictuelle et Contractuelle,* 5th ed., Vol. I, 1957, No. 526.

power, his "engagement" in the world and among other men. A stone does not bear any liability if a murder is committed beside it; a man does. By his decision not to interfere or to intervene, he participates in the murder.

The duty to rescue was recognized by some European legislation, which imposed criminal sanctions as early as the middle of the nineteenth century. The Netherlands, for instance, incorporated it in its legislation in 1866. However, the greatest movement of recognition occurred between 1925 and 1935. At present the duty to rescue seems to be imposed in most European countries, whether Western or Eastern, most recently in Belgium in 1961. In France, the recognition of the duty to rescue occurred late and under tragic circumstances. In 1941, after fifty hostages had been killed as a reprisal for the murder of a German officer, a statute was passed on October 25, obliging citizens to intervene for the prevention of crimes and the rescue of persons in danger.[3]

After the Liberation, the government, by an Ordonnance of June 25, 1945, declared the 1941 statute void, but made new rules which were really improvements to, and not a repudiation of, the 1941 rules. The 1945 provision may be found in Articles 61, 62, and 63 of the Penal Code. They have hardly been changed since their introduction. Article 63 was only slightly amended by a statute of April 13, 1954, which provided for more severe penalties.[4]

Some of these provisions are of small interest to us,

[3] For a comparative study of the duty to rescue, see: Note, "The Failure to Rescue: A Comparative Study," 52 *Col. L. Rev.* 631 (1952); Dawson (*supra*, note 6); Reda Ahmed, *"L'Omission de Porter Secours en Droit Comparé"* (Paris thesis, 1954). *Adde:* Penal Code of Belgium, Article 422 *bis*, added by a statute Jan. 6, 1961; Penal Code of the RSFSR, Article 127, 128, 129 (*supra*, note 1).

[4] See Dalloz, *"Répertoire de Droit Criminel,"* Vol. I, v⁰ *Abstention Délictueuse*, by L. Hugueney, and annual *Mise à Jour;* Goyet, *"Droit Penal Special,* 7th ed. by Rousselet and Patin, Nos. 227 et s., (1958).

protection of property, for instance, in the case of a fire or of a threat of fire.

A Before the 1941 and 1945 statutes, the question whether mere omission was a civil tort, giving the victim a right to damages, had been the subject of much discussion. In a decision made in 1924, the French Supreme Court (*Cour de Cassation*) stated that "if everybody is liable for his negligence, mere omission can justify liability only to the extent to which the person to whom it is imputed had a duty to accomplish the fact which has been omitted." Even after this *dictum,* the law remained, to a great extent, uncertain.[5] The circumstances in which such a duty was to be recognized were open to question. The effect, and perhaps even the aim, of the dictum of the *Cour de Cassation* was to imply that failure to perform a mere moral duty could not be considered as a civil tort. On the other hand, there was an indisputable duty to accomplish the fact omitted, when the duty was a statutory one. But such a duty could certainly also be a professional one, and there the matter was open to discussion.

The impact of the 1941 and 1945 statutes on the civil consequences of a failure to rescue was twofold.

First, when the failure to rescue constitutes a crime, it can no longer be disputed that civil liability is incurred. The person who could have rescued the victim and did not do so must pay for the consequences of his failure. Of course, the causal connection between tort and damage does not appear here in its usual setting. Even before the law was passed, however, it could already be strongly argued, on the basis of human liberty, that such causal connection existed.[6] Since causal connection is now undisputed in the application of penal law, it can no longer be disputed in the application of civil law.

Furthermore, the change in criminal law has brought with it a larger change in attitude toward omission. A number of cases have led to broader *dicta* than that of

[5] 1 Mazeaud-Tunc, No. 544.
[6] 1 Mazeaud-Tunc, No. 527.

1924. It is now recognized that the criterion of fault in cases of omission, as well as in cases of commission, is behavior different from that of a reasonable man, careful and mindful of others, in similar circumstances. Therefore, even when circumstances are such that a failure to rescue does not constitute a crime, civil liability will be incurred whenever it is the judgment of the court that a reasonable man, careful and mindful of others, would have acted and, as the case may be, would have rescued the victim or prevented the damage.[7]

B If we now assume that somebody faced with a man in need of rescue, or with a property threatened by fire, has acted like the Good Samaritan, or has done the work of a fireman, three sets of problems may arise from a point of view of civil liability.

1 The Good Samaritan may be accused of mistaken behavior, having brought harm to the rescued person. It may be a mistake to place a man with a broken leg on the back of a mule. It may even be a mistake to place such a man in a normal car. Nowadays, it is considered wiser, at least in normal circumstances, just to call an ambulance.

The Good Samaritan is fairly well protected from such reproach under French law. A great number of cases have decided that circumstances should be taken into account in judging his behavior. Of course, good will in itself is no justification. The French fabulist, La Fontaine, has illustrated the danger of stupid friends, and a really stupid Good Samaritan might incur civil liability. However, if the Good Samaritan has given medical treatment to the victim, the courts will not compare his behavior with that of a physician, but with that of an ordinary man.[8]

This choice of criterion is not the only protection he is afforded by the law. The courts will take into considera-

---

[7] 1 Mazeaud-Tunc, No. 544. (For the last cases, see the 6th ed., published in Fall 1965).

[8] 1 Mazeaud-Tunc, No. 429, referring to Ferdinand F. Stone, "Tort Doctrine in Louisiana: The Concept of Fault," 27 *Tul. L. Rev.* 1, 11–12 (1952).

tion the emergency conditions under which he has acted, and the emotion created within him by this emergency—an emotion which may excuse some mistakes.[9]

Among recent cases, attention may be drawn to the decision of the Paris Court of Appeal of June 27, 1964.[10] At a circus, during the performance, a person suffered a heart attack. There was no physician and a mere nurse went to help him and gave him some injections. The asepsis was not perfect and the person, although he recovered from the heart weakness, developed an abscess. He brought action against the circus and against the nurse. The Court of Appeal sustained the action against the circus for its failure to have a physician, but dismissed the action against the nurse. The reason was the following: "Unforeseen circumstances, in which the nurse was brought to intervene in the absence of a physician, and which gave her the feeling that she should try to do something and do it immediately, do not permit her intervention to be considered a fault, even if the future has shown that it was imperfect."

Finally, if the Good Samaritan is a physician, he is relieved, by the particular circumstances, of his normal duty to obtain the consent of the patient or of his family before giving medical treatment. This dispensation is so obviously justified that it is hardly mentioned in the judicial decisions.[11]

2 The Good Samaritan may have suffered some damage or incurred some expense in his attempt to rescue a

[9] 1 Mazeaud-Tunc, Nos. 488 et s., esp. No. 496; Dalcq, *"Traité de la Responsabilité Civile,"* Vol. I, Nos. 351 et s., (1959). Cpr. Nguyen Xuan Chanh, *"La Notion de Faute de la Victime en Droit Français et en Droit Anglo-Saxon Comparés,"* 1 the *Asian Comparative Law Review* 257, 274–277 (1963). Cpr. also, in the case of damage suffered by the rescuer, the dictum in Civ. 2e civ. 11 juill. 1962, D. 1963. 40 note Azard, *Gaz. Pal.* 1962.2.282, *Rev. Trim. Dr. Civil* 1963.358 note Tunc.
[10] J.C.P. 1964. II. 13893 note Esmein, *Gaz. Pal.* 1964.2.424.
[11] See, however, *Journal des Tribunaux,* 1965, p. 130.

person or to protect a property. Tw
must still be considered.

It may be that the damage was br
ness or stupidity of the Good Sa
Good Samaritan should then bea
the damage or the expense. Ho
rightly, will again consider the circu
of the Good Samaritan should not
which would have been possible
of the circumstances.[12]

Assuming that the Good Samarit
for clumsiness, our courts will a
demnity. They can do so on three

First, when the person who ne
for it or accepts it, our courts fin
an implied contract, under whic
rescue or help undertakes to inde
contract is implied in any kind o
cases of rescue but also when so
cepts assistance, for instance, for
mud or the ditch.[13]

Furthermore, when the need f
result of a fault, the damage suf
gives help is considered the cons
other words, the act of helping
connection between the fault an
the helper.[14]

[12] Riou, *"L'Acte de Dévouemen*
Droit Civil, 1957, p. 221 et s., No
1499; 1 Dalcq, Nos. 351 et s. (*supr*
Civ. 2e. civ. 11 juill. 1962 (*supra,*
[13] Civ. 1er civ. 27 mai 1959,
J.C.P. 1959 II. 11187 note Esmein
aud, *Rev. Trim. Dr. Civil* 1959.73
D. 1962. som. 131, *Gaz. Pal.* 1962
Trim. Dr. Civil 1963.327; Civ. 2e
[14] 2 Mazeaud-Tunc, Nos. 1499,
20); 1 Dalcq, Nos. 351 et s. (*su*
et s.; Tunc, note D. 1956.354; Go

An interesting example is provided by a case decided by the Paris Court of Appeal on April 18, 1955.[15] A truck, through the negligence of its driver, was hit by a train and pushed along the railway track for a distance of about a quarter of a mile. While the truck was on the track, two passers-by, who had seen the accident and who thought that the truck driver might still be in his cabin, decided that he should be rescued immediately, before another train came along, and therefore went up alongside the truck. At that moment, another train coming from the opposite direction and hidden from their view by the truck hit the latter once more. The truck, in turn, hit the two rescuers and killed them. The Court of Appeal considered that the widows of the rescuers had an action against the driver of the truck, who came out of the adventure quite safely, and against his employer.

In order to understand the importance of this ground for action, one must bear in mind the interpretation given to Article 1384, Paragraph 1. Under this provision, everybody is liable for the damage caused by the thing which he owns or which is in his "custody," unless he can show that the damage was caused by an act of the victim or of a third party, or by a fortuitous event. Therefore, whenever an accident is caused by the intervention of a thing, the owner or "custodian" of that thing bears the presumption of liability and, in most cases, has to indemnify the rescuer for the damage he has suffered.[16]

Assuming that the rescuer or the helper cannot base an action either on the implied contract or on the tort of the

---

[15] D. 1956.354 note Tunc, J.C.P. 1955. II. 8774 note Esmein. See also Grenoble, 7 déc. 1959, D. 1960.213 note Goré.

[16] See, for instance: Civ. 2e civ. 11 juill. 1962 (*supra*, note 9). Compare the Swiss Statute of Road Traffic (1958), Art. 58, Para. 3: the owner of a car involved in a traffic accident must indemnify a rescuer. See Oftinger, *"L'Evolution de la responsabilité civile et de son assurance dans la législation suisse la plus récente,"* in Mélanges Offerts à René Savatier, p. 723 et s., 730 (1965). A similar provision may be introduced into French law.

person in need of rescue or help, he will still have an action of *negotiorum gestio*. According to this institution, the person who voluntarily interferes in the business of another person, the latter being unable to take care of himself, must be compensated for all damage suffered or all expenses incurred, whenever his intervention has been a useful one.[17]

As each of these bases for action is liberally construed, there is practically no case in which, at the present time, the courts will find themselves unable to indemnify the rescuer.

3   The third problem might raise greater theoretical difficulties than the second one but it occurs much more rarely. The Good Samaritan, in order to perform his duty, might use or destroy something which is the property of another person. He might even injure somebody—either the person who was about to commit a crime or a passer-by.

A first question is again whether the Good Samaritan has not committed some fault. It is clear that there is no fault involved in the infliction of injury or even death on somebody who was about to commit a serious crime, when this would have been inflicted by a reasonable man in the same circumstances. The question is one of proportion between the evil avoided and the evil committed.[18] When, however, a third party is a victim of the Good Samaritan, the courts are more prone to find a fault on the part of the Good

---

[17] See Amos and Walton's *Introduction to French Law*, 2nd ed. by Lawson, Anton and Neville Brown, 192–94 (1963); Dawson, Negotiorum Gestio: "The Altruistic Intermeddler," 74 *Harv. L. R.* 817, 1073 (1961). On the possibility of applying the rules of *negotiorum gestio* in the circumstances under discussion, see Dawson (*supra*, note 1); Riou, *op. cit.*, No. 21; 2 Mazeaud-Tunc, No. 1499. Cpr. Art. 95 of the Fundamentals of USSR Civil Legislation (1961), and Art. 449, Para. 2, and 472, of the RSFSR Civil Code (1964). In exceptional circumstances, the Good Samaritan might be able to base an action, against the rescued person or his insurer on unjust enrichment: see Riou, *op. cit.*, Nos. 20, 22.

[18] 1 Mazeaud-Tunc, No. 489.

Samaritan. This does not mean that he will always have to indemnify the third party. He will be discharged from any liability if he has acted according to the behavior of a reasonable man in similar circumstances. The injury suffered by the third party may, for instance, be the result of an unfortunate combination of circumstances. Or the Good Samaritan may have damaged the property of the third party, but may have acted to save a life or to prevent a serious disaster, such as a fire. In such circumstances, the third party may find it harder to obtain indemnification. Still, a certain number of courts may be open to a move not against the Good Samaritan but, as justice requires, against the beneficiary of the intervention.

No difficulty arises when the beneficiary of the intervention was in need of this intervention by reason of his own fault or by reason of a thing which was under his control, in which case Article 1384, Paragraph 1, may again be applied. Otherwise, the circumstances may justify an action on the basis of unjust enrichment or *negotiorum gestio.*

Finally, it is generally recognized that the normal rules of unjust enrichment can be enlarged in this case. The person who intervened to rescue may have been faced with conflicting duties. In order to perform some legal or moral duty, he may have been obliged to disregard some rule of the law. Such circumstances could justify another exception to the normal working of the rules of unjust enrichment, and a very broad application of them.[19] Some codes have considered it necessary to make special provision for these circumstances. For instance, Article 2045 of the Italian Civil Code of 1942 provides that, when somebody has caused damage which was necessary for his own protection or for the protection of somebody else, and when he had not created the danger in question and could not have avoided it otherwise, the victim of his damage may

[19] Pallard, *"L'Exception de nécessité en droit civil,"* Nos. 209, 210 (1949); 1 Mazeaud-Tunc, No. 488-2.

obtain an indemnity, the measure of which is left to the discretion of the judge.

Similarly, while Paragraph 1 of Article 449 of the RSFSR Civil Code of 1964 provides that, as a principle, the damage caused in case of emergency must be compensated by its author, still Paragraph 2 of the same article permits the court, considering the circumstances, to place the compensation upon the beneficiary of the intervention, or to exonerate from the compensation, entirely or in part, the author of the damage and the beneficiary of his action.

III   THE APPLICATION OF THE LAW
      AND ITS IMPACT ON SOCIAL BEHAVIOR

On paper, the French law appears satisfactory. What are its consequences in practice? This question is obviously much more difficult to answer than the others. However, by reading the court decisions and the newspapers, and by observing daily life, it is possible to give an answer that one can hope to be reasonably sound, even if it cannot be clear-cut or supported by statistics.

First, it appears that, even before the statutes of 1941 and 1945, the Good Samaritan was not uncommon. Certainly we are all prepared to be Good Samaritans, within limits. Very probably, we do not wish to be put to too much trouble, or to be led into too much expense for the sake of helping somebody else. But, as long as we are not too inconvenienced, we are ready to help; and French law did nothing to inconvenience the Good Samaritan.

The only complaints that were heard from Good Samaritans concerned administrative red tape and, exceptionally, police suspicion. Apparently it sometimes happened that somebody who had put an injured and bleeding person into his car—incidentally thus allowing his upholstery to be spoiled—and had rushed off with the feeling that a few minutes could make the difference between life and death for the injured person, would finally arrive at the hospital to be met by a placid doorkeeper who would refuse to admit the injured person without knowing his name and all the details which would enable him to fill in a form and establish who was going to pay for the medical care. Exceptionally, a Good Samaritan was even suspected by the police; in some cases it may have been unpleasant for him, but in no case, as far as we know, was a Good Samaritan jailed for somebody else's crime.

Anyhow, it does not seem that administrative red tape or police suspicion were ever strong deterrents to rescue. Today, at any rate, there are not any noticeable deterrents. The red tape has been eliminated, except perhaps in exceptional cases, and the police, if they have suspicions, work more discreetly to clarify the matter.

Against this background, one might think that the 1941 and 1945 statutes were almost useless. As a matter of fact, however, they seem to have received a surprising amount of application, particularly in the years following 1945. Unfortunately, it is not possible to be very specific in this connection. The observer may be misled by the fact that the law reporters, or even the newspaper reporters, paid special attention to the new statute and gave an account of nearly every decision made for its application. It would, therefore, be most interesting to know how many sentences of punishment were given immediately after the enactment of the law, and to consider whether the number of sentences decreased after some years of application. Unfortunately, the statistics published by the Ministry of Justice do not give any precise figures for the first ten years of application, and the figures published after that do not reveal any trend. One may remark, however, that in 1954 the French legislators considered it useful, as has already been said, to increase the penalties for the crime of failure to rescue.

If we are unable to detect a trend, we can at least give the figures for the application of the act, as they appear in the 1962 statistics of the Ministry of Justice. During the year 1962, a total number of 214,918 sentences were pronounced by the criminal courts, including 103,127 sentences to jail. The crime of failure to denounce a criminal

was responsible for only seven sentences to jail and for no
sentences to fine. Failure to rescue was responsible for
only fifty-two sentences to jail and twelve to fine. These
figures are perhaps higher than we should like them to be,
but they are really very small when compared with the
total number of sentences for 1962.

Another figure which should be mentioned is that concerning sentences for "hit-and-run" crimes (it should be
borne in mind that the crime is committed whenever
someone leaves the scene of a traffic accident, even when
nobody is hurt in the accident). Here the number of sentences seems to be unfortunately high: 986 sentences to
jail and 1,260 sentences to fine, *i.e.* a total of 2,246, or
slightly more than one per cent of the total number of
sentences for 1964. The number increases from year to
year in the statistics of the Ministry of Justice. However,
the number of sentences does not appear to increase faster
than the number of cars on the road in France. No trend,
therefore, is perceptible.

Turning again to the failure to rescue, it would be interesting to know the facts behind the figures. What kind
of people were sentenced? Why did they deserve punishment? What caused them to act as they did? The general
picture is very hard to give. On some occasions the provisions have been applied to classical cases of refusal to
rescue: an excellent swimmer, fishing or talking to friends
by a river, is told that somebody has fallen into the water
but refuses to go to the trouble of taking off his suit and
diving in. Sometimes a crime is incidental to another one:
a hunter shoots at somebody by mistake, but, having discovered his error, does nothing for the victim in order to
evade his liability. Sometimes also the provisions have been
applied to persons who, technically, cannot be sentenced
as accessories but, morally, are accessories to a crime.

Many other circumstances may explain the failure to rescue. In one case, for instance, somebody was being given a
free lift in a car. The driver hit a person on the road and
his passenger saw that he had done so. However, when
they both got out of the car at a restaurant a few miles

farther on, the passenger did not dare to call the police, even without giving his name, to tell them that somebody was lying in the road in need of help. Sometimes, to take another example, the failure to rescue may be explained by anger at the person in need of help—for instance, if he is a victim of his own drunkenness. In a recent case the family of a drunkard had refused to let him in when he came back home late at night. They wanted "to give him a lesson." On the following morning they found him dead at the door.

However, two sets of cases deserve special consideration: refusal on the part of a physician to answer an emergency call and failure to rescue somebody injured on the road.

More often than not, the question arises whether the law should be applied to physicians or nurses who have refused to give care to a patient. The defense of the physician or nurse may vary from one case to another. Usually, however, the physician explains that he was extremely busy at the time, or extremely tired, or even that he had flu or a cold, and that he had not understood that the patient was in urgent need of help. He underlines the fact that physicians receive many calls from patients, or relatives of patients, declaring that help is urgently needed, while, in fact, these patients could have waited without any danger, and the priority should have been given to others. Sometimes he also contends that the patient was not a regular client and that therefore he had considered that the rules of professional ethics prevented his taking care of him.

From a statistical point of view, the courts, in most cases, consider the defense of the physician to be a valid one. In fact, it is probably justified in most cases, at least when it relates to a failure to understand the measure of the emergency. It perhaps has less chance of being justified when it relates to the duty to abstain from taking the client of a colleague. One may suspect that a physician, particularly in a small community where everybody knows everybody, is irritated when he receives an inconvenient call from somebody who has never called him before—especially when the call occurs at night—and that, in such circumstances, he may not show the greatest willingness to rush to this patient, even when the latter is really in need of a physician and cannot reach his usual one. Recently a physician was jailed the day after he had refused to go, during the night, to the victim of a traffic accident—even though he maintained that he had been told an ambulance had already been called. The physicians of the region made very strong protests and their colleague was released a few days later.

Similar incidents, however, have had good results. The physicians of cities or parts of cities are now organizing themselves more and more, so that one or a few of them will always be available to answer emergency calls while the others enjoy the necessary rest.

As far as the rescue of traffic victims is concerned, the 1941 and 1945 statutes do not appear to have had much effect because there was no great need of a change in behavior. It is hard, therefore, to detect any real impact of these statutes on social behavior. At least it can safely be stated that French law, considered as a whole, is in no way a deterrent to Good Samaritan behavior in this field. Some factors outside law must, however, be mentioned, as they certainly have some bearing on social behavior.

Some of these factors make it easier than previously to be a Good Samaritan. For instance, the police are now well organized to render emergency assistance, and telephone booths are reasonably numerous. Therefore, even though the Good Samaritan may sometimes have to give some emergency aid to the victim of a traffic accident, he is told that, in many circumstances, if he is not a physician, the best he can do is to leave the victim where he is and just rush to call the police. This is certainly easier than putting a bleeding person into one's car.

Nevertheless, it has happened a number of times that a person injured in a car which has run into a tree has spent a long time without receiving any assistance, although many other cars have been passing. It is difficult to know exactly what explains such behavior. It seems that the accidents occurred without any witnesses. Later on, therefore, when

Rewards for the Rescue of
Human Life?

JOHN P. DAWSON*

Official sources of American law have done their best to
discourage Good Samaritans. The altruist who renders a
service to another, without request or authority and for
purely unselfish motives, is apt to be described in English
as "a mere volunteer" or, still worse, "an officious intermeddler" as a prelude to denying him all recovery. In
most of the legal systems of western Europe, on the other
hand, he will probably be described merely as "the manager of another's affair" and the impulse will be both to
praise and to reward him. The difference in terminology
reflects a considerable difference in attitudes. The difference is mainly due, of course, to the survival in western
Europe of the conception of *negotiorum gestio* that was
originally developed in Roman law and that the Anglo-
American common law has on the whole rejected.

The "management" of the affairs of others, as it appears
under modern legislation in western Europe, can take many
forms—the sale or leasing of another's property, discharging
his obligations, supplying support to his dependents, and
so on. Here I propose to concentrate on a single type of
unsolicited intervention, the preservation of human life.
Through this concentration one misses the wide sweep of
negotiorum gestio doctrines, the complex ways in which
they help to solve specific problems, and their effects on
the thought of whole societies in which mutual aid is declared by law an approved ideal. But there is some virtue
in selecting an intractable problem, which provides a severe
test of our basic convictions and marks most sharply the

* Professor of Law, Harvard University Law School.

contrasts in approach between Anglo-American law and the systems inspired by Roman law.

Emphasis will be placed mainly on German law,[1] though some incidental references will be made to Switzerland and France.

I   THE "EXPENDITURES" THAT ARE REIMBURSABLE

From the time of their earliest emergence in Roman law sources and through most of their later history the rules of *negotiorum gestio* were justified essentially by a moral ideal that placed a high value on disinterested service to others. But it is interesting to note that the discourse of lawyers for centuries was mainly concerned with aid or protection to economic interests. The preservation of human life or health was mainly discussed in connection with slaves or with support to dependents for which parents or husbands were primarily liable. It was not until the twentieth century that sustained attention was given to the broader question whether, in the absence of existing legal duty, we are keepers of our brothers' lives as well as of their property. When this question emerged, the rules of *negotiorum gestio* did not provide a ready solution.

[1] The decisions of the German Supreme Court as it was constituted until 1945 will be referred to here by the form of citation usually employed in Germany for the principal series: R.G.Z. for civil cases and R.G.St. for criminal cases. Similarly, the decisions of the Supreme Court of Western Germany since World War II will be cited B.G.H.Z. for civil cases and B.G.H.St. for criminal cases. The *Juristische Wochenschrift*, in which many decisions are reproduced, will be cited J.W. and the new series starting in 1947, the *Neue Juristische Wochenschrift*, will be cited N.J.W. Other German reports and periodicals will be referred to without abbreviation.

To avoid confusion, decisions of the Swiss Supreme Court will be cited by the full title of the principal series: *Entscheidungen des Bundesgerichts*. The principal series of French law reports will be cited by the usual abbreviations: D. for *Dalloz*, S. for *Sirey*, *Gaz. Pal.* for *Gazette du Palais*.

Negotiorum gestio did not originate as a branch of the law of unjust enrichment, though even in the classical period of Roman law there was some connection between them and the connection grew closer as time went on.[2] In the modern codified systems of Europe the closest connection of *negotiorum gestio* is with the law of mandate, which one can roughly translate as agency. Through express incorporation by reference the rules for mandate are made to govern the claim of the *gestor* for reimbursement. Where the activities of the *gestor* do not serve the principal's interest or conform to his "actual or probable will," the rules for restitution of unjust enrichment operate as a surrogate and any resulting enrichment can be recovered. But in the life-saving cases that will be considered here, it is only in cases of deliberate suicide that intervention by the stranger will not be likely to meet these tests. If they are met, the *gestor* is treated like an agent and he will have reimbursement for such "expenditure" (*Aufwendung*) as is necessary and appropriate.[3]

In Germany after 1900 the question first arose in situations where emergency aid was in fact requested, but without any prior bargaining that might define the limits of

[2] The connections developed by the mediaeval Romanists between *negotiorum gestio* and unjust enrichment are briefly sketched in Dawson, *Unjust Enrichment: a Comparative Analysis* 64–78 (1951).

[3] The relevant provisions of the German Civil Code are:
Article 683. If undertaking the management of the affair corresponds to the interest and the actual or probable will of the principal, the manager can demand compensation for his expenditure in the same manner as an agent . . .
Article 684. If the requirements of Article 683 are not met, the principal is obliged to surrender to the manager all that he has acquired through the management, in accordance with the legal rules for restitution of unjust enrichment. If the principal ratifies the management undertaken, the manager has the claims provided by Article 683.
Provisions similar in substance, though differently phrased, appear in the Swiss Code of Obligations Art. 422.

the liability assumed by the rescued person. A Reichsgericht decision of 1909 provides an example.[4] Here the defendant was a tavernkeeper whose right hand was crippled by rheumatism. Two tough-looking strangers had lingered late in his tavern and, as closing time approached, defendant asked two regular customers to stay on to help him in case any trouble arose. After closing time had been announced and the strangers refused to leave, defendant grasped one by the shoulder with the object of ejecting them both. Both attacked him and defendant, wounded in the ear, cried out: "I am wounded, throw them out." The regular customers, who had stayed on as he had requested, rushed to his aid and were severely wounded by defendant's assailants, using a knife and a beer glass as weapons. After the unwelcome strangers had been convicted of assault and sent to jail, the injured customers sued the tavernkeeper for indemnity for their injuries. But the Reichsgericht dismissed their action, reasoning as follows. Ordinary tort liability was clearly excluded, for the tavernkeeper was in no way at fault. The fact that physical injury was easily foreseeable should lead to the inference, not that he had guaranteed them against injury but that the intervenors were consciously assuming the risk of physical injury. Even if it were conceded that they were managing defendant's "affair," the sacrifice of their health or physical integrity was not an "expenditure" for which they were entitled to compensation. The court argued that "expenditure" within the rules for mandate meant (1) an *economic* outlay that (2) was *voluntarily* made. Physical injuries incurred in protecting the tavernkeeper were not only not an economic sacrifice but they were wholly unintended, for the last thing the plaintiffs desired was to be cut up by glass and a knife. The plaintiffs argued that by his call for help defendant had tacitly undertaken to indemnify them and that if he not intend this, good faith

---

[4] Reichsgericht, April 5, 1909, [1909] J.W. 311, no. 7. [*The Reichsgericht was the highest appellate court in Germany at the time of the decisions referred to in this article.* Ed.]

required that he make his intention clear in advance. But the court disposed of this by saying that a man in great danger who calls for help cannot be expected to enter any such formal disclaimers; his call for help is involuntary and no legal consequences one way or another should be attached to any such reflex action.

In a comment on this case one author criticized the distinction drawn between economic loss and physical injury to rescuers. He argued that if the customers of the tavernkeeper had had their clothing torn in the scuffle, if they had held up an umbrella instead of an arm to ward off a blow, the sacrifice would be economic. It would also be involuntary in the same literal sense, that the consequence was not planned and in itself was extremely unwelcome. But in all these cases it could be contended that the loss was caused inevitably by the rescuer's decision to attempt the rescue, a decision made of his own free choice. If claims for physical injury were to be rejected, some more persuasive ground was evidently needed than a narrow definition of "expenditure."[5]

In fact this narrow ground was soon abandoned in cases where the request for aid could be somehow construed as creating an express contract of mandate. A finding of fact that a mandate existed, if supported by some evidence, will ordinarily be exempt from review by the Reichsgericht. As a result, private persons were allowed in two cases to recover for physical injuries in aiding police officials, at their request, in apprehending (1) a criminal and (2) a dog infected with rabies. The lower courts had made unassailable findings of fact that the police officers in these cases had contracted on behalf of the cities that employed them to indemnify their helpers for all foreseeable injuries. But to support this result it was necessary for the Reichsgericht to hold as a matter of law that "expenditures" under the law of mandate could include physical injuries to the policeman's helpers, however reluctant the helpers may

---

[5] Hoeniger, *Hilfe in Lebensgefahr,* 35 Archiv fuer Buergerliches Recht 272 (1910).

have been to incur them.[6] From this it was not a very long step to the conclusion that, where a private person was killed in guarding a dangerous prisoner at a policeman's request, his surviving widow and children could recover from the state for loss of support. Again the result rested on express mandate and the only question was one of fact —could a tacit contract of indemnity be inferred from an express request by a police officer to a private person to assist him where great danger could be foreseen?[7] A broad reading of "expenditure" was then confirmed in another tavern-brawl case in 1937. Here a customer was allowed to recover for the loss of a finger which was bitten off by a drunk whom the tavernkeeper had asked the customer to exclude from the tavern.[8] All these cases rested on a theory of mandate, but the expanded conception of "expenditure" that they established could apply equally well to sacrifices or injuries incurred in the course of unsolicited intervention, since the Code used the same term (*Aufwendung*) for both.

[6] Reichsgericht, March 31, 1914, [1914] J.W. 676, no. 4; Nov. 28, 1918, 94 R.G.Z. 169. Similarly, Febr. 26, 1920, 98 R.G.Z. 195 (injuries to a private person in putting out a fire, after being called on for help by the local mayor). The contrary decision on quite similar facts, Nov. 19, 1928, 122 R.G.Z. 298, by a different Senate (the Sixth) did not return to a narrow reading of "expenditure" but emphasized the absence of fault in either mayor or city and concluded that the injured person's status as a volunteer fire-warden precluded any tacit guarantee by the state against injuries in performing his public duty.

[7] Reichsgericht, Dec. 20, 1924, [1927] J.W. 441, no. 7.

[8] Reichsgericht, Nov. 2, 1936, [1937] J.W. 152, no. 2. In Reichsgericht, Jan. 5, 1931, [1931] J.W. 3441, no. 10, the question whether an "expenditure" was involved was pushed aside, since the lower court had found a tacit agreement to indemnify a neighbor's son against injuries in lifting a horse.

II THE DUTY TO AID IN THE CRIMINAL LAW

In the meantime there had been important developments in the criminal law that had some relevance to the problems of civil liability. The German Criminal Code of 1871 had made it a criminal offense for a private citizen to disobey the police when they requested the citizen's aid "in cases of accident, common danger, or necessity."[9] By legislation of the Nazi regime in 1935 this provision was greatly expanded. Refusal of aid requested by the police was made merely a particular instance of a much broader crime, punishable by money fine without limit or imprisonment up to two years and defined as refusal of "aid in cases of accident, common danger or necessity where there is a duty to aid according to the sound feeling of the people" (*gesundes Volksempfinden*).[10] By an amendment of the German Criminal Code, Article 330c, adopted in 1953, the characteristically Nazi phrase, "the sound feeling of the people," was omitted as a standard and the wording was rearranged to read as follows:

> Whoever does not render help in cases of accident, common danger or necessity although help is required and under the circumstances is exactable, and in particular is possible without danger of serious injury to himself and without violation of other important (*wichtige*) duties, will be punished by imprisonment up to one year or with money fine.[11]

[9] Criminal Code Art. 360, no. 10.

[10] Law of June 28, 1935, [1935] *Reichsgesetzblatt* I. 842. The phrase *gesundes Volksempfinden* was of course a favorite expression of National Socialist mysticism. It was used in another well known clause in the same enactment, the amendment to Article 2 of the Code (*id.* I. 839), which authorized extension of rules of the criminal law by analogy, wherever the offense, though not previously punishable, deserved punishment according to the *gesunde Volksempfinden*.

[11] Kohlrausch & Lange, *Strafgesetzbuch mit Erläuteraungen*

It is a point of considerable interest that similar legislation
has been adopted in most of western Europe. In Holland
as early as 1886 the Criminal Code provided for imprisonment up to three months and money fine up to 300
florins for one who refused aid to a person "in danger of
death" if aid could be given "without reasonable fear of
danger to himself or another" and if the death of the person in distress followed.[12] Similar provisions for criminal
liability for refusing aid to persons "in peril" or "in danger of death" were adopted in Turkey in 1926, in Italy
in 1930, in Poland in 1932, in Denmark, Rumania, Norway, Portugal, and Russia.[13] The draft proposals of 1934
for revision of the French Criminal Code included a

605–6 (4th ed. by Lange 1956), gives the text with a brief
historical account.

[12] Dutch Penal Code Art. 450 (Tripels, *Les codes neerlan-
dais* 726 (1886)), translated in Seavey, Keeton & Keeton, *Cases
on Torts* 157 (1957). Article 446 (Tripels 725) also provided a
money fine of not more than twenty-five florins for one who
refused assistance demanded by public authorities in cases of
"danger to the general security of persons or property" or in
cases of flagrant delict where assistance could be given without
"immediate danger." These provisions are discussed in 2
Noyon, *Het Wetboek van Strafrecht, verklaard* 671, 681 (6th
ed. 1954).

[13] Turkish Criminal Code Art. 476 ("wounded or otherwise
in danger of his life"); Italian Criminal Code Art. 593
("wounded or otherwise in peril"); Polish Criminal Code Art.
247 ("in a situation directly endangering life"); Danish Criminal Code Art. 253 ("evident peril to life"); Rumanian Criminal
Code Art. 489 ("in danger of death"); Norwegian Criminal
Code Art. 387 ("evident and immediate danger of death");
Portuguese Criminal Code Art. 2368. The Norwegian and Portuguese provisions appear in Cohin, *L'Abstention Fautive en
Droit Civil et Pénal* 252–53, 256 (Paris thesis, 1929). The
Portuguese provision applies only to cases of the person in dan-
ger who has been "attacked with violence."

The effects of Russian legislation are discussed by Hazard,
Soviet Socialism and the Duty to Rescue, appearing in this
volume at page 160.

clause authorizing criminal punishment of a person who could, "without prejudice or risk to himself or his near relatives," give aid to a person in peril if this person for lack of aid has died or suffered serious bodily injury. This clause was not adopted in France until 1941, and it was then included as one of a group of measures introduced by the Vichy government under pressure of the German occupying forces in France.[14] But again, as in Germany, when the matter was reconsidered by the French government after liberation from the Nazis, legislation of 1945 retained these basic provisions, with penalties reduced but with coverage extended.[15]

One question inevitably raised by legislation of this kind is whether the standard of conduct defined by the criminal law is carried over to the law of tort so as to permit recovery of damages against the person who commits a crime in refusing aid. I have found no German decisions that permit this translation of criminal into civil liability.[16]

[14] The Law of Oct. 25, 1941 appears in [1942] D. Législation 33. Article 4 contains the provision on the duty to aid. The history is discussed by Tunc in [1946] D. Législation 33 and Magnol, [1946] *Semaine Juridique* I. 531. A review of the French legislation and decisions applying it appears in Note, *The Failure to Rescue: A Comparative Study,* 52 Col. L. Rev. 631 (1952).

[15] Article 63 of the Criminal Code, introduced by decree of June 25, 1945. The text is given in [1947] D. Législation 130. Imprisonment up to three years and fine up to 50,000 francs are provided for one who "voluntarily abstains from giving to a person in peril assistance that he can give without risk to himself or to third persons either by his own action or by securing aid." This provision omits the previous requirement that the person in need shall have lost his life or incurred serious bodily injury for lack of aid.

[16] In the systematics of the German Civil Code the question is whether Article 330c of the Criminal Code is a "protective law" within the meaning of Article 823(2), Civil Code, which allows damages for violation of "a law whose purpose is the protection of another person." In a discussion heavily impregnated with Nazi philosophy, Weimar, *Schadensersatzpflicht bei*

In one trial court decision in France, however, the accused in a criminal case had walked away from the scene when his son-in-law fell through ice into a deep canal. The accused also refused, despite the son-in-law's "peril of death," to join with a third person in handing out to him a nearby iron bar to which the son-in-law might cling. For this unkindness, excessive even in a father-in-law, the accused was sent to jail for three years. But the son-in-law had apparently managed to scramble out of the icy water, for he appeared in the action as *partie civile* and recovered 25,000 francs from his impervious father-in-law.[17] The general conclusion that the standards of the criminal law define fault for the purposes of damage liability has the strong support of the leading modern French authors on tort liability.[18] It may be, therefore, that through the indirect route of the criminal law French courts will reach a solution of the problem, much discussed in our own law, of tort liability for refusal of aid in emergencies.[19]

The problem with which we are now concerned, however, cannot be resolved merely by reverting to the standards of the criminal law or the law of tort. The problem is—what should be done if the rescuer complies with duty or

---

Schädigungen durch Unterlassen, [1937] Deutsches Recht 77, argued that Article 330c was a "protective law" but without citation of any decisions. One small clue is that the standard commentaries on the Civil Code, such as those of the "Reichsgerichtsräte" (10th ed., 1953), Soergel (8th ed. 1952), and Palandt (19th ed. 1960), do not list Article 330c among the "protective laws" in their discussion of Civil Code Art. 823(2).

[17] Aix Trib. Corr., March 27, 1947, [1947] D. 304. But in Bethune Trib. Corr., Oct. 19, 1950, [1951] *Semaine Juridique* II. 5990, difficulties in proving causation led to denial of damage recovery to a husband whose wife had died in childbirth after the accused, a physician, had delayed for 3¼ hours in attending her. The accused was convicted for refusing aid but the court could not find that she would have lived if the accused had come promptly.

[18] 1 H. & L. Mazeaud & Tunc, *Traité de la responsabilité civile*, no. 526 (5th ed. 1957).

[19] Harper & James, *The Law of Torts*, § 18.6 (1956).

rises beyond the limits of duty and in the effort incurs some sacrifice? Should altruism be its own reward and should the rescuer himself assume all the risks? In one's approach to these extremely difficult questions one cannot ignore the value judgments that are expressed in the criminal law. It seems unlikely to me that in the United States we will seek to express our own sense of the value and promise of human life by invoking the sanctions of the law of crime. Yet it is a most impressive fact that in the largest part of free western Europe the duty to aid in the saving of human life and health is now enforced by the criminal law. It may well be that the thought and aspiration that have clustered around the ancient heritage of *negotiorum gestio* had some part in preparing the minds of Europeans for these extensions of the criminal law. Lacking this heritage, we may suffer from defective vision. The problem of the self-sacrificing rescuer will be troublesome whatever may be the state of the criminal law; some civil remedy might be awarded even though the criminal law had laid no duties upon him. But in countries where the refusal of aid has become a crime, there has clearly been some added pressure toward finding a remedy for the person who complies with or exceeds his duty.

III   THE RESCUER AS UNSOLICITED "MANAGER"

The incident that produced the great German case on the subject occurred on July 7, 1939.[20] One B. was driving a car in which defendants, husband and wife, were passengers. B. drove off the road and in his effort to return to the road caught the wheels in a gutter, with the result that the car drove off an embankment into a stream that was fifteen feet deep. The men in the car succeeded in escaping and reaching the bank; but Frau Bl., one of the two defendants, though she escaped from the car, could not swim and had difficulty keeping her head above water. She cried loudly for help and was heard by two persons who were at work

[20] Reichsgericht, May 7, 1941, 167 R.G.Z. 83.

nearby. Both hurried up and one of them, G., sprang into the water. He held up Frau Bl. long enough for the driver of the car to return to the water and rescue her, but G. then drowned. The action was brought by the widow and children of G. to recover for loss of the support of their deceased husband and father. They asked for the widow a life annuity of 720 marks a year and for each of the children, until their eighteenth year, 120 marks a year. The trial court and the intermediate court of appeal declared that the action against the two defendants, Herr and Frau Bl., was in principle well founded.

The intermediate court of appeal started from the premise that the call for help by Frau Bl. was not an offer of agency and had in itself no legal consequences. With this the Reichsgericht agreed, citing the tavernkeeper case that has already been referred to.[21] The court of appeal also concluded that the rescuer, G., had managed the "affair" of both the rescued person and her husband, that his action conformed to the interest and probable will of both, and that both defendants were therefore jointly liable to reimburse the rescuer for his "expenditure." Again the Reichsgericht agreed, saying that it must ordinarily be taken for granted that a husband will approve measures necessary to save his wife's life; still more must this be true of the wife herself. No difficulties arose from the fact that G. himself did not actually accomplish the rescue, since his intervention was useful in holding up Frau Bl. until the driver of the car could reach her. The problem came in finding some Code or statutory provision which could determine the measure of recovery. The court of appeal used two theories, somewhat intermingled: (1) a tacit agreement to indemnify, of the kind that could be inferred in cases of express mandate, and (2) the "idea of community" that underlay the duty-to-aid provision of the amended Criminal Code (Article 330c). From the second theory it followed that recovery by G.'s survivors should not be conceived as damages but as an "equitable indem-

21 Cited *supra,* note 4.

nity" or adjustment governed by standards of good faith (Article 242, Civil Code). The Reichsgericht rejected both these modes of analysis, saying as to (1) that there was no room for implication of a promise to indemnify where the intervention was for legal purposes wholly unsolicited, and as to (2) that the provisions of the amended Criminal Code could not be carried over for this purpose. The Reichsgericht concluded that the remedy to be awarded rested precisely and exclusively on the Code provisions for *negotiorum gestio*.

This made the problem in some respects harder, for the plaintiffs had demanded annuities of the type provided by the Code for the survivors of person wrongfully killed through the defendant's fault and no fault existed in the present defendants. The Reichsgericht pointed out, however, that the course of decision in express mandate cases had already enlarged the concept of "expenditure" to include sacrifices of health and physical integrity. The rules for reimbursement of agents in the Code section on mandate were expressly incorporated by reference in the Code sections on *negotiorum gestio*. The result was that there existed a "gap" in the Code, and it was necessary to carry over by analogy the wrongful death provisions, with their specific rules for annuities to survivors, despite the absence of fault in the defendants. (Incidentally, it should be noted that there appeared nowhere in the case a finding that B., the driver of the car, had been negligent, and the effects of his possible liability were not considered.) The court justified the analogical extension of the wrongful death provisions by arguing that any other result would contradict good sense. For if the rescuer, G., had lived but had suffered some physical injury the decisions in the express mandate cases had committed the court to awarding him full indemnity. "It is unthinkable that merely because he has made the greater sacrifice of his life, the defendants should be free from all duty of indemnity."

The Reichsgericht then tangled with another problem, which has some interest of its own. By a statute passed in 1928 accident insurance had been made payable to any

person who was injured when, "without being legally
obligated to do so, he saves or undertakes to save another
from present danger to life, with danger to his own life,
body or health."[22] This provision had been amended and
somewhat expanded in 1939.[23] The object of such legislation was plainly to cast on the public insurance system
liability for injuries incurred by persons who performed
such acts of self-sacrifice, even though they were not engaged at the time in working in an insured occupation.
But there was the added difficulty that by another provision of the social insurance legislation the public insurance
system was subrogated to the rights of the insured person
against the person liable, to the extent of the payments for
which the public system became responsible.[24] Did this
subrogation provision apply (the court of appeal thought
it did not) and if it did, would it leave any margin for recovery in the present action? The Reichsgericht concluded
that it did apply, that the plaintiffs therefore could not
recover from defendants for support to which plaintiffs
were entitled from the public insurance system, but that
since public insurance would often fail to cover the full
amount of impaired earning capacity or (here) loss of
support, plaintiffs could recover in this action the margin
of difference, if any could be shown to exist. In net result,
the rescued woman and her husband were left with a joint
obligation to maintain the rescuer's widow and minor children (up to the age of eighteen years) and the claims to
enforce this obligation were merely split between the state

[22] *Reichsversicherungsordnung* Art. 553(a), added by Law of
Dec. 20, 1928, [1928] *Reichsgesetzblatt* I. 405–6.

[23] Law of Febr. 17, 1939, [1939] *Reichsgesetzblatt* I. 267,
amending *Reichsversicherungsordnung* Art. 553(a). Accident
insurance was made available to those who acted "without
special legal duty" and to those who were injured giving aid to
public officers or in the pursuit or apprehension of criminals
whose crimes were serious enough to justify imprisonment as a
sanction.

[24] *Reichsversicherungsordnung* Art. 1542.

and the rescuer's dependents, but not reduced, by the availability of social insurance.

It seems unlikely that the rescuer, G., in the case just described could have been convicted of the crime of refusing aid if he had not jumped into the water in an attempt to save Frau Bl. The question would be whether there was "danger of serious injury" to himself in the attempt. Something might depend on whether he had in fact had training in life-saving techniques, for if he had not there would surely be considerable danger in coming within the reach of a terrified person unable to swim and about to drown. If the criminal law did impose such a duty, the question might arise whether G. was managing "his own" rather than defendants' affair so that all recovery would be excluded. An author who considered this argument rejected it emphatically.[25] There certainly have been many decisions holding that if the action taken is "for" another, an element of self-interest or obligation on the side of the intervenor does not exclude *gestio*. On the other hand, where the dominant purpose is to promote some purpose or advance some interest of the intervenor himself, the device of labelling the action "his own," not another's, has been quite often used in other *gestio* situations.[26] Where the matter stands now in Germany is not altogether clear. The decision of the Reichsgericht in 1941 in the case of

[25] Feaux de la Croix, *Die Entschädigung bei Hilfeleistung in Not- und Unglücksfällen,* [1939] J.W. 457.

[26] For example, where the nominee of a political party sought to recover for his campaign expenditures against the officers of the party that had nominated him: Reichsgericht, Nov. 25, 1907, [1908] J.W. 37, no. 11; where lessees had made alterations of the leased premises to adapt them to the lessees' own needs: Oberlandesgericht Celle, Febr. 28, 1912, 27 *Rechtsprechung der Oberlandesgerichte* 143; Braunschweig, June 25, 1920, 41 *id.* 113; where a landowner repaired a collapsed storage dam and then sought to recover a share of his costs from the owner of a nearby mill who was a joint user of the water impounded by the dam: Reichsgericht, Jan. 3, 1934, 143 R.G.Z. 92.

the drowned rescuer was followed by an intermediate appellate court in a post-Nazi decision of 1949, involving an attempted rescue of an unconscious man from a pit that was filled with poisonous gas.[27] But the issues have been in part reopened by more recent cases in which recovery has been sought by automobile drivers for injuries to their automobiles in efforts to avoid collisions with children. In the most recent case of this kind that I have found, a court of appeal, faced with an action for damages against the child's parents, concluded that the driver did not act consciously to manage the parent's "affair" but responded to a reflex produced by his training; even if conscious thought was involved, the driver himself was under a duty to avoid a collision and might be civilly or criminally liable if he did not, so that the "affair" that he managed was the driver's "own."[28]

The critical question, if any civil remedy is to be awarded, is the measure of recovery. On this latter issue a Swiss decision throws some further light. The defendant in the case in question owned a dairy farm and employed the plaintiff to milk his cows. One evening defendant observed some marauders stealing wood from his wood lot and asked plaintiff to accompany him in pursuing the

[27] Oberlandesgericht Tübingen, Oct. 13, 1949, [1950] *Monatsschrift für Deutsches Recht* 160.

[28] Oberlandesgericht Koblenz, July 8, 1953, [1953] N.J.W. 1632. Discussing these cases, Roth-Stielow, *Haftung der Eltern für Verkehrsunfälle, die spielende Kinder verursachen*, [1957] N.J.W. 489, argues in general against liability of parents who are not shown to be at fault in supervising the children. He accepts the argument that for *negotiorum gestio* there must be a "voluntary sacrifice of economic value for a defined purpose," so that injury to the car or its occupants would not be an "expenditure." But he seems to end up with a distinction between injuries caused by a sudden stop and injuries caused by a "voluntary" decision to drive off the road with the result that the car hits some fixed obstacle. The psychology required for this distinction has not yet been worked out in the laboratories, so far as I know.

thieves. Plaintiff complied and was then attacked in the wood by the three thieves, received a knife wound in one eye, and lost the eye as a result. The court analyzed the case as a mandate, arising independently of the contract of employment. By the revision of the Swiss Code of Obligations, effective in 1912, the principal in cases of *negotiorum gestio* was made liable to reimburse the intervenor not only for his "expenditures" but for "other injuries to be assessed in accordance with the judge's discretion" (Art. 422, Code of Obligations). This amendment, for which there is no counterpart in the German Code, had not been inserted in the rules for mandate, but the court declared that this was an obvious oversight by the legislature which produced a "gap" that the court should fill. By calculating the impairment of plaintiff's earning capacity over the period of his life expectancy, plus the cost of a glass eye, the court reached a figure of 11,051 francs as the measure of plaintiff's loss. But the court concluded that defendant was not liable for this whole sum, since the parties incurred the danger together, "liability in the rendition of aid must stand in a reasonable relationship to the injury that is to be averted and in fairness should be much less where the injury arises in giving aid for the protection of property than when it is given in averting imminent danger to life." Under all the circumstances, the court concluded, the indemnity to plaintiff should be scaled down from 11,000 to 3,000 francs, so that defendant "will not be burdened in an amount exceeding his economic resources."[29]

[29] Bucher v. Lisibach und "Zürich" Allg. Unfall- und Haftvers. A.G., Bundesgericht, Dec. 13, 1922, 48 (II) *Entscheidungen des Bundesgerichts* 487. The court made nothing of the point that defendant, the employer, apparently carried liability insurance with an insurance company that was joined as defendant in the action.

A similar approach was used in the later case Wüest v. Haltiner, Bundesgericht, April 2, 1935, 61 (II) *id.* 95. Here the plaintiff was a farmer who climbed a tree of a neighboring farmer at the latter's request and suffered permanent injuries

This kind of discretionary adjustment, which is expressly authorized by the present Swiss Code, has been urged by authors in Germany, despite the absence of any similar provision in the German Code. In an interesting discussion in 1910 one writer argued that with sacrifices made in the salvaging of property, expenditures can be kept in some reasonable relationship to the interest served; if the expenditure is disproportionate the principal can say that the action did not correspond to his "interest" and he will then be liable only for his actual enrichment. But when salvage is attempted of human life and the sacrifice of the rescuer is of his own life or health, measurement in economic terms becomes extremely difficult. The author in question nevertheless proposed that economic factors be taken into account, in order to ensure that the person whose rescue was attempted is not burdened with a liability that exceeds his resources, so that after his life or health has been saved "life must seem no longer worth living."[30] A more recent author, relying on the analogy of maritime salvage, advocated an even more complex adjustment, in which account would be taken of the economic resources of both helper and victim, the degree of danger incurred, and the possibilities of recovery from third persons, including insurers.[31]

---

to his spine when the limb on which he was standing collapsed. The case was thought by the court to be mandate, probably gratuitous, and again Article 422 of the Code of Obligations (*negotiorum gestio*) was held applicable through judicial "gap-filling." There is no indication of plaintiff's ultimate recovery, but the lower court was directed, after estimating plaintiff's total injury, to fix "according to its fair judgment" the amount defendant must pay.

[30] Hoeniger, *op. cit. supra* note 5, at 275.

[31] Feaux de la Croix, *op. cit. supra* note 25, at 463. The maritime law of all Western countries allows recovery for successful efforts in saving vessels and their cargo that are in danger of loss at sea, with a limited provision for a reward for the salvage of human life. The law of maritime salvage is referred to in more detail later in this article.

That the French Court of Cassation is willing to take account of the availability of insurance is suggested by a decision in 1955. The case involved a car owned by one Hamoud, whose nephew, Boucif, was driving when the car turned over and caught fire. One of the passengers, Bensafi, pulled the driver, who was unconscious, out of the car but was himself so severely burned that he died soon thereafter. The widow of the rescuer sued for loss of support by herself and her children against the insurance company which had insured the owner of the car against liability. The Court of Cassation refused to set aside a judgment against the insurer which rested on the ground that the deceased rescuer was a "manager" of the insurer's affair. The Court of Cassation reached this result despite a clause in the insurance policy excluding any liability to members of the insured's family, a clause that included the rescued nephew. The court explained that the utility of *gestio* must be determined as of the moment it was initiated and it was enough that the owner might be liable to someone for injuries due to the burning of the car.[32] As critics of this strange decision have pointed out, it is difficult to conceive that in pulling an unconscious body out of a burning car, the rescuer was managing an affair of the insurance company, especially in view of the express limitation on its liability that the policy contained.[33] But earlier cases involving unsolicited efforts to stop runaway horses and a 1955 case involving *solicited* aid in extinguishing a fire indicate that French courts may be at least as willing as German courts to permit recovery under *gestio* doctrines against the rescued person himself, for personal injuries incurred by the rescuer in giving emergency aid.[34]

[32] Cie d'Assurances l'Union v. Bensafi, Cass. Civ., 1st. Ch., Nov. 16, 1955, [1956] *Semaine Juridique* II. 9087.

[33] The decision is criticized by Esmein in a note to the report, *supra* note 1; also by H. & L. Mazeaud, [1956] *Revue trimestrielle de Droit Civil* 356, and Riou, *L'Acte de dévouement*, [1957] *id.* 221, 237–43.

[34] Runaway horse cases: Trib. de Commerce de la Seine,

It thus appears that judicial decisions in Germany and France and perhaps also in Switzerland have opened some avenues for recovery by rescuers of human life, or by their dependents where the attempt at rescue proved fatal to the rescuer. In the cases in question it was assumed that there was no fault in the imperilled victim or in any third person in creating the peril that invited rescue; if there were such fault, presumably the law of tort could provide indemnity to the rescuer. In these cases it was also assumed that the rescuer was not a public officer who was required by the terms of his employment to incur personal risk in saving lives or property; if he were, different considerations would apply that need not be developed here. The essential question therefore is whether modern law should recognize a new kind of liability without fault, imposed on a private person (or his estate) who incurred imminent peril to life or health and whom another private person has attempted to rescue. In attempting to answer such a question, anyone must hesitate, for it provides a crucial test of our moral

---

April 1, 1936, [1936] 1 *Gaz. Pal.* 877, and same court, Jan. 3, 1900, [1902] S. II. 217, with a note in the latter case reviewing earlier decisions. In some of these cases the owners' fault in leaving the horses unattended might have provided an alternative ground.

Lille Trib. Civil, June 28, 1955, [1955] 2 *Gaz. Pal.* 413, allowed recovery for injuries through burning by a workman who was asked to assist in putting out a fire in a garage. The Court of Appeal of Poitiers, Nov. 28, 1952, [1953] *Semaine Juridique* II. 7565, held the owner of a truck liable for injury to the eye of the plaintiff, who helped the driver at his request to put stones under the truck in order to raise it from a ditch. The court adopted the view that had been urged by Savatier, *L'Etat de nécessité et la responsabilité civile extra-contractuelle*, in *Études de Droit Civil à la mémoire de Henri Capitant* 729, 741 (1939), that *if the rescue is successful* the rescuer can recover for all losses incurred as a result of the "state of necessity" in which the victim found himself, even without fault on his part. This decision was quashed for "lack of legal basis": Servouse v. Motillon, Cass. Civ., 1st Ch., March 21, 1955, [1955] *Semaine Juridique* II. 8714.

values and of the obligations of individuals to the community under the mounting perils of modern life.

IV   CONCLUSION

The first problem is whether the land-based rescuer should have a reward for the service itself—that is, the service of attempting rescue. It will be noted that in the life-saving cases above discussed no claim of this kind was even urged. Under the traditional rules of *negotiorum gestio* one difficulty comes from the close tie-in of *gestio* with mandate, which under the inherited Roman law tradition is presumed ordinarily to be gratuitous. In the case of mandate this presumption of course can be overcome by evidence of contrary intent. Where the service is by a highly trained professional—for example, a physician—the presumption will normally be reversed. In Germany, physicians whose intervention was considered to be justified under the rules of *gestio* have been allowed to recover at their usual rate.[35] Perhaps this notion could be extended to other kinds of "professionals," such as mountain guides whose services likewise are commonly paid for. But with rescuers of other kinds there are difficulties more serious than the restrictive effects of ancient tradition. How can one place a money value on the time, energy, and risk in carrying a body from a burning building or in extracting a drowning person from deep water, even if the rescuer is a professional life-guard? And if valuation were possible, there seems to be no compelling reason, in most of the cases that can be imagined, why the service itself should be rewarded. Here again one must hesitate, for the issue is crucial. Does the morality that

[35] Colmar, March 25, 1904, 8 *Rechtsprechung der Oberlandesgerichte* 343; Celle, Nov. 10, 1905, 12 *id.* 272. Compare Cotnam v. Wisdom, 83 Ark. 601, 104 S.W. 164 (1907), where a surgeon was found to be justified in intervening to save the life of an unconscious man injured in a street accident and was allowed to recover the reasonable value of his services in performing an unsuccessful surgical operation.

dictates mutual aid—morality that is perhaps reinforced by
the criminal law—also dictate payment for time spent and
risk incurred where the risk has not resulted in loss? At
least there has appeared no disposition in the European
sources I have consulted to reverse the presumption that
as to the service itself, aid given by non-professionals on
land will be considered to be gratuitous.[36]

Then if the problem is further narrowed to that of indemnifying the rescuer for loss to his person or property,
should the grant of indemnity be made to depend on success
—perhaps the limited kind of success that consists of keeping a drowning woman afloat until someone else can rescue her? As has already been pointed out, no such restriction is imposed by traditional doctrines of *gestio* or their
modern formulations in the European Codes. In maritime
law some degree of success is a prerequisite to recovery by
the salvor, either of property or of human life. But the
survival of this restriction in maritime salvage may be
partly explained by the common use of proceedings *in rem*,
in which liability is conceived to fall on the ship and cargo;
if nothing is saved there is nothing to which a maritime
lien can attach.[37] Perhaps such a restriction, by stimulating

[36] It is worth noting that Riou (*op. cit. supra* p. 154, note 2,
at 221) argues in general terms for the use of *negotiorum gestio*
and the *actio de in rem verso* in life-saving cases, but urges
merely indemnity for injuries to the person or the property of
the rescuer.

[37] The Brussels Convention on Salvage of Vessels at Sea,
which has been adhered to by all the principal maritime countries, is explicit in Article 2 that "Every act of assistance or
salvage which has had a useful result gives a right to equitable
remuneration. No remuneration is due if the services rendered
have no beneficial result." Article 741 of the German Commercial Code has a similar requirement. The American legislation that adopts the substance of the Brussels Convention is
discussed by Gilmore & Black, *The Law of Admiralty* 445-47
(1957).

By Article 753 of the German Commercial Code the salvor
is limited to a claim against the vessel or cargo rescued and
any personal liability of the owner is excluded. It should be

the acquisitive impulse, helps to ensure that the salvor will be more strenuous and heroic in his efforts than he would be otherwise. But surely this is the most that can be said in its defense. If the land-based rescuer voluntarily, or under compulsion of the criminal law, submits his own body or goods to the risk of loss or injury, there is no good reason why he should also assume the risk of failure. It should be enough to require that the measures used have a reasonable hope of success and that they be appropriate in meeting the apparent need—in the traditional language of *negotiorum gestio,* that the "management" be useful when begun and be conducted with due diligence.

And so we come to the ultimate, painful question—should the life-salvor on land have a civil remedy to reimburse him for his losses against the person whom he attempted by appropriate means to save from imminent peril, whether or not the attempt succeeded? My own answer is an inclusive no. To me the difficulty is not merely that American law has failed to adopt the generalizations of *negotiorum gestio;* for our own law of restitution, backward as it seems to most European observers, could be extended to fill at least part of this gap. Perhaps there would be no great injustice in allowing recovery against the victim for minor injuries to the person or property of the rescuer—medical care for frostbite suffered in a mountain rescue, or repairs to a car that is driven off the road to avoid colliding with a pedestrian. If the person rescued, inspired by gratitude, subsequently promises a reward or indemnity to his rescuer, it should be possible to find enough moral obligation to justify enforcement of the promise, even though the traditional tests of bargain consideration are not satisfied.[38]

---

noted, however, that under the Brussels Convention (Article 9), the German Commercial Code (Article 750) and U.S. legislation (Gilmore & Black, *op. cit. supra,* 471-73) the saving of human life gives rise to no claim unless it occurs in conjunction with the salvage of property.

[38] Webb v. McGowin, 27 Ala. App. 82, 168 So. 196 (1935); but cf. Harrington v. Taylor, 225 N.C. 690, 36 S.E. 2d 227 (1945).

But where no such promise has been made as a distinct ground and measure of liability, it seems grossly unjust that a drowning woman, herself without fault, should be required (jointly with her husband) to support the widow of the drowned rescuer for the rest of the widow's life, and the children of the rescuer until their majority. The injustice may be somewhat disguised by the fact that under standard German practice, employed in actions for *wrongful* death, the victim's liability is expressed in an instalment judgment and extended indefinitely over time. The dilemma remains—the claim of the rescuer or his dependents will become more appealing the greater the rescuer's sacrifice; but in the same degree it becomes more unjust to cast the whole loss on the imperilled victim, who was not at fault, who merely responded to the deep human impulse toward survival and called out for help. If any recovery at all is to be given, how can one frame doctrine that will award a little but not too much?

One solution, of course, is that employed in maritime salvage, to remit the whole matter to judicial discretion. This solution has been adopted in Switzerland, in cases that were technically analyzed as mandate but that were dealt with under the Code provisions for *negotiorum gestio*.[39] But this serves merely to transfer the problem without providing means for its solution. By what mathematics does one scale down the award—by measuring the degree of the rescuer's risk, the skill or clumsiness that he used, the usefulness to society of the life in peril? The test that has been most strongly urged has been the income and resources of the rescued person, so that the wealthy would reimburse for all losses incurred, middle-class victims would pay much less, and the impoverished victims would make merely token payments. The all-wise judge could also add to the equation the alternative remedies that the rescuer might have. The remedy could be called "subsidiary," like the *actio de in rem verso* in modern French

[39] See cases cited *supra*, note 29.

law[40]—to be awarded where no other remedies are available to the rescuer or to the extent that they fail to give full reimbursement. In that event the victim would be liable only if there was no adequate alternative remedy against third persons whose fault created the danger, against the state through social security payments, or against private insurers of rescuer or victim. If recovery were to be allowed, some such limitation would have much to recommend it, but again it would seem to add great complications without resolving the essential problem.

Are there other ways in which the costs of reimbursing rescuers can be more widely distributed or cast on others who are better able to pay than the imperilled persons themselves? The latter solution is in effect adopted in maritime salvage, where the claims for life salvage, insofar as they are allowed at all, are merged with the claims of the property salvors and normally become a charge on ship or cargo, thus indirectly upon the owner as one of the costs of his shipping enterprise. It is interesting to note that an American author, who urges more generous treatment of life salvors at sea, rejects the notion that the persons rescued should be personally liable; insofar as recovery is unavailable or insufficient under existing rules, he would create through new legislation a national fund from which grants to life salvors would be made by an independent executive agency.[41] But with life salvage on land, there will seldom be a specific fund or enterprise which can be made responsible for the rescuer's claim except, perhaps, where rescue of imperilled persons falls within the scope of employment of persons entitled to workmen's compensation. As to resort to the national treasury, it seems to

[40] 7 Planiol & Ripert, *Traité Pratique de Droit Civil Français* § 763 (2d ed., 1954); Goré, *L'Enrichissement aux Dépens d'Autrui* §§ 182–196 (1949).

[41] Jarett, *The Life Salvor Problem in Admiralty,* 63 Yale L. J. 779 (1954) (proposal for legislation that would follow and further extend the device of a national maritime fund set up by British legislation of 1894).

me unlikely that we shall follow the example of Austria and provide state funds from which grants can be made to saviors of life.[42] We would all applaud our great foundations if they gave not only Carnegie medals but cash awards to heroes or one could have recourse to the social security system, as in Germany whose legislation, already described, awards health, accident, and survivors' insurance at the normal rates to any person who "saves or undertakes to save another from present danger to life, with danger to his own life, body or health," even though the person who attempts the rescue is not employed in an insured occupation.[43] This seems, indeed, an attractive solution, for if mutual aid in the conservation of human life serves the interests of the community and even becomes a duty enforceable within limits by the criminal law, one feels a strong impulse to spread the cost over the widest possible group of contributors. But even this group is not large enough, for in truth the whole community should pay. In any event, our legislatures have so far been reluctant to include the costs of illness and disabling accident among the charges of the social security system, even for persons in insured occupations. It is not likely that in the near future these new claims will be recognized.

My own conclusion, nevertheless, is that private law remedies are misapplied when they create liability without fault in the person whose life or health is saved. Whatever merit they may have in other contexts, the doctrines of

[42] 2 (II) Klang, *Kommentar zum allgemeinen bürgerlichen Gesetzbuch* comment to Art. 1036, at p. 881 (1934), describes the Austrian legislation, initiated in the eighteenth century and expanded in the nineteenth. It gave a reward out of public funds where both victim and rescuer were in danger of their lives and the victim was saved from death by water, fire, or suffocation. The commentator (Swoboda) concluded that no satisfactory solution could be found through private law to the problem of indemnifying life salvors and that the earlier Austrian legislation providing grants from public funds should be preserved and extended.

[43] See the legislation referred to *supra* notes 22 and 23.

negotiorum gestio do not compel this result. The German decisions provide the main examples to date in which these doctrines have been applied, but I suggest that it was a purely mechanical operation to carry over the reasoning of the express mandate cases to those in which the intervention was for legal purposes wholly unsolicited. Even the extensions of the criminal law that have occurred in most of the NATO countries do not seem to me to affect this question. Perhaps it is right that the deviant individual who refuses aid when it can be rendered without serious risk should be punished by the criminal law and also made liable by the law of tort. But it seems to me a different question whether the one who conforms to or exceeds his duty should receive from another in desperate need either reward or indemnity for the aid he gives.

Perhaps this means that we must confess at this point a major failure of legal techniques. But I believe that even those who have the techniques—the doctrines of *negotiorum gestio*—should hesitate long before establishing rules of such broad reach and consequence. Remedies and doctrines of private law are ill adapted to measuring the value of human life. I see no compelling reason why they should be used to transfer the risks of our life together in a perilous world or to limit the price we all must pay for the privilege of being human beings.

The Duty to Rescue: A Comparative Analysis[1]

ALEKSANDER W. RUDZINSKI[*]

I INTRODUCTION

The duty to rescue has probably ceased to be regarded in this country as an interesting but exotic and largely academic topic—fit only for scholarly essays[2] and without practical legislative applicability. The impact on public opinion of the Genovese case and a series of similar incidents has been very strong. . . . The following remarks may therefore not be out of place. They try to present first an analysis of foreign criminal provisions regulating this difficult and controversial subject and secondly a brief discussion of the arguments militating for and against the introduction of similar legislation in this country.

In contrast to Anglo-Saxon law, which discourages interference in another person's affairs even for the purpose of saving him from imminent danger of death, thirteen European countries,[3] as of the end of the 1950s, had spe-

* Associate in Public Law, Columbia University.

1 This paper was written in the course of a research project on Comparative Communist Legal Systems headed by Prof. John N. Hazard and supported by a grant from the Ford Foundation.

2 "The Failure to Rescue, A Comparative Study," 52 *Col. L. Rev.* 631–47 (1952), John N. Hazard, "Soviet Socialism and the Duty to Rescue" in *XXth Century Comparative and Conflicts Law, Legal Essays in Honor of Hessel E. Yntema*, Leyden, 1961, pp. 160–71, John P. Dawson, *Rewards for the Rescue of Human Life? supra*, pp. 63–89.

3 Portugal 1867, the Netherlands 1881, Italy 1889 and 1930, Norway 1902, Russia 1903–17, Turkey 1926, Denmark 1930, Poland 1932, Germany 1935 and 1953, Rumania 1938, France

cific provisions in their criminal codes stipulating a duty to
rescue. Such legislation was introduced in Belgium in
1961,[4] and reintroduced in the RSFSR in 1960,[5] in both
countries without noticeable opposition. To these countries
must be added Switzerland, where several cantons (Obwalden [Unterwalden ob dem Wald], Ticino, Neuchâtel)
have general provisions concerning persons in immediate
danger, while some others (Valais, Waadt, Thurgau) restrict the duty to rescue to abandoned children and old or
sick persons. Three other cantons (Uri, Nidwalden [Unter-
walden nid dem Wald], and St. Gallen) have preserved
the medieval obligation of every citizen to take active part
in saving life and property during general disasters like
fires or floods without request by an official.[6]

Thus fifteen countries, all but one on the European con-
tinent, now recognize such a legal duty.

Before proceeding to a systematic analysis of such foreign provisions as are presently in force, let us briefly men-
tion some provisions related to but distinct from the general duty to rescue, in order to make more precise the
scope and the limits of our topic.

Special relationship vs. general human obligation. First
of all, our duty of rescue is conceived as a general human
obligation affecting every human being as such in the circumstances defined by law, even in the absence of any

---

1941 and 1945, Hungary 1948 and 1961, Czechoslovakia 1950.
The Portuguese provision appears in the Portuguese Civil Code
of 1867 still in force.

[4] Art. 422 bis of the Belgian Criminal Code added by statute
of January 6, 1961 (Art. 1).

[5] Sect. 127 of the criminal code of the RSFSR of 1960. A
similar provision was contained in Sect. 491 of the Russian
Criminal Code of 1903.

[6] Ernst Pedotti, *Die Unterlassung der Nothilfe,* Aarau, 1911,
pp. 70–81. The Swiss federal Criminal Code of December 21,
1937, does not include provision concerning failure to rescue.
This subject was left to cantonal legislation, as before. (Ph.
Thormann & A. von Overbeck, *Das Schweizerische Strafgesetz*
(21. XII.1937) 2 Bd. Zürich, 1941, p. 48.

special relationship based on law or contract between him and the person in distress, such as parent and child, husband and wife, guardian and ward, physician (or nurse) and patient, mountain guide and tourist, policeman, fireman, or lifeguard and public, shipmaster and crew or passenger, master and servant, host and guest, etc. Therefore, the various penal provisions concerning failure to fulfill obligations based on such special relationships are beyond the scope of our topic.[7]

Leaving the place of an accident. Another somewhat related provision must be distinguished. Most countries (the United States included) punish drivers for leaving the place of a traffic accident which they caused or to which they contributed or in which they were involved.[8] The punishment is for the positive act of fleeing, not for an omission. What is more important, it does not apply to accidental onlookers.

Aid during general disasters. Clearly overlapping with our topic are traditional medieval provisions concerning

[7] E.g., French Criminal Code, Art. 349, Statute of April 19, 1898 (*abandon d'enfant ou d'incapable*) Art. 357-1, 357-2 Ordinance of December 23, 1958, #58-1298 (*abandon de famille*), German Criminal Code 1871, para. 221 (*Aussetzung*), Swiss Criminal Code 1937, Art. 127 (*Aussetzung*), Polish Criminal Code 1932, Art. 243 (abandoning of child), Art. 202 (failure to care for life and health), Turkish Criminal Code 1926, Art. 473-475 (abandoning of child or invalid), Rumanian Criminal Code 1938, Sect. 454 (abandon familiar), Sect. 486 (abandoning of child or invalid). It must be stressed, however, that in spite of the general character of the duty to rescue, at least one category of persons is very often held liable in European courts, i.e., physicians, because they have, due to their professional training, the special capability of efficient and successful intervention when life is endangered, and their failure to render help when requested to do so is particularly revolting.

[8] E.g., para. 142, German Criminal Code 1871 (Verkehrsflucht), Art. 128, Swiss Criminal Code 1937, Sect. 489 Rumanian Criminal Code 1938, para. 228 Czechoslovak Criminal Code 1950, Art. 377 (1) Hungarian Criminal Code 1948, Sect. 259 (3) Hungarian Criminal Code 1961.

the legal duty to render aid and save lives during *general disasters* such as earthquakes, floods, major explosions, forest, village, or town fires or shipwrecks. Such catastrophes affect simultaneously a whole group of persons and create a clear state of emergency for all of them. People under such circumstances are usually solicited by official or private leaders to take part in life-saving operations. A refusal or failure to join under such critical circumstances has a greater eloquence, indicating a more serious rupture of the social bond than failure to respond to the lonely victim's cry for help, but there exists no neat boundary between the two categories. A stormy sea may throw two or three men overboard, leaving the rest of the crew and the boat intact or only slightly damaged. Several statutes regulate both categories jointly in the same provision.[9]

Prevention of crime. Finally, our duty to rescue must be carefully distinguished from provisions dealing with a duty of citizens to prevent crime by intervention or report to authority.[10] The provision concerning duty to rescue is directed toward saving human life, *not* exclusively nor directly toward preventing crime; it refers as well to rescue from a danger created by accident. Vichy France introduced the legal obligation to render aid as part of a special legislative effort to combat the activities of the anti-Nazi underground. It introduced on October 25, 1941, by statute, a penal provision punishing anyone who, being able without risk to himself or others to prevent a crime or an offense against the integrity of the body, voluntarily abstains from so doing. This was coupled in the same statute

---

[9] Sect. 387 Norwegian Penal Code 1902, Art. 253 Danish Criminal Code 1930, Sect. 330c German Penal Code amendment 1935, Art. 422 bis Belgian Penal Code amendment 1961. See also the original Art. 475, #12 of the French Code pénal of 1810, no longer binding in France but reflected textually in the new Belgian Art. 422ter.

[10] E.g., Art. 63 French Criminal Code amendment 1941 and 1945, Art. 18 Polish decree of June 13, 1946 (so-called "small criminal code").

with the duty to render aid to persons in danger by personal action or by soliciting aid.

In spite of this rather unsavory origin of the duty to rescue in France, the postwar French government retained, by ordinance of June 25, 1945, and statute of April 13, 1954, the Vichy enactment as part of the French Criminal Code. The two duties, though contained in one article, are considered as distinct in French jurisprudence.[11]

II WHEN DOES THE DUTY TO RESCUE ARISE?

What are the factual circumstances which bring about this legal duty? First, let us consider the kind of distress or emergency encountered by the person to be rescued, and afterward, the conditions relating to the potential rescuer.

Accident or third person as source of distress. The emergency requiring rescue may arise either by (1) accident or by (2) a crime or offense or simple negligence of a third person.[12]

Examples of accidental dangers to life include: drowning while swimming or because of the capsizing of a boat or canoe, collision of two cars or other traffic accidents, biting by a poisonous snake or a mad dog, a heart attack, and the like.

[11] Code Pénal, 61 éd. Petits Codes Dalloz, Paris, 1962, pp. 40–41 and 62 éd. 1965, pp. 36–38.

[12] This applies also to the German provision of 1935, amended in 1953, in spite of its language referring only to accidents. The German Bundesgerichtshof construes the legal term "accident" (Unglücksfall) as covering not only events brought about by pure chance without human participation but also events caused deliberately or negligently by third persons. (Kohlrausch-Lange, Strafgesetzbuch, 43 ed. Berlin, 1961, p. 671 decision BGH St. 3.66 concerning an assault. The German Criminal Code, besides covering both these sources of distress, combines our legal duty toward individual persons with the traditional obligation discussed above of taking part in rescue operations during general calamities (Para. 330c "bei Unglücksfällen oder *gemeiner Gefahr* oder [gemeiner] Not").

Only danger to life. The Netherlands, Norway, Denmark, Poland, Czechoslovakia, and the RSFSR restrict the duty to rescue to situations involving sudden and imminent danger to human *life*, thus by clear implication excluding situations endangering only human bodily integrity or the lives of animals.[13]

The same direct danger of death has been circumscribed in Rumania[14] by specifying the finding of a wounded person as a clear indication of such a danger.

An interesting basic interpretative decision was rendered by the Polish Supreme Court in 1961. It stresses the requirement of the immediacy of the danger to life and that the latter must have arisen suddenly, taking the endangered person by surprise and placing him in a helpless position or at least in a situation where outside help is urgently needed and indispensable. In other words, such a danger must arise at once in a developed and advanced form at a moment and under circumstances which cannot be foreseen.[15]

Suicide controversial. Thus, the question arises whether

[13] Art. 450 of the Dutch Penal Code 1881 (*danger de mort dont une autre personne est subitement menacée,* Sect. 387 of the Norwegian Penal Code 1902 (a person whose life is in obvious imminent danger), Art. 253 of the Danish Criminal Code 1930 (any person who is in evident danger of his life), Art. 247 of the Polish Criminal Code 1932 (a man who is in a situation immediately endangering his life), Art. 227 of the Czechoslovak Penal Code 1950 (a person being in danger of death), Sect. 127 of the RSFSR Criminal Code 1960 (a person being in a situation endangering his life).

[14] Sect. 489 of the Rumanian Criminal Code 1938 ("a seriously wounded person or in danger of death" *Ugolovnoie zakonodatelstvo zarubiezhnikh sotsialisticheskikh gosudarstv. Rumynskaia narodnaia respublika*), transl. M.A. Gelfer, Moskva, 1962, p. 280.

[15] Resolution of January 19, 1961, VI KO 43/60, *Państwo i Prawo,* June 1961, item 4, p. 1062, answering a legal question requiring fundamental interpretation of the law pursuant Art. 390, Para. 1 of the code of penal procedure.

the legal duty to rescue embraces also cases where the danger to life was deliberately created by the endangered person himself, through attempted suicide. The problem transcends the boundaries of statutory provisions and touches on basic moral values of the Western Judeo-Christian and Mohammedan civilizations. Is every person free and authorized, morally and legally, to put an end to his own life? The Brahmans not only allowed it, but honored a person who voluntarily freed himself from his body; the ritualistic character of the Japanese hara-kiri is well known. Suicide seems to have been respectable also in ancient Rome. Judaism and Christianity, as well as Islam, consider suicide as sinful, even as a crime equivalent to murder. This condemnation is no longer shared by the Western secular individualist, and suicide has long ago ceased to be punishable in most Western countries. Nevertheless, most countries still consider help given to a person in committing suicide as a criminal offense. The *moral* duty to prevent an attempted suicide is still widely accepted, and policemen are under a *legal* obligation to do so.

The existence of a legal duty of casual witnesses to prevent a suicide is rather controversial, even where the general duty to rescue is legally binding. The German Bundesgerichtshof has made contradictory decisions on this point.[16] The question could be rephrased thus: the underlying assumption of our duty obviously is that the endangered desires help and rescue, and, if able to do so, calls out for help. If he obviously does not wish to live, is help *against* his will still obligatory for an accidental onlooker? Probably not, if the onlooker's behavior does not transcend sheer passivity and if we accept the premise that each person is legally authorized to dispose of his own life. But a contrary view may also be adopted, based on the premise that the law, while not punishing suicide, still puts human

---

[16] Quoted in Kohlrausch-Lange, *Strafgesetzbuch,* 41 ed., Berlin, 1956, p. 606, partly based on the requirement of accident (Unglücksfall) in the text of Para. 330c of the German Criminal Code, amendm. 1935 and 1953.

life beyond and above the disposal of the individual, that the duty to rescue is introduced by public law in the *public interest*, overriding the desires of the would-be suicide. Emphasis may be put on the existence of imminent danger of death where suicide has been attempted.[17]

Danger to life and limb. Several countries extend the legal duty to rescue beyond the imminent danger to life only, including also any serious danger to bodily integrity and health; among them are Germany,[18] France,[19] Belgium,[20] Italy,[21] Turkey,[22] and Hungary.[23] This broader formulation originated in Article 389 of the Italian Criminal Code of 1889.[24]

Apparent death. A logical extension of our duty to preserve human life may be found in the Italian provision (also adopted by Turkey) covering the finding of a seem-

---

[17] Ernst Pedotti, *Die Unterlassung der Nothilfe*, Aarau, 1911, p. 123–24, 162.

[18] Sect. 330c of the German Criminal Code, amendm. 1935 and 1953 (Unglücksfälle) and Kohlrausch-Lange, *op. cit.*, p. 607 (Leib oder Leben von Menschen).

[19] Art. 63, code pénal, statute of April 13, 1954, *"une personne en péril"* see the cases quoted in Petits Codes Dalloz, Code Pénal, 62 éd., Paris, 1965, p. 37, #3, particularly Crim. May 31, 1949, D.1949.347, Jan. 21, 1954, D.1954.224 and Dec. 17, 1959, D.1960.398.

[20] Art. 422 bis Belgian Penal Code, statute of January 6, 1961 *"à une personne exposée à un péril grave."*

[21] Art. 593, Criminal Code of 1930, *"una persona ferita o altramenti in pericolo."*

[22] Art. 476, Criminal Code of 1926, "a person wounded or otherwise in danger." Also the Polish 1963 draft of a new criminal code extended in its Art. 216, para. 1, the duty to rescue to situations where a person is in danger of major bodily injury or of grave disruption of health.

[23] Sect. 259 (1) Criminal Code of 1961 "an injured person, victim of an accident or a person in a situation which directly endangers life or corporeal integrity."

[24] This Art. 389, in turn followed an ancient police regulation of Tuscany; see Code Pénal d'Italie (30 Juin 1889), trad. Jules Lacointa, Paris, 1890, p. 175.

ingly dead human body.[25] There is usually some probability in such a situation that prompt and competent first aid and assistance may still save life.

Only violent attack. Portugal limits the duty to rescue to situations where "a person has been attacked by a third person using violence" against the rights of the former. "Any person present during aggressions of this kind is obliged to render help to the person attacked without transgressing the limits of self-defense."[26] It must be stressed that the Portuguese provision appears in a *civil* code and the failure to come to the aid of the attacked results in liability for damages (*sera passible de dommages-intérêts*). An analogous but much broader provision encompassing any kind of danger to health and property was introduced into the Czechoslovak Civil Code of 1964 (see p. 111 below). These are apparently the only instances of a *private* law claim for rescue. All others are public law provisions of a criminal law or administrative law nature. Their private law implications and consequences (if any) are at best indirect and have to be demonstrated.

III PROTECTION OF HUMAN LIFE OR
     PUNISHMENT OF CALLOUSNESS

The intimate relationship between legal duty and the realm of ethics results in an interesting problem as to whether an outsider is still legally obliged to render help when the danger to life of the person threatened is so great that death is reasonably unavoidable and certain, or may already have occurred. Obviously, since our offense can only be committed intentionally, the crucial factor is whether the accused potential rescuer knew that death could no

[25] Art. 593 Italian Criminal Code 1930 and Art. 389 of the Italian Criminal Code of 1889 *"trovando un corpe umano que sia o sembri inanimato."* Art. 476, Turkish Criminal Code of 1926 "finds a body appearing to be dead."

[26] Art. 2367 and 2368 of the Portuguese Civil Code of 1867 dealing with self-defense. This code is still in force.

longer be averted and that assistance was thus already
futile. The purely objective state of affairs, that is, the
medical chances of survival of the person in danger at the
moment when the accused failed to act, is relevant only
insofar as it was known to the latter at that time. Therefore, the dichotomy between protection of human life, or
the punishment of a callous disposition, as two mutually
exclusive purposes of our legal provisions, strictly speaking
does not exist. The incompatibility of those two goals
would become real only if our offense could be committed
and punished irrespective of intention, by sheer objective
failure to act when action was objectively possible. Then
and only then could instances arise of a penalty being imposed for failure to assist, not out of indifference or malice,
but out of honest judgment that any help would come too
late and be of no avail.

Basically, the purpose of our provision must be defined
as protection of human life in the public interest *through*
punishment of a callous attitude of witnesses and outsiders
in emergencies. The German court decisions during the
Nazi period were perverted in putting excessive emphasis
on evil moral disposition as the target of the legal provisions. That view was obviously in line with the ideological
tendency of Nazism to punish not only for acts prohibited
by law but also for wrong convictions, views, and attitudes.[27]

Nevertheless, the question just discussed returns through
the back door in court practice, particularly in France,
Poland, and Germany, in connection with the interpretation
of the statutory concept of danger to life. Can a man
whose death is *certain* and *imminent* still be considered as
being in danger and therefore the coming to his aid still a
duty? A 1953 French decision of the Cour de Cassation

---

[27] *"Bestrafung der rücksichtslosen Gesinnung"* (punishment of the ruthless disposition) decision E 74.200 quoted in
Kohlrausch-Lange, *op. cit.,* p. 605. See also *"Gesinnungsstra-
frecht"* (penal law directed against disposition [mentality]
ibid.)

answered this question in the affirmative.[28] The Polish Supreme Court in 1949 took the same position.[29] These controversial decisions apparently arise from the conviction that the judgment of a casual witness, or even of a physician, may be wrong, and therefore all possible means must be applied to save life. Only clear evidence of death relieves this obligation.[30]

Dead body. Naturally, other purposes of public policy (public health and prosecution of crimes) are served by some legislative provisions which include both the finding of a dead human body and encountering a seemingly dead person.[31] Clearly in such cases the only duty is to report to the authorities.

IV WHO IS BOUND TO RENDER ASSISTANCE?

Witnesses only. Portugal, the Netherlands, Italy, Turkey, and Rumania, by clear language of the law, restrict the duty to rescue to outsiders *witnessing* or *finding* a person in distress.[32] Norway and Denmark achieve the same

---

[28] Criminal Code, March 23, 1953, D.1953.371; *"un délit d'attitude devant une situation apparente,"* Belley, Oct. 22, 1953, D.1953.711. In 1955 Art. 63, al. 2 was considered inapplicable when the accident resulted in immediate death of the victim, Crim. Feb. 1, 1955, D.1955.384.

[29] Sentence of January 31, 1949, To K909/48, *Państwo i Prawo.* August 1949, pp. 131–32, discussed in *Kazimierz Buchała, Przestępne zaniechanie udzielenia pomocy w niebezpieczeństwie grożącym życiu człowieka, Państwo i Prawo,* Dec. 1960, p. 1001.

[30] The German Bundesgerichtshof excludes liability when the victim (of a traffic accident) is already dead, unless danger still exists for other persons, sentence BGH St. 1.266 Kohlrausch-Lange, *op. cit.,* 43 ed., Berlin, 1961, p. 672.

[31] Italy, Art. 593 (*corpo umano que sia . . . inanimato*), Turkey, Art. 476 (dead body).

[32] Portugal, Art. 2368, Civil Code 1867 *"Quiquonque est présent,"* the Netherlands, Art. 450, Penal Code 1881 *"Celui qui, étant témoin,"* Italy, Art. 593, Penal Code 1930 (Art. 389,

result by implication, requiring respectively that the danger of life must be "obvious"[33] or "evident."[34] German courts apply the German provision in the same restrictive sense.[35]

Everyone informed. Poland, France, Belgium, and Hungary extend the duty to rescue to every person, even those not present, who become (reliably) *informed* of the danger to another person's life. The new Russian provision introduced in 1960, patterned closely on the Polish prewar text in impersonal description of the critical situation, may be assumed to follow the same line.[36]

The Polish Supreme Court was quite explicit, stressing in the above-mentioned interpretative resolution of 1961 that, contrary to other legislation, the Polish Criminal Code of 1932 did not limit the duty to render aid to persons witnessing the event but "transferred this problem into the field of evidence," meaning the problem of awareness of the danger to another person's life.[37]

French courts have convicted physicians deliberately failing[38] to visit a sick person in danger of death[38] or failing

---

Penal Code of 1889) *"chi, trovando,"* Turkey, Art. 476, Criminal Code 1926 "Whoever finds," Rumania, Sect. 489, Criminal Code 1938 "who seeing . . ."

[33] Norway, Art. 387, Criminal Code 1902, transl. Harald Schjoldager, Sweet & Maxwell, London, 1961, American Series of Foreign Penal Codes #3 p. 152.

[34] Denmark, Art. 253, Criminal Code 1930, transl. Copenhagen, G.E.C. Gad Publishers, 1958, p. 103.

[35] Kohlrausch-Lange, *op. cit.* p. 608, decision BGH St. Gr. Sen. 6.152 only witnesses of accident duty bound.

[36] The Russian Criminal Code of 1903 contained in its Art. 491 a provision clearly restricting the offense of "abandoning in danger" to persons *witnessing* the danger threatening the life of another person. This limitation has not been repeated. The official commentary (B.S. Nikoforov, *Nauchnoprakticheskii kommentarii ugolovnogo kodeksa* RSFSR, Moskva, 1964, pp. 287–89) is silent on this point.

[37] Resolution of January 19, 1961, VI KO 43/60, *Państwo i Prawo,* June 1961, item 4, p. 1063.

[38] Crim. May 31, 1949, D.1949.347.

to investigate for themselves the gravity of a danger brought to their attention.[39] A director of a hospital was convicted for failure to come to the rescue because he refused a patient admission to the hospital when a physician had found the patient to be in a dangerous condition.[40]

The new Belgian statute stipulates expressly that the legal duty to come to the aid of, or to obtain aid for, a person exposed to a grave danger exists both when one has ascertained by himself the situation of such person and when such a situation has been described to him by those who solicit his intervention. His failure to intervene will, however, not be punished if the circumstances of the request could make him believe that the appeal is not to be taken seriously.[41]

More than one potential rescuer. A situation may easily arise where more than one person is witnessing an accident or criminal attack. Are all equally bound to render help? This kind of situation has been regulated sensibly in the Polish draft of a new Criminal Code of 1963. It provides that no offense is being committed when there exists a strong possibility of prompt and effective aid by another person or institution whose duty to render aid is obviously greater, or when the potential rescuer, having good reasons for it, was convinced that such a strong possibility exists. Furthermore, the Polish draft excludes liability of a person who fails to come to the rescue of another when he failed to act out of a well-founded fear of criminal liability for an offense threatening himself or his next of kin.[42] Naturally a criminal offense connected with the present emergency is meant.[43]

[39] Montpellier, February 17, 1953, D.1953.209.

[40] Trib. corr. Douai, Dec. 20, 1951, D.1952 Somm. 53.

[41] Art. 422 bis Belgian Penal Code statute Jan. 6, 1961.

[42] Art. 211, Para. 2 and 4, *Projekt kodeksu karnego. Komisja Kodyfikacyjna przy Ministrze Sprawiedliwosci. Wydawnictwo Prawnicze, Warszawa,* 1963, p. 42.

[43] However, a driver's causing of a traffic accident naturally does not relieve him of the legal duty to rescue. See Art. 254, Para. 2, *ibid.,* p. 51.

The Polish draft code of 1963 is the only legislative text known to the present writer dealing explicitly with the presence of more than one potential rescuer. But the principle which it enunciates—namely, that the general duty to rescue incumbent upon the accidentally present outsider is *supplementary* to and less stringent and demanding than legal obligations based on a special relationship to the person endangered (parent, guardian) or on public office (policeman, fireman) or in some countries on the particular profession of the potential rescuer (physician)[44] is

---

[44] The legal position of *physicians* in this respect differs in European countries. In France, until World War II, they were free to refuse medical assistance, more or less as attorneys-at-law are free to take a case or reject it. There was not even disciplinary responsibility before the medical corporation (Marco R. Cohin, *L'abstention fautive en droit civil et pénal*, Sirey, Paris, 1929, p. V). Now physicians are a frequent target of punishment for failure to rescue under Art. 63 Crim. Code (amendment 1945) (see several sentences quoted in Code Pénal, 59 éd., Dalloz, Paris, p. 41). In Germany a special legal duty of physicians to come to the rescue, based on their medical profession, is still controversial in the courts (Kohl-rausch-Lange, *loc. cit.* 43 ed. Berlin, 1961, pp. 672–73). They may incur disciplinary sanctions meted out by autonomous medical corporations. In prewar Poland refusal, in the absence of serious obstacles, by a physician of assistance in cases where delay threatened life or health, constituted a special offense punishable by state administrative authorities. In places where around-the-clock emergency medical service was available, no such duty existed. Disciplinary action by the autonomous medical chamber took place independently (Art. 17 [i] decree of Sept. 25, 1932, on medical practice, J. of L. #81, item 712). An analogous provision restricted to cases where life is endangered or permanent disability threatens has been in force in Poland since 1950 (Art. 12, statute on the medical profession of Oct. 28, 1950, J. of L. #50, item 458). All physicians are under this special administrative obligation because of their medical profession *in addition* to the general criminal law duty pursuant to Art. 247 of the Criminal Code 1932 and to disciplinary responsibility. In Communist and in welfare-state countries freedom of contract is no longer the exclusive or even

taken for granted and is embodied in legislation and court practice in Europe.[45]

V RISK TO RESCUER EXCLUDING DUTY

The degree of risk which will relieve the potential rescuer of the duty to act varies from country to country. This feature has great moral and practical importance. Obviously, demanding heroism and heavy sacrifice from an average stranger, who accidentally happened to be present when the emergency arose, would be not only futile and unrealistic but could be even considered an objectionable attempt to deprive deeds of genuine heroism and self-sacrifice of their moral excellence and high merit by turning them into routine compliance with law.

Risk of life. Rumania seems to come near to such an extreme. Only danger to the *life* of the potential rescuer or other persons relieves him of the obligation to save life. He has, however, an acceptable alternative, immediately to inform the organs of authority.[46] Thus the problem of excessive demands is avoided after all.

Serious risk. Norway, Denmark, Germany, Russia, and Belgium stipulate *serious* (or special) danger or sacrifice to the person of the potential rescuer or other persons. (The German provision adds "the violation of one's own important obligations" by the rescue action as a justification of passivity.[47]) This serious danger must threaten the

---

the main source of the relationship between physician and patient. It is therefore not surprising that the Czechoslovak Criminal Code of 1950 and the Hungarian of 1961 introduce heavier punishments for failure to rescue for those, who, because of their profession, were obliged to render aid. (Para. 227, alinea 2 and Sect. 259 [3] resp.).

[45] See above, "Special Relationship . . . ," p. 92.

[46] Sect. 489, Rumanian Criminal Code 1938.

[47] Sect. 387, Norwegian Criminal Code 1902 "without any *special* danger or sacrifice to himself or others," Art. 253, Danish Criminal Code 1930 "without *particular* danger or sacrifice to himself or others," para. 330c German Criminal Code

person of the rescuer or of other bystanders, that is, their own life and health, not their property alone.

A lesser (not serious) amount of danger to life and limb has to be faced by the potential rescuer. This seemingly harsh requirement of the law exists in its undiluted form in Norway and Denmark, where the only kind of rescue demanded by law is personal intervention to save life. Only lack of ability or power to do so justifies inaction.[48]

In Germany the requirement of rendering aid is in addition qualified by a provision that coming to the aid "can be expected from him under the circumstances" (*"ihm den Umstanden nach zuzumuten . . . ist"*) which brings judicial and indirectly social appraisal into operation.

In Russia the law provides an alternative to personal intervention, namely, informing immediately the proper institution or person about the necessity of help. In Belgium the law requires the outsider either to come to the aid or to procure aid. Thus an excessive unreasonable demand seems after all not to be made.

In Portugal, the Netherlands, Italy, Turkey, Poland, Czechoslovakia, and France the requirements concerning the amount of risk the rescuer is bound to face are the lowest. In Portugal and France intervention is obligatory only when no risk for the rescuer is involved; in Portugal he apparently need not even risk his property.[49] In

---

amendment 1935, 1953 *"ohne erhebliche eigene Gefahr und ohne Verletzung anderer wichtiger Pflichten,"* Sect. 127, RSFSR, Criminal Code 1960 *"bez serioznoy opasnosti dla sebia ili drugikh lits,"* Art. 422 bis Belgian Penal Code amendment 1961 *"sans danger sérieux pour lui-même ou pour autrui."*

[48] Norway, *loc. cit.* "to help according to his ability," Denmark, *loc. cit.* "to the best of his power."

[49] Portugal Code Civil, *loc. cit. "un risque,"* France Code Pénal, *loc. cit. "sans risque pour lui ni pour les tiers."* In France the cases quoted in Code Pénal, 62 éd., Petits Codes Dalloz, Paris, 1965, p. 38, indicate that the risk for the rescuer must affect his person and not his property, Rouen, March 31, 1949, D.1950. Somm. 9; Crim. Dec. 30, 1953, D.1954.333; Comp. Trib. corr., Orléans, Nov. 29, 1950, D.1951.246.

the Netherlands, Poland, and Czechoslovakia the danger justifying abstention must be of a personal nature. Italy and Turkey are silent on this point because the duty stipulated in these countries confronts the potential rescuer with a clear-cut choice: render aid personally *or* inform the proper authority. Thus there is no necessity to fix the degree of risk which the rescuer is duty bound to brave.

VI   WHAT OBLIGED TO DO?

Personal action. The duty to rescue consists primarily in *personal action* removing the danger to life threatening the person in a critical situation. Depending on the kind of emergency, it may consist in preventing the final blow to his body by putting an attacker to flight, or stopping a machine run wild, or removing the endangered person from the railroad tracks or from the river. It may also be the provisional application of a tourniquet to stop his bleeding, or the inducing of artificial respiration. Or both kinds of action may be necessary—external, to prevent final blows to the victim, and internal, to prevent further collapse of his organism. Obviously such actions are legally required only to the extent that the accidental outsider is capable of them under the circumstances.

Obtaining help. Personal action is, however, not the only form of assistance required by law. The Netherlands, France, and Belgium explicitly require either personal intervention or the *obtaining* of help from other persons.[50]

---

[50] The Netherlands, Art. 450, *loc. cit., "néglige de lui prêter ou de lui fournir l'assistance,"* France, Art. 63, *loc. cit., "s'abstient . . . de porter . . . l'assistance que, . . . il pouvait lui prêter, soit par son action personelle, soit en provoquant un secours,"* Belgium, Art. 422 bis, *loc. cit. "s'abstient devenir en aide ou de procurer une aide."* It is interesting to note that the French Cour de Cassation decided in 1954 that the alternative language just quoted does *not* create for the witness of the danger or the person informed about it an arbitrary option between two kinds of assistance. The law creates a duty to intervene in a manner imposed by the emergency and even when

It seems reasonable to assume also that the countries requiring simply that help be given to the person in danger (Portugal, Poland, Germany, Hungary, Czechoslovakia) consider that getting other persons to perform the rescue operation satisfies the demands of the law. After all, not every witness is physically able or competent to master by his own action a dangerous situation. If he succeeds in inducing others to do so, his duty of giving aid is certainly fulfilled. It would be absurd to punish him. If he tries to influence others and fails, he will have to prove that that was all he was able to do under the circumstances. One of the means to instigate help by others consists of notifying the proper authorities or institutions about the urgent need of speedy aid.

Notifying authority. The legal situation is significantly different in Italy, Turkey, Rumania, and Russia, where the law expressly formulates an *alternative* duty either to render help *or* to inform immediately the proper authority.[51] Here the potential rescuer is faced with a *choice:* either to undertake personal intervention or to inform the next policeman or emergency station. Either course satisfies his duty; only complete passivity makes him criminally liable.

VII   CRIMINAL FEATURES

The failure to rescue represents, in fourteen European[52] countries, a *criminal* offense. In the Netherlands it is pun-

---

necessary by the cumulation of both kinds of assistance. Crim. July 26, 1954, D.1954.666. A driver was punished because, although able to transport a wounded man, he limited himself to informing a gendarme. Trib. corr. Bayeux, June 22, 1954, D.1954.603.

[51] The Russian sect. 127, *loc. cit.,* speaks about "proper institutions or persons," obviously meaning emergency first-aid stations with ambulances in cities.

[52] We take the liberty of including Turkey in that European group because the Turkish Penal Code of 1926 was part of the imposition of European institutions and law on Turkish society by Mustafa Kemal Pasha and was based on the Italian Crimi-

ishable only in the event that the death of the person in distress actually resulted from the failure. No such restriction of criminal liability exists in the other thirteen countries. However, in Norway, Italy, and Hungary a higher penalty is explicitly prescribed if death was caused.

Intention to abstain. This point seems to be connected with the conscious and deliberate character of the offense. The potential rescuer must be conscious that danger threatens another person, that aid is urgently needed, and that he can give it without serious risk. Failure to act must be *voluntary and intentional;* the intention being simply to remain passive, not to bring about death or injury to the person in danger.[53] Such a requirement of penal responsibility follows clearly from the fact that in all criminal codes (except Norway's) which use the tri-partite (crimes, felonies, and misdemeanors) or the dual (felonies and misdemeanors) division of criminal offenses, the offense has been placed in the first or second category, and not considered to be a mere misdemeanor—thus eliminating punishment for mere disobedience to law irrespective of the act's voluntary or involuntary character.[54] Only Norway treats the offense as a mere misdemeanor.

Result not essential. Our offense is classified as *delictum mere omissivum,* or a *formal* offense of inaction (omission); both these terms mean that to its perpetration the mere fact of (voluntary) inaction is sufficient, irrespective

---

nal Code of 1889. From this source (Art. 389) it took over almost verbally its provision (Art. 476) dealing with our subject. See Code Pénal, Le Législation Turque, John A. Rizzo, Constantinople, 1927, p. 135; Dr. Naci Sensoy and Dr. Osman Tolun, *Das Türkische Strafgesetzbuch,* Gruyter, Berlin, 1955, p. XIII.

[53] About the intentional character see, e.g., Resolution of the Polish Supreme Court of Jan. 19, 1961, *loc. cit.,* p. 1064, Kohlrausch-Lange, *op. cit.,* p. 608 #VI, W. Makowski, Kodeks Karny, vol. III, Warszawa, 1922, pp. 141–42.

[54] The French Art. 63 Penal Code unnecessarily contains explicitly the term *"s'abstient volontairement."*

of any effect or lack of it.[55] The nearest analogy is the offense of failure to leave the place of a riot despite official request.

The offense is committed at the moment when the time during which rescue was possible and necessary has fruitlessly elapsed. Fruitlessly means without any action being undertaken by the bystander. The offense is therefore punishable even in the event that the person in danger finally managed to save himself.[56]

Penalties. Penalties range from a fine only (Turkey) through a fine or simple detention (Denmark), fine or imprisonment (Norway), prison or fine (Germany), correctional labor or social censure or applying measures of social influence (Russia), arrest or fine (Italy), detention and fine (Netherlands),[57] imprisonment and fine or one of them (France, Belgium), imprisonment or arrest (Poland), to deprivation of liberty only (Rumania, Czechoslovakia, Hungary).

The longest prison term provided by law for the offense can be found in France: up to five years. Next in severity comes the Polish Criminal Code of 1932: up to three years. The most lenient upper statutory limit of three months is in force in the Netherlands, Denmark and Italy (detention), and in Rumania (prison).

---

[55] Only the Netherlands is, as mentioned above, an exception. There a death must result for the inaction to become an offense. It is, therefore, there a *delictum per omissionem commissum,* a *material* offense of inaction (omission).

[56] See the French case of the son-in-law who fell through ice into a deep canal. His father-in-law walked away and refused to join with a third person in handing out to him a nearby iron bar. The son-in-law, nevertheless, was saved and recovered damages from his father-in-law, who was sentenced to three years in jail. Trib. corr., Aix, March 27, 1947. D.1947.304 as noted in Dawson, *supra* p. 72.

[57] As stressed above, the failure to rescue is punishable in Holland only if death resulted. Therefore, this penalty (up to three months) seems rather light.

VII PRIVATE LAW ASPECTS

Civil claim of the victim. A detailed and thorough presentation of the private law aspects of the duty to rescue arising from public (criminal) law would require a separate study. Therefore, only a sketchy presentation of the main problems and their tentative solutions will be included here.

As stressed above, Portugal was the first country to introduce a specific private law provision in its Civil Code of 1867 (still in force), establishing a civil claim by a person violently attacked (and therefore authorized to use force in self-defense) towards any person present at such an aggression for help in repelling the attack, if it can be done without exposing the rescuer to a risk. The reluctant bystander who fails to assist is subsidiarily liable for damages (*perdas e danos*).[58]

This provision obviously deals only with part of our problem, namely, with situations where the danger was created by an illegal attack of a third person, and not by an accident. It leaves open also the question of civil claim, if any, which the rescuer may have against the victim of the accident (or his heirs), for damages suffered when rescuing.

The new Czechoslovak Civil Code of 1964 introduced, alone among European codes, a sweeping *civil law* duty, not only to rescue human life but, more broadly, to prevent any bodily injury, and even any damage to health and to property. Such a duty is imposed on "everybody" and consists of an obligation to notify the appropriate authorities of the danger of serious damage as well as a duty to intervene actively if action is urgently needed to avert the damage in an emergency situation. Only if serious circumstances prevent his intervention or if by intervening he

---

[58] Art. 2368 of the Portuguese Civil Code of 1867, Code Civil Portugais, tr. Fernand Lepelletier, Paris, 1894, p. 437, Códige Civil Português Actualizado por A. Rochade Gouveia, Lisboa, 1958, p. 364.

would expose himself or persons close to him to a serious danger does the duty to intervene cease.[59]

This broad civil law obligation to prevent death, injury, and damage before they arise supplements in Czechoslovakia the criminal provision requiring rescue in cases where human life is in instant danger. There is also an explicit civil law sanction attached. He who failed to prevent damage by not notifying the competent authority or by failing to intervene, where these steps would have prevented imminent damage, may be ordered by a court to contribute to the payment of damages to an extent determined by the circumstances, if such compensation cannot be recovered from those initially responsible for the damage.[60] In other words, civil liability for failure to rescue, though a subsidiary one, exists in Czechoslovakia beyond any doubt, and such claims seem to be encouraged. The passive onlooker, as a substitute for the actual wrongdoer, is held responsible for damages suffered by the victim, as in Portugal.

In other countries the legal position of the victim who was injured and disabled and failed to get aid from a potential rescuer has to be decided in the first place according to general principles of each national legislation governing torts.

In countries where the duty to rescue remains of a purely *moral* character, tort liability for abstention from acting in the face of danger to another person's life could be based, if at all, only on provisions, if any, along the lines of Paragraph 826 of the German Civil Code (BGB) of 1900, and Article 41, al. 2 of the Swiss Code of Obligations of 1911. These provisions create liability only in those who *deliberately,* in a manner contrary to good morals, create damage to another person. Naturally one difficulty always remains —to prove in a specific case that death or injury which actually occurred *resulted causally* from the omission; i.e., from the inaction of the potential rescuer. For continental

---

[59] Sect. 416, Czechoslovak Civil Code 1964.
[60] Sect. 425, Czechoslovak Civil Code 1964.

jurists the causality of omissions does not present the highly paradoxical character which is self-evident to natural scientists. Many jurists have adopted their own modified social concept of causality in civil and criminal matters, still hotly debated, but covering omissions as well. Such liability seems nevertheless farfetched and rather theoretical.

In countries where the *legal* duty to rescue is established by public criminal law, the tort liability of the potential rescuer would seem to be based on more solid ground. The principle that a violation of a legal duty creates civil liability of the person guilty of such violation forms the basis of tort law in a number of continental countries such as Germany, Switzerland, Czechoslovakia, and RSFSR (principle of liability for illegal action).[61] But even there it was for several decades controversial. A Swiss monograph published in 1911[62] tried to argue that the only legal duties which create tort liability are those which affect persons concretely specified in advance, and which can therefore be relied upon to be fulfilled. The public law duty to come to the aid of a person in distress is a purely accidental obligation. Only chance decides whether anybody at all will be placed in such a situation. Thus, it concludes, a potential rescuer is not liable for damages to the victim.

This line of reasoning would equally apply to all private law claims *erga omnes* (so-called absolute rights) as, e.g., the right of the owner of a piece of real estate to forbid

---

[61] Para. 823, al. 1 BGB, Art. 41, al. 1 Swiss OR (*widerrechtlich*), Sect. 420 CSSR Civil Code 1964 (violating a legal obligation), Sect. 403 RSFSR Civil Code 1922 and Sect. 444, RSFSR Civil Code 1964. Basically the same idea is known to common law of torts (J. A. Jolowicz and T. Ellis Lewis, *Winfield on Torts*, 7th ed., London, 1963, p. 19). Naturally illegality of the damage-creating action is also one of the routine grounds of liability in countries like France where it is based on the broader fault principle (Art. 1382, Code Civil 1804) and Poland (Art. 415, Civil Code 1964).

[62] Ernst Pedotti, *Die Unterlassung der Nothilfe*, Aarau, 1911, pp. 168–69.

trespassing. The only significant difference is that a prohibition valid against everybody forbids certain actions, whereas the duty to rescue demands positive action.

Another much better argument was put forward by the same author. It would be unacceptable to hold the potential rescuer liable in the same manner as the man who caused the emergency.[63] This objection is well taken but not decisive. The third man who by his action brought the danger and the injury about is naturally directly liable for the whole damage done to the victim. The civil liability of the potential rescuer in such a situation can at best, if at all, be only *subsidiary* and only for a *part* of the damage, if it can be established that his intervention was obligatory and would have prevented part of the damage or injury. Obviously this argument is pointless in a situation which arose out of an accident.

There may be, however, situations where the potential rescuer may reasonably raise an objection to a claim for damages by the victim or his heirs, namely, that the victim acted recklessly or negligently by exposing himself to a situation or conditions which made it probable that a danger to his life might arise, e.g., swimming in a swollen river in a rapid current in spite of his poor swimming ability. Even under the continental doctrine concerning contributory negligence the claim of the victim against the potential rescuer seems rather tenuous under such circumstances.

In Germany the situation is even more negative. Paragraph 823 (2) of the BGB allows damages for violation of "a law whose purpose is the protection of another [person]." The question whether Paragraph 330c of the German Criminal Code represents such a "protective law" seems to be decided by the courts and by authoritative commentators of the German Civil Code in the negative, and no positive court decisions are known.[64]

---

[63] *Ibid.*, p. 169.
[64] Achilles-Greiff, BGB, 20th ed., Walter de Gruyter, Berlin,

But aside from third-person causation of the injury, and contributory negligence of the victim, the liability for damages of the potential rescuer who fails to act has been acknowledged by legal doctrine in France.[65] The claim of the victim is usually handled as part of the criminal proceedings against the potential rescuer, the victim demanding recovery of damages as *partie civile* (the injured party in criminal proceedings).[66]

Claims of the rescuer. The claims of the rescuer against the person saved by him for recovery of damages suffered during the rescue or for compensation for bodily injury due to the rescue forms the reverse side of the private law coin.

Such claims have been handled by the German courts as an instance of implied mandate or of a *negotiorum gestio*. The latter institution, virtually unknown to Anglo-Saxon common law, consists of the management of another's affair or affairs without authorization (mandate) by the person interested, but with the intention of serving the latter's interests.[67] The *negotiorum gestor* is entitled to the reimbursement of his expenses, even if his efforts, reasonably made, remained unsuccessful. The pre-World War II German Supreme Court (*Reichgerichtshof*) extended in relation to rescuers the scope of "expenses" to cover also bodily injuries suffered as a result of the action to save life.[68]

Another method of dealing with the problem at hand

1958, p. 442; see also commentaries quoted by Dawson, *supra*, fn. 16.

[65] Dalloz Répertoire de Droit Civil, Vol. II, Paris, 1952. *Faute, Abstentions fautives,* #57, p. 735 and H. & L. Mazeaud & Tunc, *Traité de la responsabilité civile,* Vol. I, #526, 5e éd. 1957.

[66] E.g., Aix Trib. Corr., March 27, 1947, D.1947.304 quoted by Dawson, *supra*, pp. 71–72.

[67] Adolf Berger, *Encyclopedic Dictionary of Roman Law,* The American Philosophical Society, Philadelphia, 1953, pp. 593–94.

[68] Dawson, *supra*, pp. 64–68, 73–75.

centers around the concept of the state of necessity or emergency (*Notfall, Notstand, état de nécessité*) and is based on the principles developed by the law of admiralty concerning general average (distribution of losses suffered during salvage in common danger) and their application to similar situations on land. Thus, the Austrian Civil Code of 1811 provides in Section 1043: "When a person has sacrificed his property in order to prevent a greater damage to himself or *to others,* all those who profited therefrom are obliged to compensate him proportionally" (emphasis added). A reference to the law of the sea follows in the code. The new Polish Civil Code of 1964 contains a special provision along the same line. "Who suffered property damage involuntarily or even voluntarily in order to avert a damage threatening another person or in order to avert a common danger is entitled to claim compensation of losses proportionally from persons who profited therefrom."[69] The term "property damage" (*szkoda majątkowa*) covers bodily injuries also.[70]

The new Czechoslovak Civil Code of 1964, too, explicitly entitles a person who was actually averting a threatening damage to health or property (a civil law duty) to claim compensation of effectively expended costs and of damages suffered by him in such action from the person in whose interest he has acted. But such compensation shall not exceed the amount corresponding to the averted damage;[71] a ceiling has been established.

The German Weimar Republic introduced in 1928 a social security accident insurance for "any person injured when, *without being legally obliged* to do so, he saves or undertakes to save another from present danger to life, with

[69] Art. 438, Polish Civil Code 1964.

[70] Also the draft of a new Civil Code of the Soviet Tadjik Republic contains an analogous provision. See L. Maidanik in *Sovetskaia, Yustitsia* 6/1964, pp. 8 ff quoted in *Nowe Prawo,* Jan. 1965, pp. 71–72.

[71] Sect. 419, Czechoslovak Civil Code 1964.

accompanying danger to his own life, body, or health.[72] An analogous provision omitting the underlined qualification would represent encouragement for potential rescuers rather more reliable than a private law claim.

Another public law method of stimulating life-saving equally worth considering is that of cash rewards from public funds to those who, risking their lives, saved others from imminent death. Such funds could be federal, state, local, or donated by great foundations. Austria, following the example of the Prussian eighteenth-century *Allgemeines Landrecht* applied and still applies such a policy, considering with good reason private law claims as inadequate for indemnifying life-savers.[73]

That a civil law claim against the rescued, (who as a rule is a faultless victim of an accident) may, when pushed too far, result in obvious injustice became evident in a decision of the German *Reichsgericht* of May 7, 1941. The widow and children of a rescuer, who saved a woman from drowning in a stream but drowned as a result, sued the rescued woman and her husband, who managed to escape from the water, for loss of support from their deceased husband and father. An annuity was granted to the widow and another for each child until his eighteenth year.[74] The rescuer made the supreme sacrifice and left wife and children in need. But to burden the faultless victim of an accident, even though she owes her life to his heroic deed, with the whole obligation to support the widow for the rest of her life and the orphans until their majority seems unfair. Such a duty should at least be shared by society as a whole.

[72] Art. 553a of the German Reichsversicherungsordnung added by statute of Dec. 20, 1928, RGB1. I, 405–6, extended in scope by statute of Feb. 17, 1939, RGB1. I, 267.

[73] Swoboda in Klang, *Kommentar zum allgemeinen bürgerlichen Gesetzbuch,* Vol. II, part 2, 1934, comment to para. 1036, p. 881.

[74] Reichsgericht, 167, R.G.Z.83 for a detailed legal analysis of the case see Dawson, *supra,* pp. 73–77 and 86.

Liability of rescuer for damage done. We must at least touch upon the question of whether the rescuer is responsible for damage done by his action to the person rescued or to his property or to third persons. In countries where life-saving has become a legal duty, required in the public interest, the rescuer will certainly have the right to assert that what he did was not only authorized by law but required. Therefore, only a clear and deliberate transgression of what he was obliged to do, an irresponsible, reckless, or foolish intervention, or an explicit legal provision could establish his liability.

The new Czechoslovak Civil Code of 1964 is quite outspoken on this point. "Anybody who has caused damage when averting an imminent threat [to health or property] not caused by himself shall not be liable for the damage unless the threat could have been averted under the given circumstances in another manner or if the consequence caused is obviously as serious or more serious than the one which had threatened.[75]

Thus the exemption from liability is here not complete, but doubly qualified. The first qualification, making the Good Samaritan liable for damage done by his action, if the danger could have been averted in another manner (and possibly the second one, too), seems to discourage rescue action and to be unfair to the rescuer. Emergency situations are not conducive to a detached calculation and well-balanced choice between several ways of action. They call for instant courageous and effective steps.

The Civil Code of the Republic of China, in its General Principles of 1929, specifically exempted "a person acting for the purpose of defending his own rights or the rights of another person against any imminent unlawful infringement" from a liability "to make compensation." Only if the limits of "necessary defense" have been exceeded is a reasonable compensation due.[76] A similar exemption from liability for damages applies under this

---

[75] Sect. 418(1). Czechoslovak Civil Code 1964.
[76] Art. 149 Civil Code of the Republic of China 1929.

Chinese code to "a person averting an imminent danger threatening the body, liberty, or property of himself or of another person." Both qualifications of such exemption spelled out in the Czechoslovak Civil Code of 1964, discussed just above, can be found in the earlier Chinese code.[77]

IX IS THE INTRODUCTION OF SUCH A
     LEGAL DUTY DESIRABLE?

Before discussing arguments pro and con, let us stress the non-controversial aspect of the problem. There seems to be unanimity in this country about the very high place of human life on the scale of values we cherish. Nor is there any dispute about the high praise and admiration due to those who heroically saved a human life when it was critically imperiled. There will probably be few who would insist that the present legal situation under common law, strongly discouraging a potential rescuer and treating him as an officious intermeddler, who may even become liable if he makes things worse by his intervention,[78] is entirely satisfactory, and that no change in the legal situation should be introduced to encourage rescue in emergencies.

Whether a *penal* provision establishing a legal duty to do so is the proper means to this end is a controversial question.

1 *Basic value arguments.* Let us first take up the arguments based on basic values and principles. It seems true that a legal duty to rescue would run against the traditional cult of rugged individualism, but only when the latter is being understood as approval of selfishness and total lack of consideration for the fate of others—in other words, "every man an island unto himself," "every man for him-

---

[77] Art. 150 Civil Code of the Republic of China 1929.
[78] Grant Gilmore and Charles L. Black, Jr., *The Law of Admiralty,* Brooklyn, 1957, p. 443.

self." That was more or less the tenor of the classic Manchester school of economic liberalism, with its model of the *homo oeconomicus.* It was convinced that the struggle of selfish individuals automatically produces the common good of all. This conviction was proved false long ago.

A more subtle argument stresses the fact that the duty to rescue asks for positive action which allegedly is a symptom of an absolutist or totalitarian state. The grain of truth behind this argument consists of the fact that criminal offenses by and large consist of prohibited positive actions (murder, robbery, etc.) and very seldom in prohibited omissions. But there are many positive actions that a modern state (democratic and totalitarian alike) imposes on its citizens under penalties, such as the paying of taxes, military service, education of children, vaccination, and so forth.

A serious problem is raised by the argument that a legal compulsion imposed by criminal law to save human life deprives the rescue of its ethical character, which consists of free deeds motivated and directed by one's conscience alone. Such a deed, it can be argued, is transformed from an act of charity, altruism, and courage, an act of heroism and sacrifice, into routine compliance with a rule of law, the doing of one's duty, not more nor less. The basis of this argument is the desire to keep law and ethics separate and avoid any overlapping and mixture of the two; such a neat separation is obviously impossible.

The answer to this line of reasoning depends on whether the amount of risk connected with rescue, which the law obliges the bystander to brave, can be fairly demanded from him. As we have seen above, the legislation of different countries displays a broad scale, from no risk at all, up to and including serious danger to health. An excessive demand stipulated by law may be tantamount to legislating the type of religious morality which demands human perfection. Such an attempt would not only be self-defeating and practically ineffective but also objectionable on ethical grounds.

The problem thus boils down to whether even the more

moderately circumscribed legal provisions analyzed above represent excessive, and therefore unfair, demands. It seems to the present writer that it is not morally unfair to expect an average man in present-day, highly organized and integrated modern society to chance a sacrifice of property and some moderate impairment of health when faced with a dying fellow human being. This conviction, like all moral judgments, is not subject to scientific proof. Such a demand, while being ethically unobjectionable in general, may still be unjust in relation to persons with a timid disposition. Therefore, a modification of the Italian, Turkish, Rumanian, and Russian approach seems most appropriate and just.

Choice of actions. The potential rescuer should have a *choice.* Either to intervene personally or, if he is not able to do it, or the risk is too great, to procure help from others better qualified and/or whose duty to rescue has priority over his own. One such alternative consists of notifying the police or an emergency hospital service. Only total passivity would be punishable.

Moral minimum. Such provision would represent a demand limited to the moral minimum. A total separation of the domain of morality from the sphere of law does not exist in fact and a tendency to keep them separate certainly does not imply that they should be patently different in content and acting at cross purposes, morality praising and extolling the same kind of behavior which present common law in this country and Great Britain tries to discourage.

The undeniable fact is that law and morality partly overlap in all but the most primitive societies where they merge and are both permeated by religious ideas. The legal duty to rescue is by no means the only ethical requirement of human perfection of yesterday, which has become today a legal obligation of everyone. The prohibition of usury, the nullity or voidability of flagrantly exploitative contracts, the prohibition of child labor and sweatshops, the introduction of workmen's compensation, social security, unemployment benefits, and fair-employment regulations are obvious examples. And developments are evidently running in this direction. Obviously, purely moral considerations are not the only driving force and the only motive behind this evolution. The social interest, the common good of society, as presently understood, are the goals pursued. But the impact of moral convictions exercised on those legislative enactments should not be underestimated. The general label which is being attached to this broad trend clearly present on both sides of the East-West ideological divide is of less importance. We call it "welfare state" or "social solidarity" or "the Great Society," while in the Communist-oriented countries it goes by the name of "socialist humanism" or "the transition from socialism to communism." From the sociological point of view it seems to be connected with the order a fully developed industrial society needs to function smoothly and to prevent inner tensions from erupting and thus disrupting society. There is certainly nothing Marxist or Communist about the legal duty to rescue. Its origin is clearly Judeo-Christian in ethics and West European in law.

2 *Practical arguments.* The somewhat stale objection often heard, that such legislation will prove ineffective because you cannot legislate morality, has been mentioned above. It represents at best a half-truth. Only if the moral requirements transformed into legal duties are excessive, too radical and abruptly introduced are they likely to prove ineffective. Otherwise, law quite successfully modifies human attitudes, reinforces moral impulses, and awakens the indifferent and passive. In our big cities there are a lot of people in need of such stimulation. The important fact is that fifteen continental European countries, ten of them sharing our political, social, and economic system, live under such a legal provision, some of them for longer than three score and ten years, and accept it as a matter of course. The duty to rescue seems to have spread recently from country to country. Belgium accepted it in 1961 from France, and Russia reintroduced it a year earlier. No ob-

jections that it would be unworkable were heard on those occasions.

A final remark: the enactment of a legal provision along similar lines is clearly needed in this country. It will most probably help to cut down the number of cases where people witnessing their neighbors dying and crying for help look the other way and do nothing. More than such enactment will be needed to overcome the fear of "getting involved," but a legal provision such as those discussed in this paper is one of the measures necessary to reach this goal.

X A TENTATIVE DRAFT

This paper might not be complete without a tentative text of a draft proposal concerning a penal provision regulating the duty to rescue:

> Art. . . . Whoever, witnessing an obvious and imminent danger threatening the life of another person, fails to come to his aid either through his personal intervention or by providing aid by others or does not notify immediately the proper public officer or institution, although he could do one of those things without reasonable fear of danger to his person or to others, shall be punished by imprisonment of up to . . . , or a fine of up to . . . , or both.

Criminal liability would here be restricted to persons present on the spot.

The critical situation of the victim includes only imminent and obvious danger to his life, excluding that to his health only.

The risk justifying passivity by the potential rescuer covers any risk to him or to others, affecting life, limb, and health. Risk of property loss could not serve as justification.

The intentional character of the offense is implied. It could as well be clearly expressed in the language of the provision by the addition of the word "deliberately" before "fails." Whether such inclusion is necessary depends on the legislative technique of a penal code into which the above provision would have to be incorporated.

APPENDIX

1 *Portugal*

Civil Code of July 1, 1867 (still in force) 4-me partie. La Violation des Droits et sa Réparation. Livre Ier—De la responsabilité civile. Titre II. De la responsabilité civile jointe à la responsabilité pénale. Chapitre I De l'imputation de responsabilité.

Art. 2367. Quiconque a été attaqué par un tiers avec violence, de telle sorte que ses droits puissent être lésés, qu'il soit privé de la jouissance de ces droits acquis, ou troublé en quelque façon dans cette jouissance, est autorisé à repousser la force par la force, pourvu qu'il ne dépasse pas les limites d'une légitime défense.

Art. 2368. Quiconque est présent à des agressions de cette nature est tenu de porter secours à la personne attaquée, sans dépasser les limites de la légitime défense; et quiconque, ne devant courir un risque, s'abstient de s'opposer à ces violences, sera subsidiairement passible de dommages-intérêts.[1]

2 *Switzerland*

A. *St. Gallen*—Penal Statute of Dec. 10, 1808.

Art. 67. Wer bei Unglücksfällen, Feuers und Wassersnoth Hülfeleistung versagt, soll je nach dem Grade der aus der Entziehung derselbem hervorleuchtenden Bosheit zu einer Geldstrafe von 15 Fr bis 75 Fr. verurtheilt werden.[2]

---

[1] Code Civil Portugais traduit par Fernand Lepelletier, Paris, 1894, p. 437. The French translation was checked against the Portuguese original and on that basis the phrase "courir aucun risque" changed to "un risque" and the omitted word "subsidiarement" added (subsidiariamente). The original speaks about "perdas e danos" (losses and damages).

[2] Gesetzessammlung für den Kanton St. Gallen. V Bd. St. Gallen, 1868, p. 7.

B. *Unterwalden ob dem Wald* (also called Obwalden) Penal
police statute April 20, 1870 (Polizeistrafgesetz).

Art. 136. Wer ohne eigene Gefahr einen in *dringender Lebensgefahr* befindlichen Menschen zu retten im stande ist und
es ohne sattsame Entschuldigung unterlässt, wird, wenn der
Andere darüber das Leben verloren oder einen bleibenden
Nachteil an seiner Gesundheit erlitten hat, mit Freiheitsstrafe
von 14 Tagen bis 8 Monaten oder mit einer Geldbusse bis 300
Franken bestraft.

Art. 137. Wer, ausser dem Falle des Art. 136, Personen in
einem lebens-oder gesundheitsgefährlichen, schleuniger Hülfe
bedürftigen Zustande findet und ohne genügende Entschuldigung
wegen sebsteigener wesentlicher Gefahr es unterlässt, denselben
die erste notwendige Hülfe nach Möglichkeit zu verschaffen,
wird an Geld bis zu 150 Franken gebüsst oder verfällt in
angemessene Freiheitsstrafe.[3]

C. *Ticino*—Statute of 1873.

Chi potendo, senza grave pericolo e grave danno proprio,
salvar altri da un urgente pericolo o da un grave danno immi-
nente, o, potendo allontanare o sospendere il pericolo e il
danno, rifiuta, od ommette di dare avviso alla persona peri-
colante, o all' autorità o al pubblico, o di prestare soccorso, é
punito colla multa dal primo al terzo grado (5-250 Frs).[4]

3   *Netherlands*

Penal Code, March 3, 1881. Contraventions relatives aux
individus en détresse.

Art. 450. Celui qui, étant témoin du danger de mort dont une
autre personne est subitement menacée, néglige de lui prêter
ou de lui fournir l'assistance qu'il peut lui donner ou procurer
sans crainte raisonable d'un danger pour sa personne ou pour
d'autres personnes, est puni, si la mort de la personne en détresse s'en est suivie, d'une détention de 3 mois au plus et d'une
amende de 300 florins au plus.[5]

4   *Italy*

A. *Penal Code of June 30, 1889* Titre IX. Des Délits contre

[3] Landbuch für den Kanton Unterwalden ob dem Wald.
I Bd. Offentliches Recht, Sarnen, 1899, pp. 276/7.
[4] Ernst Pedotti, *Die Unterlassung der Nothilfe*, Aarau,
1911, p. 77.
[5] Code pénal des Pays-Bas (3 mars 1881) traduit par
Willem-Joan Wintgens, Paris, 1883, Imprimerie Nationale,
p. 121.

la Personne. Chap. V. De l'abandon d'enfants et d'autres personnes incapables de veiller sur elles-mêmes ou bien en péril.

Art. 389. . . . .

Encourt la même peine [une amende de 15 à 500 livres] celui qui, trouvant une personne blessée ou de toute autre manière en péril, ou un corps humain qui est ou paraît inanimé, omet, quand cela ne l'expose à aucun dommage ou péril personnel, de prêter l'assistance nécessaire ou d'en donner immédiatement avis à l'autorité ou à ses agents.[6]

B. *Penal Code of October 19, 1930.* Titolo XII. dei delitti contro la persona. Cap. I. dei delitti contro la vita o l'incolumità individuale.

Art. 593. Ommissione di soccorso.

. . . Alla stessa pena [la reclusione fino a tre mesi o la multa fino a lire 120.000] soggiace chi, trovando un corpo umano che sia o sembri inanimato, ovvero una persona ferita o altrimenti in pericolo, omette di prestare l'assistenza occorente o di darne immediato avviso all' Autorità.

Se da siffatta condotta del colpevole deriva una lesione personale, la pena è aumentata; se ne deriva la morte, la pena è raddoppiata.[7]

5 *Norway*

Penal Code, May 22, 1902, as amended March 1, 1961. Misdemeanors against persons.

Sec. 387. Punishment by fines or imprisonment up to three months shall be imposed upon anybody who omits, although it was possible for him without any special danger or sacrifice to himself or others, to:

1. help according to his ability a person whose life is in obvious and imminent danger, or

2. prevent by timely report to the proper authorities or otherwise according to his ability, fire, flood, explosion or similar accident which endanger human lives.

If anybody dies due to the misdemeanor, imprisonment up to six months may be imposed.[8]

---

[6] Code Pénal d'Italie (30 Juin 1889) traduit par Jules Lacointa, Paris, 1890, Imprimerie Nationale, p. 175. Art. 389 was inspired by Art. 97 of an old regulation of Tuscany on repressive police powers and by Art. 450 of the Dutch penal code [above under #3], *ibid.*

[7] Codice Penale e Codice di Procedura Penale, Ulrico Hoepli, Milano, 1963, p. 119.

[8] The Norwegian Penal Code, translated by Harald

6 *Russia*

A. Penal Code, March 22, 1903. Part XXV. Abandoning in danger.

Art. 491. Any person who, witnessing a danger threatening the life of another person, does not report it to the competent authority or who does not render or furnish aid in spite of being able to render or furnish it without reasonable fear for himself or others—if as a result death or very grave bodily injury of the person in need of aid occurred—shall be punished by arrest up to one month or a fine up to 100 rubles.[9]

B. *RSFSR*—Penal Code, October 27, 1960.

Sec. 127. Leaving in danger. The failure to render aid which is necessary and is clearly required immediately to a person in danger of death, if such aid could knowingly be rendered by the guilty person without serious danger to himself or to other persons, or the failure to inform the appropriate institutions or persons of the necessity of rendering aid, shall be punished by correctional labor tasks for a term not exceeding six months or by social censure or shall entail application of measures of social pressure.[10]

7 *Turkey*

Criminal Code, March 1, 1926. Chapter 5. The Crimes of Leaving Unattended Children, Persons Unable to Take Care of Themselves and Persons Who Are in Danger.

Art. 476. . . . Whoever comes upon [finds] a person wounded or in danger [of life], or a dead [human] body or one appearing to be dead and fails to render any possible aid [to him] or fails to notify the proper office or a government official immediately, shall suffer the same punishment [a heavy fine of 5–50 liras].[11]

Schjoldager, Sweet & Maxwell Ltd., London, 1961, The American Series of Foreign Penal Codes, 3, Norway, p. 152.

[9] W. Makowski, *Kodeks Karny,* vol. III, Warszawa, 1922, p. 141, text checked with Code Pénal Russe, traduit par E. Eberlin, Paris, A. Pedone, 1906, p. 142.

[10] *Soviet Statutes and Decisions, A Journal of Translations,* Fall 1964. Vol. I, #1, Criminal Code of the RSFSR, p. 60.

[11] Turkish Criminal Code, English translation, Headquarters, U. S. Air Forces in Europe. Office of the Staff Judge Advocate, 1960, p. 142; text corrected by comparison

8 *China*

Civil Code of the Republic of China, May 23, 1929. Book I. General Principles. Chapter VII. Exercise of Rights.

Art. 149. A person acting for the purpose of defending his own rights or the rights of another person against any imminent unlawful infringement is not liable to make compensation, provided that, if anything is done in excess of what is required for necessary defense, a reasonable compensation is due.

Art. 150. A person acting for the purpose of averting an imminent danger threatening the body, liberty or property of himself or of another person is not liable to make compensation, provided that the act is necessary for averting the danger and does not exceed the limit of the damage which would have been caused by the danger.

In the case provided in the preceding paragraph, if the person so acting is responsible for the happening of the danger, he is liable to make compensation.[12]

9 *Denmark*

Criminal Code, April 15, 1930. Chapter XXV. Offenses of Violence against the Person.

Art. 253. Any person who, though he could do so without particular danger or sacrifice to himself or others, fails

1. to the best of his power to help any person who is in evident danger of his life, or

2. to take such action as is required by the circumstances to rescue any person who seems to be lifeless, or as is ordered for the care of persons who have been victims of any shipwreck or any other similar accident; shall be liable to a fine or to simple detention for any term not exceeding three months.[13]

10 *Poland*

Criminal Code of July 11, 1932 (still in force). Failure to render aid in danger.

Art. 247. Whoever does not render aid to a person who is in a situation endangering immediately his life, when he can do so without exposing himself or persons close to him to a personal

---

with *Das Türkische Strafgesetz* vom 1 März 1926. Dr. Naci Sensoy and Dr. Osman Tolun, Berlin, 1955, p. 108.

[12] The Civil Code of the Republic of China, English translation. Shanghai 1931, p. 41.

[13] The Danish Criminal Code, Copenhagen, G.E.C. Gad Publishers, 1958, p. 103.

danger, shall be punished by imprisonment up to three years or detention to three years.[14]

11 *Germany*

A. *Criminal Code, May 15, 1871* amendment June 28, 1935.

Par. 330c. Wer bei Unglücksfällen oder gemeiner Gefahr oder Not nicht Hilfe leistet, obwohl dies nach gesundem Volksempfinden seine Pflicht ist, insebesondere wer der polizeilichen Aufforderung zur Hilfeleistung nicht nachkommt, obwohl er der Aufforderung ohne erhebliche eigene Gefahr, und ohne Verletzung anderer wichtiger Pflichten genügen kann, wird mit Gefängnis bis 2 Jahren oder mit Geldstrafe bestraft.[15]

B. *Criminal Code, May 15, 1871,* amendment August 25, 1953.

Par. 330c. Wer bei Unglücksfällen oder gemeiner Gefahr oder Not nicht Hilfe leistet, obwohl dies erforderlich und ihm den Umständen nach zuzumuten, insbesondere ohne erhebliche eigene Gefahr und ohne Verletzung anderer wichtiger Pflichten möglich ist, wird mit Gefängnis bis zu 1 Jahre oder mit Geldstrafe bestraft.[16]

12 *Rumania*

Criminal Code in force January 1, 1938, text of February 27, 1948.

Sec. 489. . . .

Subject to the same penalty [correctional imprisonment from one to three months] is also whoever, seeing a gravely wounded person or someone in danger of death, fails to render aid to him if rendering does not expose him or other persons to danger of death or else to notify the organs of authority about it immediately.[17]

13 *France*

Criminal Code, February 12, 1810, amendment of October 25, 1941 and June 25, 1945.

Art. 63. Sans préjudice de l'application le cas échéant, des

[14] Mieczyslaw Siewierski, *Kodeks Karny i Prawo o Wykroczeniach,* Komentarz, wyd. IX, Warszawa, 1965, *Wydawnictwo prawnicze,* p. 310.

[15] Strafgesetzbuch, Ministerium der Justiz der DDR, Berlin, 1951, p. 150.

[16] Kohlrausch-Lange, *Strafgesetzbuch,* 41 Aufl. Walter de Gruyter & Co., Berlin, 1956, p. 605.

[17] *Ugolovnoie zakonodatelstvo zarubezhnikh sotsialisticheskikh gosudarstv. Rumynskaia narodnaia respublika.,* trans. M. A. Gelfer, Moskva, 1962, p. 280.

peines plus fortes prévues par le présent code et les lois spé-
ciales, sera puni d'un imprisonnement de trois mois à cinq ans
(Ord. 25 juin 1945) et d'une amende de 360 NF à 15.000 NF
ou de l'une de ces deux peines seulement, quiconque, pouvant
empêcher par son action immédiate, sans risque pour lui ou
pour les tiers, soit un fait qualifié crime, soit un délit contre
l'intégrité corporelle de la personne, s'abstient volontairement
de le faire.

Sera puni des mêmes peines quiconque s'abstient volontairement de porter à une personne en péril l'assistance que sans
risque pour lui ni pour les tiers, il pouvait lui prêter, soit par
son action personelle, soit en provoquant un secours.

Sera puni des mêmes peines celui qui, connaissant la preuve
de l'innocence d'une personne incarcérée préventivement ou
jugée pour crime ou délit, s'abstient volontairement d'en ap-
porter aussitôt le témoignage aux autorités de justice ou de
police. Toutefois, aucune peine ne sera prononcée contre celui
qui apportera son témoignage tardivement mais spontanément.

Sont exceptés de la disposition de l'alinéa précédent le coup-
able de fait qui motivait la poursuite, ses co-auteurs, ses com-
plices et les parents ou alliés de ces personnes jusqu'au quat-
rième degré inclusivement.[18]

14 *Hungary*

A. *Art. 377 Criminal Code Act. XLVIII of 1948 omitted.*[19]

B. *Criminal Code Act V of 1961*. Omission to Lend Assistance.

Sec. 259 (1). Whoever does not lend such assistance, as could
be expected from him, to an injured person, to the victim of an
accident, or a person in a situation which directly endangers
life or corporeal integrity, shall be punished with loss of liberty
not exceeding one year.

(2). Punishment shall be loss of liberty not exceeding three
years if the injured person died and his life could have been
saved by assistance.

(3). Punishment shall be loss of liberty not exceeding three
years or loss of liberty ranging from six months to five years
according to the differentiation made in paragraphs (1) and
(2), if the accident or situation directly endangering life or

18 Code Pénal, 59 éd., Petits Codes Dalloz, Paris, 1962,
p. 40.
19 See Dr. Ladislaus Mezöfy, *Die Ungarischen Straf-
gesetze,* Berlin, 1960, p. 118.

corporeal integrity was caused either by negligence or guiltless conduct of the perpetrator or if the perpetrator was by profession or also for other reasons obliged to lend assistance.[20]

15 Czechoslovakia

A. *Criminal Code, July 12, 1950.* Criminal Acts against the Life and Health. Failure to Render Aid.

Par. 227. 1. Whoever deliberately omits to render aid necessary to a person in danger of death though he can do so without danger to himself or others shall be punished by loss of liberty up to six months.

2. Loss of liberty up to one year shall be the punishment if the deed was perpetrated though due to his profession he was duty-bound to render aid.

Par. 228. The driver of a transport vehicle who, after a traffic accident in which he was involved, deliberately omits to render aid necessary to a person injured by the accident, although he can do it without danger to himself or another person, shall be punished by loss of liberty from three months to two years.[21]

B. *Civil code, February 26, 1964.* Prevention of threatening damage and undue enrichment.

Sec. 415. Everybody shall have the duty to behave so as to prevent injury to health and damage to property or undue enrichment to the detriment of society or individuals.

Sec. 416. (1) Everybody shall have the duty to notify the respective authorities of the danger of a serious damage. He shall have the duty to act if action is urgently needed for averting the damage; he shall not be obliged to do so if he is prevented from doing so by a serious circumstance or if he would thereby expose himself or persons close to him to a serious danger.

Sec. 418. (1) Anybody who has caused damage when averting an imminent threat not caused by himself shall not be liable for the damage unless the threat could have been averted under the given circumstances in another manner or if the consequence caused is obviously as serious or more serious than the one which had threatened.

Sec. 419. Whoever was averting a threatening damage or preventing undue enrichment shall be entitled to compensation

---

[20] Criminal Code of the Hungarian People's Republic, Budapest, Corvina Press, 1962, p. 99.

[21] *Trestny zakon,* 3d ed., Tatran, Bratislava, 1952, p. 186.

of effectively expended costs and of damages suffered by him in such action also from the person in whose interest he had acted, but such compensation shall not exceed the amount corresponding to the averted damage or undue enrichment.

Liability for failure to avert damage.

Sec. 425. Any individual who failed to fulfill his duty set in the provision of Section 416, para. 1, although its fulfillment would have prevented imminent damage may be ordered by a court to contribute to the compensation of the damage to an extent appropriate to the circumstances of the case, unless the damage may be compensated otherwise. The court shall take into consideration in particular what had obstructed the fulfillment of such duty and the social importance of the damage as well as the personal and material situation of the individual who had failed to do his duty.[22]

16 *Belgium*

Criminal Code amendment January 6, 1961. De quelques abstentions coupables.

Art. 422 bis. Sera puni d'un emprisonnement de huit jours à six mois et d'une amende de 50 à 500 francs ou d'une de ces peines seulement, celui qui s'abstient de venir en aide ou de procurer une aide à une personne exposée à un péril grave, soit qu'il ait constaté par lui-même la situation de cette personne, soit que cette situation lui soit décrite par ceux qui sollicitent son intervention.

Le délit requiert que l'abstenant pouvait intervenir sans danger sérieux pour lui-même ou pour autrui. Lorsqu'il n'a pas constaté personnellement le péril auquel se trouvait exposée la personne à assister, l'abstenant ne pourra être puni lorsque les circonstances dans lesquelles il a été invité à intervenir pouvaient lui faire croire au manque de sérieux de l'appel ou à l'existence de risques.

422 ter. Sera puni des peines prévues à l'article précédent celui qui, le pouvant sans danger sérieux pour lui-même ou pour autrui refuse ou néglige de porter à une personne en péril le secours dont il est légalement requis; celui qui le pouvant, refuse ou néglige de faire les travaux, le service, ou de prêter le secours dont il aura été requis dans les circonstances d'ac-

[22] Bulletin of Czechoslovak Law #1-2/1964, The Act No. 40/1964, C. of L. The Civil Code, pp. 122–23, 125.

cidents, tumultes, naufrage, inondation, incendie ou autres calamités, ainsi que dans le cas de brigandages, pillages, flagrant délit, clameur publique ou d'exécution judiciaire.[23]

[23] Les Codes Belges, vol. II. Matières Pénales, 30 éd., Bruxelles, 1961, p. 110.

Compensation and the Good Samaritan

NORVAL MORRIS*

The lesson of the parable remains firm and clear, but the passage of 2000 years has changed both the theory and practice of Good Samaritanship. On a modern superhighway, it is often positively anti-social *not* to pass by on the other side if a domino-sequence of tailgate collisions is to be avoided; to pass by and then to contact the nearest highway patrol for aid for the injured person is often the wiser course. To pick up the injured man, to put him in your Detroit donkey, and to take him to a hotel and pay for his board, committing him to the care of the hotel proprietor, is, in our complex social organization, an exercise in the wildest imagining. There are, thus, for us, important societal aspects to Good Samaritanship, a battery of complex social organizations through which the Good Samaritan should often best proceed—ambulance services, casualty wards, and social services to assist the injured person and his family. Good Samaritanship is no longer only an expression of individual empathy, of a one-to-one brotherhood; it has important societal and legislative aspects.

Professors Gregory and Tunc have excellently dealt with the Anglo-American and continental aspects of the problem. My friend Professor Waller tells me that he proposes to discuss in particular misprision of felony and other criminal law aspects of volunteering or not volunteering to assist a potential victim of a crime of violence, or to assist the police in the exercise of their duties when they need

* Julius Kreeger Professor of Law and Criminology, The University of Chicago.

such assistance. This happily leaves to me what I consider the single most important issue of immediate practical significance. I refer to the question of the compensation of those who are injured when assisting the victim of a crime of grave personal violence, or who are injured when assisting the police to prevent such a crime or to arrest a felon.

Morally and legally this issue is of central importance. Looking at Good Samaritanship in terms of social organization, is it not essential that society through its statutory law and administrative practice should at the very least say to the potential Good Samaritan: "Even though we may not compel you to assist your fellow citizen threatened by a crime of personal violence, or to assist the police when need exists, nevertheless, if your sense of human identity with your fellow citizen, of brotherhood, is such that you *do* assist him and suffer substantial loss thereby, we shall, as a community, share that loss with you"?

If it be replied that the criminal and not the total community should be compelled to compensate not only his victim but the Good Samaritan who came to his victim's assistance and was injured thereby, I would agree, but would point out that in most legal systems we have had no great success with providing such compensation, either by civil process or by compensation assessed at the time of the criminal trial. Our experience has generally been that such processes are inadequate, particularly after the state in the criminal trial has denuded the criminal of whatever assets he had. If the criminal *can* so compensate, it is wise in some cases to provide that he should; but this is a rare situation and a society which values Good Samaritanship cannot rely on this mechanism alone.

State compensation schemes are, in my view, essential if we are sincere in this matter of Good Samaritanship. The New Zealand Criminal Injuries Compensation Act of 1963 and the somewhat similar though less far-reaching scheme in the United Kingdom of 1964 provide experimental patterns which it is our clear obligation to emulate and further to develop. Each of these schemes covers the Good Samaritan coming to the aid of a potential victim of a crime of violence or assisting the police in the prevention of such a crime or arresting such a criminal. The Administrative Board, under the New Zealand scheme, which assesses and pays compensation to the injured Good Samaritan, is then subrogated to his rights against the criminal, and may in the few cases where it is appropriate to do so recover damages from the criminal.

Some seek to justify a state compensation scheme of this nature by reference to the assumed failure of the state's obligation to provide physical security for its citizens; to my mind, this is an error. Crime is endemic in our society and to justify compensation in terms of a failure or fault of societal organizations is unreal. But since crime is endemic, and since it is chance in many instances which defines who shall be the victim of crime, and a combination of chance and high moral qualities which define who shall be the injured Good Samaritan, it is surely proper that the society which is so organized that crime is endemic should share in the financial aspects of the loss to the Good Samaritan. We cannot bear the knife ourselves, but at least we can diminish the financial loss to the Good Samaritan, and to those who are financially dependent upon him, from the fact that he bore it for us. The analogies with workmen's compensation legislation and with compulsory third-party motor vehicle insurance are of some relevance; perhaps a closer analogue in this country are the extensive medical and social welfare provisions of the Veterans Administration legislation, by which the community shares in the loss to individual Good Samaritans (and their dependents) who have suffered for us from the external aggression of war; we should likewise share the loss to Good Samaritans who suffer for us from the internal aggression of crimes of personal violence.

I do not want to attempt here detailed analysis either of the New Zealand Act or the United Kingdom scheme. Both provide workable modest systems of compensation for the types of situations we have in mind. They provide maxima of compensation which should preclude the possibility of Good Samaritanship being manipulated as a technique of financial gain. Both direct that the claimant's behavior be taken into account when compensation is being assessed, and any excessive or immoderate Good Samaritanship can, as it should, work to reduce compensation. They provide, also, adequate techniques of minimizing the likelihood of success of fraudulent claims.

I well realize that the argument I have been offering for the financial compensation of certain Good Samaritans by the state does not by any means cover the whole issue of Good Samaritanship. It applies only where crime is involved and even then is confined to crimes of serious personal violence. But the situations where Good Samaritans have not stepped forward to assist the Kitty Genoveses, and the other victims of crimes of personal violence, whose solitary agony while their fellows hurry by on the other side of the road, or perhaps worse, stand there gaping, are exactly the situations in which the community through its law should promptly and clearly speak. Whether or not this makes any difference to the incidence of Good Samaritanship, we should so organize the community that we minimize the financial loss to the citizen who is prepared to act on his sense of expanding human brotherhood. It happens that to do so would not be a very expensive undertaking and that financially such schemes are well within the financial reach of countries no less wealthy than New Zealand and the United Kingdom. We face a question of societal Good Samaritanship and not a question of the budget. The case for cautious experimentation along the lines that New Zealand and the United Kingdom have pursued seems to me overwhelmingly strong morally and compelling also in terms of sound practical politics.

It is so easy to talk about the failure of others; of how Good Samaritanship seems to be a dying art among others. There is another parable, something about a mote and an eye, which seems to me to have relevance. Perhaps we should first talk about ourselves, and our failure to provide even minimum conditions financially to protect those amongst us who *are* willing to act the Good Samaritan.

Rescue and the Common Law : England and Australia

LOUIS WALLER*

Listening to Professor Tunc speaking about the provisions
in the French *Code Pénale*[1] reminded me of what Mait-
land once said when he was discussing the attitude of
common lawyers at that time to foreign law. He described
their attitude as one of ". . . very complete and traditionally consecrated ignorance."[2] Perhaps in this university,
where Professor Rheinstein carries out his great work,
that complete and traditionally consecrated ignorance has
been removed. By listening to the description which Professor Tunc gave of the French system, we may be led to
consider at least partial emulation. If nothing more, at
least the provisions of the French *Code Pénale* enunciate,
with the curious force that only the criminal law has, a
community attitude about certain sorts of misbehavior,
about certain sorts of omission in the circumstances which
he has mentioned to us. And whether or not the law leads
to direct, individual changes of heart, it at least continues
to serve as a *public enunciation* of what ought to be done
and a *public denunciation* of what is considered reprehensible. There is general agreement today that the criminal
law has a strong didactic purpose. It serves to teach, in its
own terrible fashion, the canons of right and wrong to
the community. In his unique and lucid fashion, Edmond
Cahn has pointed to this purpose by writing: ". . . Laws

* Sir Leo Cussen Professor of Law, Monash University, Australia.

[1] Art. 63. See Tunc, A., Recueil D.H. (1946) L.33 ff.

[2] Quoted in Gutteridge, H.C., *Comparative Law* (2nd ed.,
1949), p. 24. And see *loc. cit.*, pp. 23–25.

deserve our special attention because they enunciate the society."[3]

In the general discussions which take place about duties to help our fellows in distress, one often hears certain political cries being uttered. Those who oppose the introduction of provisions such as those which now exist in many European criminal codes raise the banner of "creeping socialism," and the cry of the "dictatorial state." It is important to remember, when we hear these catch cries, buttressed as they are by reference to the history of certain provisions—to the fact that the French provision was introduced by the Vichy regime, and that the German provision was introduced in 1935—that proposals for such introduction into the respective penal codes were made well before actual introduction took place. More important still, let us remember that when times changed after May 1945, both France and Western Germany retained these provisions as part of the criminal law of democratic states.[4]

My main aim is to provide some Anglo-Australian footnotes to Professor Gregory's vivid description of the common law's attitude to Good Samaritans. But first I must make one comment about the American experience. Professor Gregory made the very important point that at least the law ought not to put barriers in the way of those who want to come to the rescue. And he has described a number of disturbing cases. I wonder what Mr. Gerald Young, a citizen of New York, thought if and when he read the descriptions of the fate which overtook Kitty Genovese in 1964. Mr. Young came into contact with the law in a very literal sense one Friday afternoon in Manhattan. He saw two large men, dressed in plain clothes, seize a young boy, nearly pull his trousers down, and attempt to wrestle him to the ground. He leaped from a crowd which

[3] *The Predicament of Democratic Man* (1961), p. 75.

[4] See Dawson, John P., *"Negotiorum Gestio:* The Altruistic Intermeddler," 74 *Harv. L. Rev.* 817, 1073, 1101–8, esp. 1105–6 (1961); "The Failure to Rescue: A Comparative Study," 52 *Col. L. Rev.* 631, 639–40 (1952).

had gathered and landed several blows on one of these large men. Indeed he fought so strongly that he managed to break one man's knee cap. It turned out that both these men were plain-clothes policemen attempting to arrest the young boy in respect of some street offense. In these circumstances Mr. Young was prosecuted, under the provisions of the New York Penal Law, for third-degree assault.[5] It was clear—or at least it was never successfully controverted—that Young believed all the time that he was engaged in rescuing a young boy from two large bullies and that he had no knowledge that both men were police officers. The Supreme Court, Appellate Division, quashed his conviction before the magistrates on the basis that his honest and reasonable belief about the event rendered his conduct legally and morally innocent. Young thought he was saving someone from an unlawful and dangerous assault; the circumstance that he was in fact interfering with the police did not make him deserving of criminal punishment.[6]

Regrettably, a majority of the Court of Appeal reinstituted the conviction and, in so doing, they enunciated a reason of policy which we, in our present context, must find most disturbing. The court said, "We feel that such a policy" [a policy which would result in the freeing of Young in these circumstances] "would not be conducive to an orderly society."[7] As well, the court transformed the crime of third-degree assault, with which Young was charged, into a crime of strict responsibility, wherein any honest and reasonable belief an accused might have had about the circumstances and his own conduct was quite irrelevant.

It is important to remember that there were several dissents in this particular case. The dissenting opinion points out that, besides the doctrinal difficulties produced by the

---

[5] People v. Young, 210 N.Y.S. 2d 358 (App. Div., 1962); rev. 11 N.Y. 2d 274 (C.t. App., 1962).

[6] 210 N.Y.S. 2d 358 (1962).

[7] 11 N.Y. 2d 274 (1964), *per curiam.*

New York Court of Appeal's decision, public interest is not promoted.

Froessel, J., with whom Van Voorhis, J. concurred, said:

Although the majority of our Courts [sic] are now purporting to fashion a policy 'conducive to an orderly society,' by their decision they have defeated their avowed purpose.

What public interest is promoted by a principle which would deter one from coming to the aid of a fellow citizen who he has reasonable ground to apprehend is in imminent danger of personal injury at the hands of assailants? Is it reasonable to denominate, as justifiable homicide, a slaying committed under a mistaken but reasonably held belief, and deny this same defense of justification to one using less force? Logic, as well as historical background and related precedent, dictates that the rule and policy expressed by our legislature in the case of homicide, which is an assault resulting in death, should likewise be applicable to a much less serious assault not resulting in death.[8]

It is perhaps improper for an Australian temporarily visiting this country to point out this sort of case to Americans. But in an investigation about the law and Good Samaritans we should not overlook these—and I use the word advisedly—*perverse* judgments which do nothing more than raise barriers before those who would come to the rescue of their fellows in distress.

Let me turn now to developments in England and Australia. Speaking at large, one can say that both parliamentary and judicial legislation in the past few years has had two results. On the one hand, some barriers that are in the

---

[8] 11 N.Y. 2d 274, 277. The reference about homicide is to New York *Penal Law*, S.1055. There are critiques of the decision in 63 *Col. L. Rev.* 160 (1963), and 111 *U. Pa. L. Rev.* 506 (1963). Similar cases have been presented in Australia and England; R. v. Reynhoudt, 107 C.L.R. 381 (H. Ct. of Aust., 1962), esp. 385, *per* Dixon, C.J.; and R. v. Mark, [1961] Crim. L. Rev. 173, which mirrors Young's case exactly.

way of those who would be Good Samaritans have been
removed—the encouragement to Good Samaritanship, using the felicitous phrase which Professor Norval Morris
has coined—and, on the other, there has been the proscrip-
tion of those who do not, in certain carefully specified circumstances, move to assist someone in trouble. I shall
briefly describe the removal of barriers first.

No one has yet mentioned some of the really terrible
cases which have arisen under the general rubric of assisting the helpless. There have been cases where members
of the medical profession want desperately to render assistance but are prevented (or *think* they are prevented)
from so doing not by any physical barrier but rather by
the impossibility of obtaining the appropriate consent to
the use of a specific medical treatment, or of medical
treatment generally. Suppose a small baby or a young child
is desperately ill; a blood transfusion is medically necessary in order to save life; and yet the parents, because of
religious conviction, refuse to consent to this particular
procedure. Cases of this sort have arisen in the last few
years in the United States.[9] In 1959 there were two such
cases in New South Wales and Victoria.[10]

In New South Wales the doctors were able to move
with sufficient speed to have the child in question declared
a ward of the state, thereby taking it out of the care and
custody of its parents, and henceforth the necessity for
obtaining their consent in order to protect the doctors from
criminal and civil liability was removed. In Victoria, re-

[9] See Trescher, R. L. and O'Neill, T. N., "Medical Care for
Dependent Children: Manslaughter Liability of the Christian
Scientist," 109 *U. Pa. L. Rev.* 203 (1960). See also Erickson
v. Wilgard, 252 N.Y.S. 2d 705 (1962); Application of President
and Directors of Georgetown College, Inc. 331 F. 2d 1000
(U.S. App. D.C., 1964), reh. den. 331 F. 2d 1010 (U.S. App.
D.C. *en banc,* 1964), Cert. den. 84 S. Ct. 1883 (1964); Raleigh
Fitken-Paul Morgan Memorial Hospital v. Anderson and anor.;
201 A. 2d 537 (N.J., 1964), Cert. den. 84 S. Ct. 1894 (1964).
[10] R. v. Jehu, *Sydney Morning Herald,* 24–30 March, 1960;
12 April, 1960.

grettably, there was not sufficient expedition. The child died, and its father was subsequently successfully prosecuted for manslaughter in that terribly unhappy situation.[11] In both states the legislature moved, after these cases, to introduce specific legislation. Its effect is that, should it again happen that a parent decline or refuse to give consent to a life-saving blood transfusion (or cannot be found), the transfusion may lawfully be administered without the doctor or the hospital in any way running the risk of civil or criminal liability.[12]

[11] R. v. Jehu, note (10) *supra*. The accused was convicted of manslaughter "with the strongest recommendation for mercy as possible." He was released upon entering into a bond to be of good behavior for five years.

[12] The Medical (Blood Transfusion) Act, 1960 (Vic.) provides:

(1) Where—

  (a) any person legally entitled to authorize a blood transfusion upon a child—

    (i) has failed or refused to authorize a blood transfusion upon the child when requested so to do; or

    (ii) cannot be found after such search and inquiry as is reasonably practicable in the circumstances of the case; and

  (b) any two or more legally qualified medical practitioners have agreed—

    (i) as to the condition from which the child is suffering;

    (ii) that a blood transfusion is a reasonable and proper treatment for the condition; and

    (iii) that without a blood transfusion the child is likely to die—

then any legally qualified medical practitioner who performs a blood transfusion upon the child shall, if he has had previous experience in performing blood transfusions and before commencing the transfusion assures himself that the blood to be transfused is suitable for the child, be deemed for all purposes to perform the transfusion with the authority of a person legally entitled to authorize the transfusion.

(2) In this section—

  . . . . .

We have slowly, in England and Australia, come to recognize that the Good Samaritan who is injured in his attempts to help is entitled to recover damages in a civil
action from the person who carelessly created the situation
of peril. Indeed, the rule in both countries is now the
same as that stated by Professor Gregory for the United
States.[13] Today, if a man carelessly puts *himself* in peril,
one who comes to his rescue in those circumstances can
successfully recover damages from the careless victim.[14]

Indeed, if one reads some of the *dicta* that have been
uttered recently by eminent judges in England, they clearly
reveal an attitude of encouragement to rescue. This was
particularly apparent in the judgment which Lord Denning,
M.R., delivered a couple of years ago in a case already the
subject of much critical comment: *Videan v. British Transport Commission.*[15]

In that case a hypothesis, long-posed by English law
teachers, actually occurred. The young child of a stationmaster, who happened to be standing on the station
platform, wandered onto the railway track. A motor trolley
was driven too quickly along the track; the driver ignored
frantic signals from the platform. At the last moment the

(b) "Child" means any person who is or appears to be
under the age of twenty-one years.

The Public Health (Amendment) Act, 1960 (N.S.W.) contains similar provisions.

[13] The leading case is Haynes v. Harwood [1935] 1 K.B.
146 (C.A., 1934). The Court of Appeal was clearly influenced
by an article by Dr. A. L. Goodhart, "Rescue and the Voluntary
Assumption of Risk" 5 Camb. L.J. 192 (1935), which contained a survey of the developments in America.

[14] Baker v. T. E. Hopkins & Son, Ltd. [1958] 3 All E.R.
147, aff'd. [1959] 1 W.L.R. 966 (C.A.); Chapman v. Hearse
[1961] S.A.S.R. 51 aff'd. 106 C.L.R. 112 (H. Ct. of Aust.,
1961), and Note, 35 A.L.J. 331 (1962); Dwyer v. Southern,
[1961] S.R. (N.S.W.) 869. See Fleming, J. G. *The Law of Torts*
(3rd ed., 1965) 165–67.

[15] [1963] 2 Q.B. 650 (C.A.), and Notes, 79 L.Q.R. 586
(1963); [1963] Camb. L.J. 193; 37 A.L.J. 335 (1963).

stationmaster (who was also, you recall, the child's father) jumped and threw the child aside, but was himself killed. The Court of Appeal decided that the British Transport Commission (the employers of the trolley driver) owed no duty to the child, who, since he was unlawfully on the track, was characterized as a trespasser. Nevertheless, the commission *was* liable to his father, who had come to the rescue.

The reasoning in the decision produces real difficulties.[16] For instance, the court decided that the trolley driver could not be expected to foresee a child on the track, but that he could be expected to foresee his father, *qua* stationmaster, leaping down to deal with an emergency. But these difficulties I shall not pursue. I bring the case to your attention in order to point out the atmosphere in which these sorts of cases are presently decided in England and to underscore the proposition that it reflects a policy of favoring the rescuer.[17]

Let me now turn from those specific legislative and judicial responses which have had as their purpose the removal of barriers in the face of, or the encouragement to, Good Samaritanship, and turn to those which have resulted in the creation either by courts or legislatures of sanctions for those who do not come to the rescue. Perhaps here the most interesting development is what some would call the resuscitation, and others the creation *de novo,* of the crime of misprision of felony.

Misprision of felony may be defined as the concealment of any information about a felony from the law-enforcement authorities by one who has a reasonable opportunity to make such disclosure. Professor Morris bears some re-

---

[16] But see Fleming, *op. cit.,* at p. 166, who supports the decision.

[17] See especially [1963] 2 Q.B. 650, 669, per Denning, M.R.; Whoever comes to the rescue, the law should see that he does not suffer for it. It seems to me that, if a person by his fault creates a situation of peril, he must answer for it to any person who attempts to rescue the person who is in danger. He owes a duty to such a person above all others.

sponsibility, or deserves some credit, for this resuscitation. Prosecutions for misprision were almost unknown in England and Australia, but one was launched in New South Wales in 1955 and he wrote a careful note about it.[18] I am sure that it was his note, referring to the elements of the offense, which helped to produce the important case of *R. v. Crimmins*[19] in Victoria.

There the accused was shot in the course of a brawl in Melbourne and taken to hospital, where he was questioned by the police. He readily admitted that he had been shot and that he knew the name and the probable address of his attacker. But he refused to say who the man was and where he could be found. His reasons were ones mentioned in earlier papers in this volume. He told the police that he would "cop it sweet" if he spoke, and his phrase can be worked out even by Americans. Crimmins was charged with misprision of felony in that he did not reveal to the police all that he knew about the purported felony, the circumstances of which were "shot home to him." He was duly convicted and his conviction supported by the Full Court of the Supreme Court of Victoria. The court held that the offense was committed by mere neglect to reveal, even though the accused thereby gained no benefit—except perhaps his life—by his silence.

R. v. Crimmins might have been regarded by those critical of the imposition of duties to inform on the public at large as a mere Victorian aberration, had it not been for the decision of the House of Lords in *Sykes v. Director of Public Prosecutions*[20] some three years later. In *Sykes's*

[18] R. v. Hosking (Q.S., N.S.W.); note by Norval Morris, [1955] *Crim. L. Rev.* 291.

[19] [1959] V.R. 270.

[20] [1962] A.C. 528 (1961). The House of Lords has heard more criminal appeals in the five years since 1960 (when the Administration of Justice Act made it possible to initiate such appeals without the *fiat* of the Attorney-General) than it did in all years between the passing of the Criminal Appeal Act, 1907 and 1960. At the same time its recent work as a Court of Criminal Appeal has been the subject of very severe criticism. See

case the House of Lords reached the same decision as the
Supreme Court of Victoria had reached. Their Lordships
decided that the crime of misprision of felony was known
to the law, that it consisted of neglecting to inform the
authorities of any felony—(and here, of course, the ancient
distinction between felony and misdemeanor takes on once
again a new lease of life)—of which you know or probably
of which you suspect. It is true that the offense is cast in
very broad terms, and this, of course, is one reason why
so much criticism has been directed at the decision. If one
ignores the qualifications which some members of the
House of Lords sought to introduce, it seems to impose a
duty to reveal to the authorities minor offenses which, because of historical accident or legislative prescription, happen to be cast as felonies.

Lord Denning, in particular, attempted to establish
boundaries within which the ordinary citizen could keep
quiet without incurring criminal sanctions.[21] His Lordship
said that there were "just limitations" to the duty to disclose or inform, and that people in well-established privileged relationships would not be guilty of misprision if they
kept confidences. However, he continued with these dra-
conic sentences:

> But close family or personal ties will not suffice where
> the offence is of so serious a character that it ought to be
> reported. In 1315 it was held that it was the duty of a
> brother to raise hue and cry against his own brother . . .
> and in 1938 a mistress was found guilty of misprision for
> shielding her lover. . . .[22]

There is still much opposition in England and Australia

---

e.g., Seaborne Davies, "The House of Lords and the Criminal
Law," 6 J.S.P.T.L. 104 (1961).

[21] [1962] A.C. 528, 564–65.

[22] [1962] A.C. 528, 564. See the critical appraisal by Glazebrook. "How Long, then, is the Arm of the Law to be?"
25 *Mod. L. Rev.* 301, 317 (1962).

to the continued existence of this kind of offense.[23] The American experience clearly buttresses this opposition. In 1940 the Supreme Court of Michigan[24] reiterated the statement made by Marshall, C. J., in *Marbury v. Brooks*[25] that

> It may be the duty of a citizen to accuse every offender, and proclaim every offence which comes to his knowledge; but the law which would punish him in every case for not performing this duty is too harsh for man.

The Michigan court held that misprision was "wholly unsuited to American criminal law and procedure as used in this State."[26] On the other hand, misprision of felony is a federal offense,[27] but more than mere non-disclosure must be proved by the prosecution. It must prove some positive act of concealment by the accused.[28]

But while the criticisms about the *extent* of the duty to inform have point, this may surely be said in support of the revival or rebirth of misprision of felony: in England and Australia people will read in their newspapers and hear on their radios that people are prosecuted, and perhaps convicted and punished, for failing to tell the police about serious offenses.[29] Perhaps this knowledge that the criminal

---

[23] See especially Seaborne Davies n. 20 *supra* and Glazebrook, n. 22 *supra*.

[24] People v. Lefkovitz, 294 Mich. 263 (1940).

[25] 20 U.S. 556 (1820).

[26] See Note, 8 *U. Chi. Law Rev.* 338 (1940), and see Commonwealth v. Lopes, 61 N.E. 2d 849 (Mass., 1945).

[27] U.S.C., S. 5390.

[28] See U.S. v. Farrar, 38 F. 2d 515 (1st Circ., 1930), aff'd. 281 U.S. 624 (1930); Bratton v. U.S., 73 F. 2d 795 (10th Circ., 1934); and Neal v. U.S., 102 F. 2d 643 (8th Circ., 1939). The A.L.I. *Model Penal Code* contains no provision dealing with non-disclosure; see comments, Tent. Draft No. 9 (1959), 209.

[29] There have been several reported prosecutions in England and in Victoria since 1961. See, e.g., R. v. King, [1965] 1 W.L.R. 706 (C.C.A.); R. v. Wootton, (Melbourne) *Age,* 17 June, 1965.

calendar contains this crime of omission to inform may persuade some people who at some time see a violent assault committed on some helpless victim to call the professional rescuers in our society—the police, the fire brigade, or the civil ambulance. Perhaps one of the watchers, who sees a young girl (like Miss Genovese) attacked, will reach for his telephone because he knows that he is obliged to call the police and may be labeled a misprisor should he neglect so to do. We are a generation concerned and disconcerted by sheep-like apathy in the face of our fellows' anguish and distress. As I said earlier, the criminal law serves, inter alia, to educate and remind. In the emergency of the moment, it may serve as a spur to action.

We are all familiar with legislation in our various jurisdictions which already exists to spur assistance, in one life situation, by using the prod of the criminal law. For instance, Sec. 80 of the Motor Car Act 1958 (Vic.)[30] imposes a duty on any person, the presence of whose motor car on a highway has caused an accident, immediately to stop and render such assistance as he can. The penalties now proscribed for failure to render such assistance are quite stringent, particularly for him who sins more than once. It is important to notice that this duty to assist is imposed even on a driver who has not been at fault in respect of the accident. The statute simply proscribes neglect to render assistance.[31] This provision is significant because it points out that such a section can be drawn to impose criminal liability for neglect to assist in certain circumstances. Courts have not found it unduly hard to work out the limits of its application. So again we ought to consider whether the creation of criminal liability in other specified circumstances, carefully delineated like those, might be of some real importance in encouraging assistance

---

[30] As amended by the Motor Car (Amendment) Act, 1961, which increased the penalties for breach of the duty to stop.

[31] See, e.g., the Uniform Traffic Act, Illinois Rev. Stat. 1950, C.95½, sec. 135.

and in enunciating the community's attitudes toward what people ought to do in such cases.[32]

The last specific response to which I want to advert is one that was contemplated hypothetically by Professor Gregory. I say "specific" because it springs again from particular incidents which apparently shocked the community and focused its attention on something that, of course, had occurred on many previous occasions.

In 1962 an inquiry into a mass resignation of doctors on the staff of a hospital near Sydney revealed that medical aid had been unavailable to a badly injured man brought to the hospital, who subsequently died. At the same time as reports of this incident were appearing in the press, the following letter was published.[33]

> About midnight on March 24, my baby was very fretful and wouldn't settle down. His body felt red hot, and he appeared to be having trouble with his breathing. After a short time, he became worse, and my husband and I decided to take him to a doctor. . . . In the early hours of Saturday morning I phoned my doctor's answering service, but he wasn't available, and on stating how serious I thought things were, I was directed to the nearest doctor or hospital.
>
> The doctor was very annoyed at being disturbed—for that he cannot be blamed I suppose—but in an emergency these things must be done. . . .

[32] See the provision in the *International Convention for the Safety of Life at Sea*, 1948 which provides:
The master of a ship at sea, on receiving a signal from any source that a ship or aircraft or survival craft thereof is in distress, is bound to proceed with all speed to the assistance of the persons in distress, informing them if possible that he is doing so.
[33] *The Sun* (Sydney), 9 January, 1962. And see *The Herald* (Melbourne) 16 January, 1962. The debates on the amending legislation are illuminating: N.S.W. *Parliamentary Debates*, 3d Ser., Vols. 45 and 46.

The baby by this time was a dreadful color and had been moaning and gasping. However, all this doctor was interested in, was who was my doctor and why didn't I see him. I explained how I had phoned and was told to consult the nearest doctor or hospital, but still he raved on that I should see my own doctor. It was useless arguing, so I got up to go and I told him if my baby died it would be his fault. With that he slammed the door in our faces. . . .

Arriving back, it must have been around five on the Saturday morning, we knew our baby was far from well. But all that could be done was to wait for surgery hours and see our own doctor, and surgery hours started at 9 a.m. So straight away, my husband rang a children's hospital, we rushed down, and even then, until a whole rigmarole was completed, he couldn't be admitted. It was 11.30 a.m. when that did happen, and by 10.30 that night my baby was dead. The autopsy showed double pneumonia caused by some virus which is very sudden. . . .

After discussions initiated by the Minister of Health in the New South Wales government, and the lapse of some twelve months, the Medical Practitioners (Amendment) Act was introduced in 1963. It amends the definition of what shall be considered "infamous conduct in any professional respect" by any medical practitioner, as follows:

[If he] *refuses or fails, without reasonable cause,* to attend within a reasonable time after being requested to do so, upon a person for the purpose of rendering professional services in his capacity as a medical practitioner *in any case where he has a reasonable cause to believe that such person is in need of urgent attention* by a medical practitioner; but shall not be guilty under this paragraph of such conduct if he causes another medical practitioner to attend as aforesaid.

Now, of course, this provision is cast within the terms of legislation controlling the practice of the profession of medicine. But we would be blind to ignore the circumstance that it is as much a penal provision—and perhaps a penal provision of a very dreadful sort as far as doctors are concerned—as would be a like provision in the Crimes Act of New South Wales. Upon a conviction of infamous conduct, a medical practitioner may find himself reprimanded, suspended, or struck from the roll and unable to practice his profession for the rest of his life.

There will be difficulties in interpreting the phrases which are emphasized in this particular section. The section employs general terms and thus demands case-by-case interpretation. But there is nothing novel in that; it is in the nature of statutory control of action through words. When the section was first introduced indeed, it carried the words, "proof whereof shall lie upon the registered person," after the first appearance of the phrase "without reasonable cause." These words were ultimately excised as the result of criticism that the burden of proving his innocence had been cast upon the accused doctors. But in the discussions which this novel legislation provoked, it became apparent that many people, including many doctors, thought that it was not a bad provision to add to this particular sort of statute.[34] While it was hoped that, by and large, it would be a completely unnecessary provision, it clearly served this announcing and denunciatory purpose which I have previously mentioned.[35] If legislation proscribing neglect to assist is enacted in respect of doctors, why not in respect of people generally?[36]

[34] Mr. Sheahan, M.L.A. (Minister of Health), who piloted the bill through the Legislative Assembly, stated that the provision resulted from "a recommendation from the doctors themselves" made at a meeting he called after the incidents mentioned in the text: See *Debates,* Vol. 45, p. 3807.

[35] See "Doctors and the Onus of Proof," 37 *Aust. L.J.,* 38; also *The Bulletin* (Sydney) 13 April, 1963.

[36] See "Good Samaritans and Liability for Medical Malpractice," 64 *Col. L. Rev.* 1301 (1964). The American pattern has been to enact legislation protecting doctors from suit in cases where they assist in emergencies. The N.S.W. legislation dis-

We have been reminded, in the course of the still current controversy about the proper ambit of the criminal law, that that large question has already been argued by nineteenth-century champions. The present debate about the propriety of punishing immorality as such, joined between Lord Devlin and Professor Hart,[37] is a reiteration, sometimes in identical terms, of the debate which was joined between John Stuart Mill and Sir James Fitzjames Stephen nearly a hundred years ago.[38]

Our questions of today, about the imposition of duties not to be heroic but at least to be a decent member of the community, have been debated over and over through the centuries. The parable of the Good Samaritan is 2000 years old. One hundred and fifty years ago, Jeremy Bentham, in his proposed Criminal Code, urged the addition of many more "duties of beneficence" than the common law then recognized.[39] At the same time Lord Macaulay, in his pellucid *Notes on the Indian Penal Code*[40] (which Ste-

---

courages frivolous or malicious complaints by providing that they must be made on oath and further provides that complainants who are neither police officers nor members of the public service must lodge a deposit with their sworn complaints. If the investigating committee (established by sec. 27 A[1]) considers that a complaint is "vexatious or frivolous," then the deposit is forfeited: sec. 27 A(4).

[37] Lord Devlin, *The Enforcement of Morals* (1965), and H. L. A. Hart, *Law, Liberty and Morality* (1963).

[38] Mill, *On Liberty* (1859); Stephen, *Liberty, Equality, Fraternity* (1873).

[39] Bentham, "Specimen of a Penal Code" in *Works* (Bowring ed., 1843) I.164:

"Every man is bound to assist those who have need of assistance, if he can do it without exposing himself to sensible inconvenience. This obligation is stronger, in proportion as the danger is the greater for the one, and the trouble of preserving him the less for the other."

See Ames, J. B., "Law and Morals," *supra*, pp. 1–21.

[40] Macaulay, *Miscellaneous Writings* (1880) IV.103,106. See also Michael, J. and Wechsler, H., *Criminal Law and its Administration* (1940), pp. 120–23.

phen saw as the common law without any of its excrescences), pointed out what he thought to be the great difficulties which attach to the prescription of duties to act in the sorts of circumstances that we are considering.[41]

I join with Professor Morris in saying that the most encouraging thing today is to find the debate being joined at large, not simply in writings on jurisprudence and the theory of legislation but in the columns of responsible newspapers and journals. I join with him in thinking that this indicates a growing awareness that there are substantial problems which all thinking people must ponder.

[41] See "The Failure to Rescue: A Comparative Study," 52 *Col. L. Rev.* 631 (1952), esp. at pp. 642–44.

The Vanishing Samaritan

ALAN BARTH*

I am not sure whether it would be more politic to begin with thanks or with an apology. But since my guilt is outweighed by my gratitude, let me say, before I say anything else, that I am grateful to you, on a variety of counts, for giving me a part in this conference.

To begin with, I take it as a very heady compliment indeed to find myself in such a goodly company of scholars —and especially, if I may say so, without any disparagement of the other disciplines represented here, in the company of legal scholars. As a working newspaperman, a large part of whose extremely active Walter Mitty existence has been spent in triumphant courtroom contests— as an heroic defender of the distressed and the desperate, a Good Samaritan of the law, so to speak—I take a particular pleasure in lecturing to lawyers. It is true that I may not be very well equipped to do this; but it is an indulgence which I have no thought of foregoing on that account.

Second, I am grateful because the subject of the conference seems to me fascinating. I have already enjoyed the morning very much. And once this learned discourse of mine is completed, I expect to have a most interesting and edifying afternoon and evening.

Third, I have some ideas I want to express to you. And this, I suppose, affords the only valid justification for traveling a thousand miles to perpetrate a monologue.

My sole misgiving revolves around my own part in the proceedings. In his extremely kind letter inviting me to come here today, Professor Kaplan suggested that I should

* Editorial writer, the *Washington Post*. The following is the luncheon address delivered at the conference.

talk about "the newsworthiness and the significance . . . of the rash of reported incidents of failure to intercede and to assist persons in physical peril which have been appearing in the press of late." And then Professor Kaplan went on to say, "We should also like to have your views on the question of whether the large number of reported incidents of this nature which one now finds in the newspapers indicates that this problem is greater than it used to be or merely better reported, and, also, your views, from a news editor's vantage point, of why this kind of an incident is actually newsworthy."

I must say that this makes it sound a little bit as though Mr. Kaplan wanted me here as a newsman rather than as an amateur jurist, legal philosopher, and roving sage. If this is the case, he is going to be disappointed; and I am going to be exposed very speedily as a rank impostor.

I might as well say at once that I don't know whether newspaper notice of Good Samaritans and of Bad Samaritans is more or less common now than it used to be. I think it is fairly frequent because stories of this sort satisfy a natural and persistent public interest.

Whether you define news by the old man-bites-dog cliché or in more sophisticated terms, the original story of the Good Samaritan seems to me to be of the very essence of newsworthiness. The report of the Commission on Freedom of the Press published nearly two decades ago—the commission was headed by that distinguished legal scholar, Robert M. Hutchins, and the report was issued by the University of Chicago Press—had this to say about the nature of news: "The word 'news' has come to mean something different from important new information. When a journalist says that a certain event is news, he does not mean that it is important in itself. Often it is; but about as often it is not. The journalist means by news something that has happened within the last few hours which will attract the interest of the customers. The criteria of interest are recency or firstness, proximity, combat, human interest, and novelty."

I suppose that the customers—the readers of newspapers

—are interested in stories about Good Samaritans because such stories mirror their best expectations of themselves, provide an account, as it were, of their own Walter Mitty lives. And I suppose that they are interested in stories about Bad Samaritans because such stories reflect their apprehensions and misgivings about themselves—afford an expression, so to speak, of their own sense of guilt.

When a man reads that someone has, like Lord Jim, missed an opportunity to be a hero, or has, in a crucial situation, behaved like a poltroon and must live with the shame of this fact all the rest of his life, he tends to say to himself, "There, but for the grace of God, go I." To say, "There, but for the grace of God, go I" is always comforting because it assumes the continuance of God's grace.

I imagine it is richly reassuring to most people to read in a newspaper about heroic or self-sacrificing conduct by their fellowmen. It lets them feel that there is at least a potential of goodness in humankind. Let me read to you a very short letter which appeared not long ago in the *Washington Post:*

> Thank God, there are still good Samaritans left in our society. I refer to the two stories that appeared on your front page on February 5. William Dent, at the risk of his own life, saved the lives of Mrs. Richard Lampman and that of her infant son; and four brave soldiers, undaunted by cold and icy waters, plunged into the Potomac River and saved the life of Dr. Paul C. Aebersold.
>
> Sincere admiration and gratitude go to them all.

No city editor with the most rudimentary knowledge of his craft would have put the stories referred to in this letter anywhere but on page one. They have much more meaning for most readers, I fancy, than the news from Viet Nam or even from Selma, Alabama.

Naturally I have been looking for news stories of this kind in recent weeks, and I have found quite a few of them. They do not always turn out happily, however. Just a month ago Representative James C. Cleveland, a forty-four-year-old war veteran serving his second term in the House, was sitting downstairs in his home near the Naval Observatory in Washington, reading the newspapers and putting the finishing touches on a Lincoln Day speech. It was about ten-thirty in the evening when his wife heard a woman scream, alerted him, and he went outside. He saw a man carrying a woman down the street in his arms. The Congressman yelled to him, hoping the sound of a human voice might frighten the man. The man put the woman down and she walked toward a car parked at the curb where another man was standing.

Suddenly the man at the car came at the Congressman, a viciously curved linoleum-cutting knife in his hand. Cleveland backed into his house, slamming the door as the attacker reached it. The man kicked at the door, then hacked at it with a snow shovel standing nearby, and finally threw the knife through a window beside the door. Cleveland called the police. The two men and the woman drove off together in the car just before the police reached the scene. "It was a very frightening experience, a very helpless feeling, too," the Congressman said.

It was not an experience, certainly, which encourages others to go out and do likewise. The moral of this tale, rather, appears to be that it is safer, if not quite so noble, to mind your own business. A great many Washingtonians, and no doubt a great many other people in a great many other places, have asked themselves what they would do—what they could do—if they heard a cry for help on a lonely street or in a wooded park late at night. It is one thing to picture yourself as Sir Galahad and another thing to picture yourself as Don Quixote.

One can call the cops, of course; and that is the sensible thing to do. The degree of inertia and apathy exhibited at the tragic Kew Gardens affair which seems to have furnished the foundation for this conference is, I should suppose, about as rare as it is abhorrent. Cowardice, I think, is much more common—much more human—than callousness.

But calling the cops may not be very effective. A woman

may be knifed to death, or robbed or raped, before the best of police forces can get there to save her. Moreover, calling the cops can hardly be effective for the intervenor's image of himself as a hero. Sensible it may be, but heroic it is not.

Let us bear in mind, however, that the original Good Samaritan extolled by St. Luke was fortunate in not arriving on the scene until after the thieves had set upon the traveler, robbed him, and beaten him half to death. The Samaritan cared for him and showed him great kindness, but he did not put himself in any peril by doing so. Perhaps this is about as much as can be reasonably asked of the ordinary mortal man.

In my newspaper research for this conference, I came upon one item which, though it is perhaps of questionable relevance, I cannot refrain from telling you about. I need hardly ask, in so literate an audience, whether you are all familiar with the comic strip known as Dick Tracy and syndicated by the *Chicago Tribune*. However, for the benefit of the few who may have been out of the country or preoccupied with professional trivia during recent weeks when the strip dealt learnedly with the constitutional rights of hoodlums, I shall recount as briefly as possible a recent episode. You had better listen attentively if by any chance you are not familiar with Dick Tracy because, believe me, this plot thickens to a pretty high viscosity.

Well, you see, there's this character called Moon Maid who is married to Dick Tracy's adopted son, Junior, and who comes from the moon and so has a couple of rather odd-looking horns on her head which store up energy from the sun and throw out a sort of laser beam capable of setting fire to anything she may point her finger at. Moon Maid goes around New York in a sort of low-cut leotard and a pair of knee-high red boots—and, of course, those horns.

Then there's a character named Matty Square—up to no good, take my word for it without asking me to go into detail—who smokes a cigar, giving puffs of it from time to time to a cat whom he carries, perpetually, it seems, on his shoulder. Matty Square is the mastermind of a gang of hoods.

All right, one of Matty Square's hoods attacks a young woman in a public place, snatching at her handbag and at the same time applying a knife to her throat. "Help, help," she cries. A large crowd looks on; no one does anything. "Them cowards aren't going to involve themselves and maybe get arrested for violating my constitutional rights," the thug says in an outburst of social commentary.

Well, ladies and gentlemen, at that point Moon Maid comes into the picture. Realizing that the cowardly crowd will do nothing, she directs her built-in laser beam at the seat of the thug's pants and sets him on fire. He drops his knife, falls to the ground, his hypodermic syringe dropping from his pocket, and as he lies there he murmurs, "Somebody violated my constitutional rights."

The strip, you see, serves a double purpose. It is at once anti-libertarian and anti-humanistic. What it says, if I grasp its message correctly, is that the average American is a coward and a slob; I think Americans, on the whole, are really not quite so bad as all that. At the same time, it derides the procedural protections of the Constitution as mere gimmicks for coddling criminals; this is in full accord, as you know, with the current right-wing theorem that the basic causes of crime are not to be found in slums or in faulty education but rather in the bleeding hearts of do-gooders—Samaritans, you might say—on the country's courts.

It strikes me as interesting—if you will permit me a somewhat parenthetical observation—that the right-wingers are always so contemptuous of their fellow Americans. They are forever assuming that everyone but themselves is a coward or a Communist; and so freedom is terrifying to them. They reject democracy and democratic institutions because they have no faith in the capacity of ordinary men for self-government.

The law in the United States, as I understand it from reading Dean Prosser on torts, has persistently refused to recognize, or at any rate to enforce, the moral obligation of common decency and common humanity to come to the aid of another human being who is in danger. Whether this absence of a duty imposed by law to aid one in peril is preferable to the European tendency to impose affirmative duties to act in such situations, I shall leave happily to the lawyers among you. I doubt that the law produces much difference in actual practice. I mean to say that I suppose the law to be more a consequence than a cause of the way people behave; and I suppose that the way people behave is to a large extent a reflection of their circumstances and their traditions.

I want to say something about the circumstances and traditions of American life as they seem to me to affect the willingness of people in this country to accept and fulfill the obligations of common decency and common humanity. It seems to me that there are three important factors tending to fragment the community and the concept of a human family mutually dependent and tied together by bonds of fraternity.

One of these—I lump them together because they are two sides of the same coin—is the urbanization and industrialization of American life.

A second is the extraordinary mobility of life today.

And the third is the degree to which specialization of function prevails all around us.

Let me say just a few words about each of these. No doubt others of you, better informed than I, will have more to say about these determining conditions of contemporary life.

Whatever may have been the dreams and preferences of Thomas Jefferson, America's economy today is industrial rather than agricultural, and the American society is overwhelmingly urban rather than rural—in residence, at least, if not in political control.

This means that we live in such physical proximity to each other that we can preserve a degree of privacy and of individuality only by a determined and contrived isolation. Very often, in consequence, we do not want to know the people who live in an identical apartment next door or on the floor above or the floor below. We want, really, not to acknowledge their existence.

A colleague of mine on the *Post*, Wolf von Eckardt—the paper's architectural editor—pointed out to me the other day a difference between European and American approaches to the city which may well explain a great deal about the difference between their legal approaches to the Samaritan problem. "Many immigrants," he wrote in an article called "Our Anti-City City Planning," "came to these shores to escape the ancient walls of their home towns and the tyranny of landlords. They brought with them the desire to own a home of their own, and the British especially brought the idea of country life as morally superior to the evils of city life. The people of continental Europe have never shared this sentiment. . . . This country was settled in search of land and its promise of unrestrained individual freedom for him who owned and tilled it. . . . European farmers live in villages, their houses huddled close together, often surprisingly far from their land. They have obviously always considered community life worth miles of travel at dawn and dusk to get to work and home. . . . But the American ideal is that of rugged pioneer individualism. American farmers made their homesteads out in the fields. They came to town only for business."

So perhaps, to some extent at least, it is a stubborn American demand for privacy that keeps us isolated from each other—encapsulated, if you like—in the very midst of our crowded metropolitan centers. "The American compact," Walt Whitman wrote, "is altogether with individuals."

The second factor, mobility, is no doubt so obvious that there is little that need be said about it. Americans live a very large part of their lives on wheels—when they are not living in the air. It used to be that a man lived out his life where he was born—in the same town and commonly, indeed, in the same house. He lived with his parents and his grandparents, his children and his grandchildren and with the same neighbors all his life, time alone producing the changes in his environment.

But few Americans are so rooted today. I'll offer you a single, shattering statistic: one out of every five Americans moves every year.

The most formative influence of all, perhaps, is the third of the factors I spoke of—the degree of specialization in our daily lives. When Benjamin Franklin became the editor and publisher of the *Pennsylvania Gazette,* he wrote his own copy, set it, printed it, and peddled the finished product to his subscribers. I haven't any idea how to set type; and if I dared to put a line of type into a form in the composing room today, the entire plant would stop working. I don't belong to the Typographical Union; I belong to the American Newspaper Guild.

We are so used to thinking of accounting as exclusively the business of accountants, of steamfitting (whatever that may be) as exclusively the business of steamfitters, of firefighting as exclusively the business of firemen that it is hardly any wonder we tend to think of law enforcement as exclusively the business of policemen.

We have come, at least much more than in times past, to mind our own business—and, not wholly without justification, to make a virtue of doing so. There is certainly something to be said for the live-and-let-live attitude of big cities as contrasted with the busybodiness and Grundyism of small towns. Ogden Nash said this very well in that poem of his about New York:

> Best of all, if you don't show up at the
>   office or at a tea, nobody will bother
>   their head,
> They will just think you are dead.

Well, I come now, at the end, to what I most want to say to you. I suppose that there is no question more full of meaning for the nature of society than the question which Cain, after he had killed Abel, asked of God—"Am I my brother's keeper?" Only where this question can in some measure be answered affirmatively can a community in any meaningful sense be said to exist.

It seems plain to me that we are less our brothers' keepers in a personal way than we used to be. There is very little, or at any rate comparatively little, of the direct kind of almsgiving that proved so gratifying to Lady Bountiful a century or more ago. We no longer, like the Cheeryble brothers, give birthday parties and handsome presents to superannuated clerks grown old and gray in our service. Missionary help to the heathen is not now very fashionable. We don't go out among our fellow men to "do good" —I have those two words in quotation marks—in the old-fashioned sense as Scrooge learned to do.

Let it be said in our behalf, however, that we have recognized and accepted a collective responsibility as our brothers' keepers in a degree never before manifested. The diminution of individual concern for the hapless and helpless has been balanced by the growth of a common concern.

However inadequate may be our public welfare programs, our old-age assistance, our aid to dependent children, our public health clinics, public hospitals, public schools, our unemployment compensation and manpower rehabilitation systems, all these constitute, nevertheless, a general acknowledgment by the community that we are our brothers' keepers.

I do not want to play Pollyanna or Dr. Pangloss to this conference, and I do not mean to suggest that we have reached the millennium. The country is full of folly, ignorance, selfishness, meanness, and evil. But before we condemn ourselves out of hand as an unredeemed collection of savages and Bad Samaritans, let us look first at the stars in our eyes.

For my part, I think we have coming up out of our colleges these days a magnificent Good Samaritan generation. You have only to look at the Peace Corps to see how warm a sense of social concern has gripped the young people of America. You have only to recall the Freedom Movement in Mississippi or the march from Selma to

Montgomery, Alabama, to observe the extent to which young Americans are regarding themselves as their brothers' keepers. Whatever the value of the civil rights movement has been for Negroes, it has provided for the white people of this country a road to redemption. And that road has been taken with magnificent spirit by the youth of the country in particular.

You may think that this or that protest movement or demonstration is wise or foolish; you may think that the kids in this or that situation are idealists or idiots; but you can hardly doubt that they are moved by a sense that they are, in truth, their brothers' keepers.

And this sense is, really, the cement of any community. Without it, individuals are only blindly colliding neutrons and protons in a senseless solar system. With it, they move together to some inscrutable destination as members of mankind.

No Response to the Cry for Help

LAWRENCE ZELIC FREEDMAN, M.D.*

We must begin any discussion of the involvement or non-involvement of the average man in the violent emergencies of others outside his immediate circle not merely by admitting but by insisting on our ignorance. Nobody so far as I know has ever adequately studied it.

We don't know whether such non-involvement has increased, decreased, or has remained essentially constant over time and generations of men. We don't know whether there are differences between cultures, between emergent societies and established societies, between cultures in which the father dominates, those in which the mother dominates, or, as in our case, the children dominate; between urban groups and rural groups, between religious, God-intoxicated Bible Belts and agnostic, cocktail-intoxicated groves of academe, even between the criminal and the conformist.

For methods, we can only apply the fragments of knowledge we do have from as nearly analogous situations as possible, we can study such external evidence as is available, and we may compare repetitious experiments in nature and try to extrapolate significant and possibly revealing differences which may expose crucial determining factors. All of these methods are fraught with potential sources of error, but here, as on that road to Jericho, when we face a strange and fearful situation, we must involve ourselves or pass on the other side of the road.

* Foundations' Fund Research Professor of Psychiatry, The University of Chicago. The preparation of this paper was aided by the Otho S. Sprague Memorial Institute.

We cannot wait for advice from the tenets of the laboratory any more than from the tenets of the Torah.

For concepts, we must make the crucial and critical distinctions between ethics and socio-legal action and between the psychological and social sciences and the psychiatric therapies.

Can ethics be investigated psychologically? It has often been asked whether morality can be legislated. Usually the question is put rhetorically, by persons who wish to prevent legal intervention into an arena of social evil, even though they cannot or dare not associate themselves with the social wrong which they deplore. Not infrequently those who ask whether morality can be affected by law reply to themselves with certitude but with some internal inconsistency that "change must come from the hearts of men," and "you can't change human nature."

So we, too, must ask whether morality can be psychoanalyzed. Since morality by predisposition and training will not lie on a couch, we must perforce analyze the conflicting motives of people who uphold or degrade her.

Human mores, whatever their context—religious, legal, social, or familial—are part of human be-ing. They can, therefore, be studied, just as any other aspect of human be-ingness can be investigated, by observing how man acts.

Let us now utilize (as best we can) a very powerful instrument for psychological research. Let us use ourselves as laboratories. A most significant factor in our fumbling efforts to study human behavior and emotions is that we are both within and outside our subject matter. Our capacity to understand others is both limited and enriched by our capacity to face ourselves honestly. While the quantitative mix of proportions is different, all human propensities—however different they may seem—are within us.

Our experiment concerns a man—you. Our method is a semantic psychodrama. Involve yourselves. A man is speeding homeward along a superhighway at seventy miles an hour—the legal speed limit is sixty miles an hour. He is moving very fast, must be alert enough to prevent accidents, to spot traffic cops. He is, therefore, vaguely tense, but there are neither emergencies nor cops and haven't been for years and he is used to scenery. So he is somewhat bored as well. But he is also a little apprehensive because at that speed he might get hurt. Furthermore, he is breaking the law and that's not quite right—even if he doesn't get caught. But going fast and defying authority even in a minuscule fashion makes him feel somewhat freer, devil-may-care, exhilarated. So our subject is (1) moving along toward his own goal, (2) vaguely tense, (3) obscurely bored, (4) slightly apprehensive about risking his own physical safety and, therefore, his responsibilities to the wife and kids at home, (5) tinged with guilt because he's violating a law, (6) somewhat concerned about being apprehended, bawled out, delayed, and possibly fined, and (7) a little exhilarated at his own power and swiftness.

He turns on the radio, half-listens, imagines himself telling the boss off and winning that argument with his wife. Suddenly the large Cadillac ahead of him swerves into the opposing line of traffic and crashes into a tiny open sports car. The driver of the sports car is thrown into an arc and crashes headfirst onto the shoulder of the road. His face is covered with blood and he lies still.

What happens?

At first—nothing. The scene is so extraordinary, so terrible, so unexpected that it takes some seconds for our driver not only to see but to comprehend what has happened. Meanwhile, at his rate of speed he has traveled several thousand feet. He has passed the scene of the accident and its prone, bleeding victim.

Now the driver must decide whether he is going to act or not act. He has already not acted—he has passed on the other side of the road. So he must react to his own non-act, which was itself a sort of decision. To intervene and help this anonymous sports-car driving victim who has intruded so unexpectedly and violently into his life, he must now, quickly, do the unusual. He must drive his car off the road onto the middle grass and either make a U-turn or run back. Although he has often edged his speed up over the limit, he has never dared to violate the rule against

U-turns and parking on the middle green. If he goes back, he'll be late for supper, his wife will be annoyed, upset, and his oldest boy disappointed because he'd promised to take him to the basketball game. He realizes now that his stomach is warm and churning and his face feels moist and flushed. It comes to him as a shock that that victim might have been himself—and he would now be half-dead or dead on the road. Terrible! Poor kids and wife. Thank God it wasn't me. What a damned heartless thought. Or I might have been in the big car which ran down that little car. Awful idea! Did I pay my last insurance premium? Did I forget to renew my license? Could I make bond? I might have killed somebody. What a hell of a way to be thinking when that man is bleeding to death back there.

Meanwhile, the car is speeding along farther and farther away from the scene of the accident.

If I did go back, what could I do? I'm not a doctor. He needs a doctor. Maybe it would be most helpful if, as soon as I get home, I phoned for a doctor and ambulance. But the state police patrol every twenty minutes. By the time I get home they would certainly have found him and radioed for help. By now a couple of dozen cars have passed him. One of them may be a doctor and has stopped to heal him. Anyone who drives a sports car on this death trap is asking for it. And that guy in the big car, what could he have been doing? He was going steadily just ahead of me. And look at all those cars going in both directions. I'm not doing anything out of the ordinary. Everybody seems to be going on his way. That must mean that somebody is helping. It would be a hell of a thing if everybody stopped anyhow. It would block traffic. The ambulance couldn't get through, and he'd be worse off—just because of morbid curiosity. We have a very efficient state patrol. Seems to me I read somewhere that amateur first-aiders do far more harm than good. By now there are probably several police cars rerouting traffic and seeing to it that he gets all the care he needs.

So our non-hero speeds home at fifty-five miles an hour

—satisfied that he's done the right thing, but a little uneasy and a little ashamed.

I chose our hapless suburbanite as an example because his experience is a more common one—one which many, if not most, of you have shared. You may correct, add, or amend this semantic psychodrama for yourself.

The chances are less that you, like the thirty-eight neighbors of Kitty Genovese, ever saw or heard a murder being committed. But, if you had, I suspect that, as may have happened to some of the silent witnesses to the Genovese tragedy, a considerable percentage of you would have denied the reality or seriousness of what you heard. You wouldn't have believed it. If nothing is happening, then nothing, obviously, need be done. And you would have gone through reactions not unlike those which I have dramatized for you.

Let us speculate, rather more systematically, on what happens when someone does *not intercede* in the crisis of another human being in trouble.

Let me say at the outset that in my view apathy and indifference are the least likely primary psychic vectors in response to such an event. The sequence as I see it is, first, the intense emotional shock—characterized predominantly, but not exclusively, by anxiety; second, the cognitive perception and awareness of what has happened; third, an inertial paralysis of reaction, which as a non-act becomes in fact an act, and fourth, the self-awareness of one's own shock anxiety, non-involvement which is followed by a sense of guilt and intra-psychic and social self-justification.

I do not assume that these things happen in such neat sequence. For all practical purposes they seem to occur simultaneously. Not all the things I am to discuss happen to everyone; when they do occur, if they do occur, their relative strength and importance appear in the unique proportions of each idiosyncratic individual. I am talking about emotions as well as ideas, fantasies as well as accurate perceptions, subjective experiences which are unconscious as well as those that are conscious.

I think that by now it is apparent that although the con-

ference from which this book grew was organized in response to widely reported examples of non-intervention—of
"Bad Samaritans"—our legal scholars are concerned with
(1) the legal risks incurred by those who do intervene in
the troubles of others and, (2) the possible legal techniques
for promoting such intervention.

I shall emphasize the psychology of those who pass on
the other side of the road—pejoratively labeled "Bad
Samaritans," with, in my view, superb literary skill, but
inappropriate historical sense, since those who elected to
continue on the road to Jericho were not Samaritans. To
label them "Bad" is to burden our discussion with unnecessarily limiting *a priori* values. To impute guilt without
a fair trial violates not only our Anglo-Saxon traditions of
justice but our universal scientific ideal of value-free ob-
servations.

The psychic motivations of the man who passes on the
other side of the road may be viewed through the refract-
ing rays of a three-sided prism. One side or perspective I
shall call I. Apprehension or fear; the second, II. Acquiescence; and the third, III. Aggression.

I APPREHENSION OR FEAR

Common sense tells us, as do the silent witnesses themselves, that they dared not intervene in the service of a
victim because they were afraid. They were afraid of the
criminal and what he might do to them then or later. Or
they were filled with great anxiety not focused on any real
person or time—simply a diffuse dread of what might happen. And for some this confrontation dissolved them into
chaotic, disorganized panic.

For many the fear was real. However, it was focused
not on the criminal but on the protective agency itself—
the police. And, indeed, along with this heightened publicity of the frozen, non-participant witness, there has been
great journalistic emphasis on the police brutality.[1]

[1] I suspect that these social phenomena, (1) heightened sensi-

Whether or not there is police brutality directed toward witnesses which warrants such fear is an empirical question for which I do not have the answer.

However, almost all the reported cases of police brutality concern policemen and allegedly criminal members of minority groups dwelling in slums rather than middle-class white witnesses. For some of these at least, the fear of contact with police may range from concern about disrupting their own lives (by involving themselves in the detecting, judging, and punishing rituals) or perhaps more frequently and unrealistically a fear of authority and authoritative figures. To explicate this we must study the development of the "normal" conscience with its never completely resolved train of unconscious complicity in nameless (and non-existent) crimes and unconscious guilt.

II   ACQUIESCENCE

The silent witness to another's distress does in a sense acquiesce in it. How can that be when the great religions and stated ideals of all cultures agree on some form of what is called the "Golden Rule" to "do unto others as you would have done unto you," and "to love thy neighbor as thyself."

One can argue that developing into "mature adults" is essentially learning mechanisms for acquiescence. As babies at home, as youngsters in school, in religious institutions, and in service clubs—learning to live in the society of men consists fundamentally of a series of repetitive lessons in acquiescence. Subjectively, for the child and for the emergent adult, social learning is experienced as a complex pat-

bility of the problem of the silent, frozen witness, (2) newspaper emphasis on police brutality, and (3) the pervading sense that there is "terror in the streets," are all linked to a common fourth referent, the migration of the rural southern Negro to the urban complexes of the North and his emergent position in our society. But this aspect of the question can only be alluded to in this report.

tern of constricting, isolating, denying, displacing, rationalizing—acquiescing mechanisms.

From another point of view, we could explore the
psycho-social ramifications of acquiescence as pre-condi-
tions for the common social welfare—cooperation, collabo-
ration, and social participation. We cannot, however, with
any logic or consistency, be overwhelmed with surprise,
dismay, and disgust when it extends also to a tolerance for
the endemic evils of our society.

But since acquiescence in the misery of other men itself
violates our sense of our own values—the human personality would be confronted with the Hegelian dilemma of
thesis—neighborly love—and anti-thesis—acquiescence in his
misery—without the confluence of psychic synthesis—a man
who can stand being himself.

To avoid this discontinuity, rather, and to achieve this
internal consistency, he must synthesize these complex alternatives by psychic maneuvers within himself. Many of
these psychic squirmings were typified in the home-bound
suburbanite whom we discussed earlier.

Cognitively there is first the lack of perception, then the
lack of belief, and finally the absence of personal involvement. Emotionally there is the simultaneous churning of
many defined and diffuse feelings of various intensity
which are almost—but not quite—brought under control by
the ultimate rationalizations.

This emotional ambivalence of the thrilling and the
chilling is especially characteristic of the initial inertia and
paralysis of action. The almost instantaneous self-protective
surge of feeling, "Thank God it wasn't me," or the more
frightening, "It could have been me," is recognized, however fleetingly, as a sort of satisfaction. Satisfaction at another's disaster is surely an unacceptable response in a
Judeo-Christian ethic—so self-congratulation yields quickly
to guilt, to recognition of anxiety, and to recuperative self-
rationalizing measures—which protects the victim from further physical harm as the result of your neglect, and yourself from further physical distress as the result of your
non-involvement.

There is, as we've seen, the lack of accurate perception of what is happening and the inability to fit so grotesque an event into any recognizable familiar scene so as to be able to respond appropriately.

There is simply a denial, a disbelief that anything so violent, so frantic, so unusual could happen to you. The event simply is not grasped or comprehended; the very reality of the strange crisis is denied.

Behaviorally, normal anxiety is most efficiently handled by some form of relevant activity. But we are not geared to reduce our anxiety by taking effective action when the very intensity and strangeness of the experience has robbed us of our usual act-specific responses to lesser stress.

This concatenation of varying pressures results immediately in a sort of internalized moratorium. What is viewed by others externally as apathy may be within the personality a massive inhibition, a paralysis of conscious feeling, willing, and mobility—not because these mutually incompatible tendencies are so weak but because they are so strong.

Let us consider for a moment the "Bad Samaritan's" relationship to the victim. The victim, as well as his criminal aggressor, intrudes himself into the life of the witness. He threatens to explode the "quiet desperation," which the marginal witness is barely containing, into noisy, public panic. Both the victim and the aggressor are strangers to the witness. When he is first exposed to them, he sees them perforce as an interacting unit, an intimate, if desperate, pattern of human relationships. Together they have disrupted his life. Together they have delivered to him the ultimate challenge, the confrontation of his own vulnerability. The witness is thus at once an outsider, and at the same time intimately involved with both. Not only his own vulnerability but his sense of personal ineffectiveness and impotency must now be faced. For this the victim is as guilty as the aggressor and for this the witness may react as strongly against him as against the aggressor. The witness somehow feels the link that binds the aggressor and his victim. He wouldn't *be* a victim if he weren't involved *somehow* with the criminal.

The victim is an ordinary but imperfect human being. The appropriate response is pity and compassion. But even pity and compassion can be directed only at someone who is less intact, less powerful, less independent than we. To feel pity there must somewhere be a feeling of contempt for the hapless object; to feel compassion there must somewhere be a fellow feeling of self-contempt for the common shared experience of vulnerability.

In Leviticus, the book of laws according to which the priest and the Levite who passed the wounded man carried out their official rituals to reconcile man with man and man with God, there were instructions concerning the treatment of the sinner, the criminal, and the sick. All were profane, unclean, and contaminated. All were to be avoided by the healthy, the intact, and the virtuous, until they had been dealt with through prescribed rituals. There were important shared elements of unworthiness and blameworthiness in their common profane state.

The victim is associated with aggressor by a common taboo—fear of contamination. Sin and sickness and crime are bad, unclean, and profane. Therefore, all connected with them are bad, unclean, and profane. Therefore all who are connected with them are taboo. The ancient fear of contamination by touch is extended and extends to all unclean, profane, bad things. Modern medicine has not discovered asepsis. It has empirically isolated and restricted the area of taboo.

III AGGRESSION

The criminal, we must realize, is not a genetic sport, a mutation, an aberration in the human species. He is an accurate reflection and expression of a part of our social complexion and our private psyches. We fear him, and one way of overcoming fear is identifying, becoming one with the person whom we fear. Aggressive, perverse, and avaricious impulses are not solely the qualities of criminals. We need only point to the nature of the content of our newspapers, the conduct of foreign policy by never-ending wars, and the fact that most murderers strike, if not their own images, their own intimates, to realize the ubiquity of the propensity for human sadism and aggression. For many silent witnesses at the scene, and for millions more who read its details with scrupulous passion, the criminal is doing our work—and silence makes us his accomplice—and guarantees that we will not lose him.

If you have followed my speculations so far, you will perhaps take one further conceptual step with me. The silent witness handles the internal inconsistencies and achieves inner harmony within himself with some of the psychic mechanisms which we have adumbrated. He achieves synchrony with society by making crime one more of the significant areas of his life that are handled by specialists—the anonymous but expert authorities. After all, we have been taught that education and charity, for example, are not proper arenas for private endeavor. We can at best advise the experts of one and contribute funds to the experts in the other. If education and charity—why not, indeed, justice as well?

CODA

If you think that I have given an overly gloomy and depressing view of human nature, that has not been my intention. Hidden aspects of human personality are not the totality of this character. They are discussed here because they go beyond the purview of what is obvious.

Furthermore, I am convinced that people do help one another, that these vast urban aggregates of people not only survive but continue to attract not in spite of their inhumanity but precisely because in unmeasurable ways people reciprocate, aid, and complement each other.

I believe that the concern over the so-called Bad Samaritan springs not from any evidence that his tribe has increased in any statistical sense—but rather it comes from our heightened sensitivity and sensibility to our common responsibility for each other.

I believe with Sherrington that "we have, because human, an inalienable prerogative of responsibility which we cannot evade, no, not as once was thought even upon the stars. We can share it only with each other." And I agree with him, too, in spite of mute and circumstantial evidence of the silent witnesses: "The loveliest friend of man is man."

In fact, we are friends and witnesses for each other, or we are—literally—nothing.

Social Sources of Levites and Samaritans*

JOSEPH GUSFIELD**

It is paradoxical that we should have met at a conference
to discuss the absence of the Good Samaritan in a month
that saw one of the greatest outpourings of mass Samaritanism in American history. The Selma-Montgomery march
and the events surrounding it demonstrated again the existence of that vital tradition of reform and intervention
in American life. The effort to protect and improve the
weak, the underdog, and the victimized has often found a
quick response in American life. Many movements of disinterested people, motivated by complex patterns of religious and moral beliefs, occupy the pages of American
history. The spontaneous and rapid assemblage of indig-
nant people from many parts of the country in Selma
during that month is certainly testimony that mass communications and the large-scale society are by no means necessarily impediments to human and moral responses.

This realization is essential to our topic. The civil rights
movement in the United States indicates quite clearly that
we cannot understand the problem under discussion by
loose statements about the absence of charity, pity, or
sympathy in the general American population. Vague references to "mass society," "modern life," or "alienation"
are contradicted by the existence of the large-scale moral
intervention that came about in Selma. To understand the
problem of moral intervention we need to be more specific
than such vague rubrics enable us to be. Our problem is

* I am grateful to David Bordua, Solon Kimball, and Walter
Phillips for several fruitful suggestions.
** Professor of Sociology, University of Illinois.

not a problem in historical morality, an effort to find out whether or not we are better or worse today than we have been in the past. It is rather a question of the specific situations which generate a concern for a problem as well as developing the behavior about which the concern is generated.

Almost every age is given to contrasting itself unfavorably with the past. We are met at once in any discussion of the Good Samaritan by an immense lack of data. That cities have been violent and that men have been violent in the past is certainly evident. Whether or not we can find more or less instances of moral intervention than have existed in past cities and societies is an insoluble problem. We are attentive to the acts of nonfeasance in considering the question of the Good Samaritan. Our law is attentive to malfeasance. We must, of necessity, ignore the very many acts of bonfeasance, the acts of heroism in which people have indeed come to each other's rescue. It is an impossible task, marked by the absence of data, to determine whether such acts have increased or decreased. Even the effort to determine the rate of crime within the United States, or within particular cities, is an enormous failure. We are simply hard put to say anything about the historical shifts in violence, in crime, or in heroic rescue. We cannot even determine the kinds of situations which first gave rise to the American law on the subject of rescue.

William Prosser, that fount of wisdom and authority on the Law of Torts, has said, "The remedy in such cases is left to the 'higher law' and the 'voice of conscience' which, in a wicked world, would seem to be singularly ineffective, either to prevent the harm, or to compensate the victim."[1] It seems doubtful that such conscience and such higher law are indeed "singularly ineffective," but it remains to us to determine the social situations which generate our belief in their singular ineffectiveness, or at least our concern for such cases in which they are ineffective, and those

---

[1] William L. Prosser, *Law of Torts,* 3d edition, West Publishing Company, St. Paul, Minnesota, 1964, p. 336.

situations in which conscience and higher law do not appear to be effective. We might almost say that the very concern with the problem is evidence of a certain amount of moral progress. We are not a cynical nation, and our anxious response to the reports indicates our lack of cynicism, our expectation that human beings must act heroicly toward each other.

SOURCES OF THE PROBLEM

This leads me to my first concern: why the problem at all? Why are we now concerned about the issue of the Good Samaritan? Since we have little evidence that in any way Samaritanism, the intervention of the disinterested helper, has in any wise increased or decreased, where does the problem originate, and why docs it pique so much interest today? Certainly once we begin to talk about it, we conjure up an immediate series of specific images and events: the Genovese case, or the recent subway beatings and murders in New York City. The *New York Times* headlined the Chicago conference as one on "the Genovese case." These are revealing because they tell us to what extent our problems originate in and through our media of communications. They are functions of our paper society. By a paper society I mean one in which a great deal comes to us via paper and exists on paper rather than the immediate event itself being one with which we are familiar. Office records, reports, newspapers, radio, and TV are a significant part of our experience.

Let us be clear about the kind of case that piques our attention. Let us refer to these as acts of "nonfeasance," instances in which people have failed to act. As I'm sure Professor Gregory would say, these range from instances in which men have acted where there would be relatively little inconvenience (such as failing to shout attention when a golf ball approaches, the golf ball having been sliced toward an innocent player) to the more striking instances in which humans fail to defend another person who is under an attack of violence, from failure to act decently to

failure to act heroically. We will confine our remarks to
the latter case, both because it is a more extreme one and
because it appears to be precisely what has attracted the
attention of lawyers and citizens. Can we demand, from
what is asked, that human beings be obligated by law to
come to the defense of other human beings who are attacked by a third party?

Perhaps the salient thing about the crimes we are talking
of here is that they are publicly visible ones.[2] Because
they occur in public places, they are more readily reported, more readily discussed, more readily reach public
attention. The priests and the Levites involved are publicly
visible in their actions and the Samaritans glaringly absent. We do not know how much that is private, how much
that exists in the confined or smaller social system of families, friends, and small neighborhoods would also pique our
curiosity and our attention if they were as visible.

A second fact about those cases which have incited
recent public interest is that they have occurred in metropolitan communities, in New York and Philadelphia.
Peculiar to American cities is their division into discreet
and segregated groups of ethnic, racial, and religious character. While these divisions are undoubtedly part of the
attractive variety and cosmopolitanism of urban life, they
are also part of the context of suspicion, distrust, and
fear in which members of different groups meet. The various communities within the metropolis do not exist in
some ranked fashion, with a clear order of dominance
and submission. As James Baldwin has noted, they are
separate countries in which the citizen is trained to look
warily once he leaves his borders.

While such segregation and mutual fear have long been
features of American cities, the separation of our cities
today into a white and a Negro component has increased

[2] See the insightful article by Arthur Stinchcomb, "Institutions of Privacy in the Determination of Police Administrative
Practice," *American Journal of Sociology*, Vol. 69, September
1963, pp. 150–60.

the magnitude of this division enormously. The fear of violence between groups is not new in American cities, but the degree and scope of these fears are, we think, new. Ignorance, suspicion, and fear between groups are not new, but the depth and width which separates white and Negro are deeper and wider than those we have seen in our cities in the past. We cannot help concluding that much of the present concern about violence and the absence of the Good Samaritan has been heightened by racial hysteria. The public attention feeds in an atmosphere already tense with racial fears, stereotypes, guilts, and hostility—the common stuff with which white and black Americans look out at each other from their distant communities. Some of my best friends are white and they react to news of violent crimes by asking if the criminal is white or colored. In this atmosphere, public attention is directed and magnified quite easily.

A third reason for increased public attention and awareness may be a shift in the locus of acts of violence so that the scene is now more visible and public. Instead of such acts being confined to specific groups and neighborhoods, where they attract less public notice, they may be moving into more public areas, where everyone must venture. The subway is too common and too publicly used an area to escape the attention of many people who greet events in other places in the city with indifference, if they ever learn of them at all. It is much too soon to make any definitive conclusions, but recent changes in crime rates and in gang warfare among New York City adolescents indicate that just such a change may be in process. Since the summer of 1964, gang warfare appears to have dwindled, especially in the Negro areas, and crime rates lessened. The civil rights movement may lead to the paradox of turning some internal violence into external violence, however. Pertinent to our subject, violence that occurs within the subcommunity, within the group, is not perceived as part of the problem of those who are outside of it. When it becomes externalized, turned on anyone, then it assumes attention in a much wider area.

We have now developed two ideas that we can carry forward. First, we have made a distinction between our concern about a problem and the factual events about which we talk. We may, and in fact probably are more concerned about human indifference at a period of time when the behavior may be less common than we think. Secondly, we have made a distinction between public events which are highly visible and less public ones which escape our attention. Whether or not the Good Samaritans are more in number and in proportions than in the past, whether or not the problem emerges because of its visibility and because of the tensions of our cities, it is there, and since it is there, we can discuss it, think about it. We become and *are* concerned about it. Let me not be the kind of scholar who answers the anxieties of laymen by saying that they don't exist. Let's then turn to the second and perhaps more compelling question: what is the social situation which appears to be connected with the Good Samaritan? What is the social situation in which the priests and the Levites take over?

SOCIAL STRUCTURE AND MORAL INTERVENTION

It is usual, in discussions of moral intervention and its absence, to ask, "Why don't people help?" We would like to turn the question around and ask, "Why do they help?" It is the intellectual bias of the sociologist to look for specific situations and expectations in analyzing human action. In the absence of data in this area, we are thrown back upon those biases. We cannot think about people in general, but about people in some social position, playing a role and expecting the rewards and sanctions that go with it. An examination of the social situation in the cases we are discussing is one way of asking if there are roles on which we can depend for heroic intervention.

Earlier I made a distinction between a public situation and a quasi-private one. Let us think of the first as an open kind of social system—one which anyone may enter, and in which the individuals have little fixed relationship to each other, are more likely than not strangers, and have no previous set of social obligations and no obligations which can extend into the future. The crowd of people waiting on a subway platform is perhaps the best illustration of this. Groups of people on the street may or may not approximate this highly public situation. The quasi-private situation, however, is much more of a closed system in the sense that those who are in it are part of a relatively fixed social pattern. They know each other, they have some kind of hierarchy of authority, some system of mutual identity. Perhaps the best illustration of a highly closed system is the relation between a husband and wife.

I think you can already begin to see that the highly closed system has two characteristics that are important for us. First, it is self-regulatory: that is, there are sanctions, there are rules, there are norms which govern its behavior. Secondly, it is a system which the stranger, the outsider, even the police are relatively reluctant to enter. However, because it is a system which has built-in authority, it contains both obligations to intervene and powers with which to make such intervention possible. A little episode from Jane Jacobs' recent book, *The Death and Life of Great American Cities,*[3] is illustrative of what I have in mind. Miss Jacobs writes of a woman in a New York City project who had been remarkably outgoing and who had made a deliberate effort to get to know the mothers of every one of the ninety families in her building. It happens that her eight-year-old son one day was stuck in the elevator and left there without help for more than two hours, although he screamed and cried. Telling the story the next day to one of her neighbors, the mother was told, "Oh, was that *your* son? I didn't know whose boy he was. If I had realized he was your son, I would have helped him."[4]

In a system that is somewhat closed, be it ethnic, class, neighborhood, any system in which there are authoritative figures and mutual obligations, intervention becomes a so-

[3] New York: Random House, 1961.
[4] *Ibid.,* pp. 65–66.

cially demanded act. Because it has a group structure, there are people charged with authority. In a public crowd this is absent. If one seeks for a leading figure, one would have to turn to the person whose dress, mien, and age indicate the responsibility for leadership. While violence can and does occur within the small system, it is more likely to be self-regulated, kept within bounds, and both to have sanctions applied later and to have systems of authority within the social system itself that can act to bring it to a close. Even the neighborhood grocer or candy-store proprietor may come to play a definitive role in a neighborhood that has an existence *qua*-neighborhood.

When we move to the more open social system, there is a most definite lack of these points of *noblesse oblige*. The very unanimity of the large group means that authoritative figures, even those of age, cannot depend upon any recognition of this for any role as intervener. People do not intervene because they are afraid that they will get hurt if they do so, and they suffer no social loss if they remain indifferent, as the recent beating of one intervener clearly indicates. They do not intervene because they have no definite set of social obligations that singles them out. Moral law does indeed operate in many cases, but we are looking at those cases in which it does not, those in which there is no role that exists that will motivate the human being to act in the situation. He cannot anticipate that his authority will be respected. He cannot anticipate that there will be moral sanctions placed upon him for not having done so. It is just the presence of these things which make police intervene, the fact that they are authoritative persons and the fact that if they don't they have failed in a professional duty or obligation.

A considerable amount of pluralistic ignorance in turn heightens the unwillingness of the individual to move. Precisely because a crowd of onlookers has little leadership or contains few people who have any obligation to seize that initiative, each can quite readily project onto the other his cynicism. He can say to himself, I am moved to act, but how do I know that this man standing next to me is also moved to act? I know nothing about him or about his motivations, and consequently I cannot depend upon the concerted action of all of us. Certainly in the Genovese case, as in the recent subway incidents, the crowd, had it been concerted and organized, could easily have stopped the crime.

The segregated structure of our cities is also part of the ethic of privacy and indifference with which urban strangers respect and ignore each other. The closed systems of family, friends, and ethnic group are not to be entered by the stranger and we must respect the private area and action of the strangers we meet in public places. We learn quickly in the big city that we must "mind our own business" or else be swamped by a multiplicity of possible events and by many a hostile response. Indifference is the other side of privacy.

So, too, the equality of American communities contributes to the unwillingness of the observer to intervene. He has learned the equality of respect for the closed systems of the segregated groups, an equality which heightens their autonomy. Neither can we depend upon a class structure in which high social position, bolstered by the internalized demands of conscience and the expectations of others, confers public authority. We have seen such processes at work in underdeveloped societies, but they are not part of American cities. Our class structure is much too fluid for that. (Apropos of privacy, we should note that the automobile is a significant privatizer. It enables us to escape many of the social sanctions to which pedestrians are heir. Even the angered motorist cannot swear at his road opponent and expect that he will be heard.)

The racial tensions that we referred to earlier must not be overlooked. They tend to make whites and Negroes mutually ignorant of each other and mutually cynical toward each other. The depth of segregation, the lack of social contacts between the two groups in our big cities mean that each can approach the other with perceptions that wall off both mutual identity and that tend to increase fear. The gifted Negro writer Saunders Redding has indicated some of this in an essay about an incident which occurred some years ago. Looking out of his office window at the edge of a white slum, he saw a young woman lurching and staggering in his back yard. She fell down in the snow, and he couldn't tell whether she was sick or drunk. While he experienced pity for her, he also experienced satisfaction from the fact that she was white, and he finally decided not to go to her aid, but saved something of his conscience by calling the police to report "a drunken woman, lying in the back yard of a house on Eighth Street." The police came, an hour later, and the next morning Redding read in the newspaper that the woman had died of exposure following an epileptic seizure.[5]

THE PUBLIC SAMARITANS

What may be the possibility for the existence of quasi-public authority, people whose formal role in the institutions provides the basis from which we might anticipate a greater degree of intervention than now found in our public situations? Certainly the problem in modern cities is in part a result of the disappearance of people whose very jobs gave them some obligation for the maintenance of public order.

"Even automation, as desirable as it may be from other points of view, has contributed to police problems. Among other things, it has opened new opportunities for the criminal and the pervert. The self-service elevator and the automatic subway train, for example, lend rapists, muggers, and other law-breakers a free hand for their molestations, in the late hours of the night, particularly. Even the coin-operated phonebox makes things easier for the thief; a foggy night in Los

[5] Charles Silberman, *Crisis in Black and White,* New York: Random House, 1964, p. 55.

Angeles has been known to veil the raiding of several miles of such installations along a single thorough-fare."[6]

One might suggest that figures such as the French concierge, the subway ticket seller, or the all-night restaurant proprietor represent valuable points around which we can institutionalize something of the functions which might otherwise be performed in the closed social system. We remember with both fear and laughter the incident in the movie *Doctor Strangelove* in which the soldier trying to call Washington in an emergency could not find the proper change for the coin box.

Perhaps we may yet see the solution to some cases like those in the New York subways or the Genovese case in the development of technological systems of monitoring or of aid which will substitute for the lack of the institutionalized human touch.

This discussion of the Good Samaritan has begun to lead us in the direction of those formal and institutional authorities who play the most definite role. Of these, of course, the police are the primary and supreme examples. They are, indeed, the hired Good Samaritans in our society. In many ways the police, both in the United States and in other countries, come to take on a multitude of functions often delegated elsewhere to a great diversity of professional and non-professional people. When I was a child growing up in the city of Chicago, there was a great wave of cases in which overtaxed mothers had called the police in the effort to get their children to go to sleep at night. A recent study by Elaine and Ian Cummings and Laura Edell is very revealing in its depiction of the many functions which police come to play, especially among the lower-income groups in our cities. Drawing on the records of the Syracuse police force, these investigators found that a good many calls which come in to the police station are calls for the kind of help and support which are often performed at other levels by psychiatrists, social

[6] Mitchel Gordon, *Sick Cities,* Baltimore: Penguin Books, 1965, p. 163.

workers, and doctors.[7] They may come to settle a quarrel
between a divorced couple, to determine whether an ambulance is needed in a case of knifing, or to return a lost
child to its home. What is interesting in these cases is the
lack among many people in the urban areas of any in-
tegration into the larger social system except through the
police.

For many, even the closed social system is lacking.
These are not the people who think of the psychiatric
agencies, the social work activities, or the great hospitals
as places to which they must immediately take their problems. Apparently neither do they have authoritative friends
or relatives. This study also is revealing in what it suggests
about the lack of resources within many aspects of the
society for the development of the kind of structured closed
system that I had reference to somewhat earlier. If the policeman is the philosopher, guide, and friend, as the authors
depict him here, where are the philosophers, the guides,
and the friends within the neighborhoods and apartment
buildings of our large cities?

This points to what seems to me to be an existent dilemma in any problem of police administration. On the
one hand, the role of the police as the major formal authorities for intervention in the society appears a necessary one in order to have a definitiveness to law and order.
On the other hand, can a society sustain itself without
that kind of latent vigilantism which emerges from functioning communities? Without some attributes of a closed
system, we multiply the demands on our formal, public
Samaritans. Such closed systems, however, are often points
of tension with the formal agents of law.

Perhaps this is behind some of the sensed antipathy between police and the would-be interveners. I took my
problem on one occasion to some friends in New York
City whom I happened to see and got a rather strange response. They were filled with cases in which they had in-

[7] "Policeman as Philosopher, Guide, and Friend," *Social
Problems,* 12, Winter, 1965, pp. 276–86.

tervened or someone else had intervened and had been met with the antipathy of police toward the intervener. They had been greeted with cynicism, with queries as to what was in it for the intervener, with a sense that for the police this was their business and that the intervener was an interloper as well. The effort of a group of Hasidic Jews to develop their own system of internal security in the Williamsburg district of Brooklyn was hardly greeted with any applause by the Brooklyn police authorities.

BONFEASANCE AND THE LAW

This concern for the citizen attitude toward the police and the police attitude toward the citizen touches upon the orientation between law and both non- and bonfeasance. Anglo-Saxon law has been deeply concerned with the protection of the rights of the individual, with seeing that his areas of privacy are maintained. Although this is a rather broad generalization, it is nevertheless sufficiently correct to give one a sense that it is only with great effort that the individual who acts can see the law as favorable to his own sense of moral intervention. For the layman, law remains a very mysterious set of activities, guarded jealously by a highly professionalized group of men speaking in a form of quasi-Latin. The intervener who acts has really no assurance that in the future his action will be interpreted in the way in which he had intended. He does not know but that there may be technicalities, traps, pitfalls, and loopholes so that what appeared to him to be the criminal may, indeed, escape punishment, or that he may not himself find that he has committed actions which are found to be legally reprehensible. Certainly the doctor who acts in an emergency, without his usual routine procedures and instruments, knows that he takes a great chance, and that his very act of morality may lead him into more difficulties than if he hadn't acted at all. Again we quote Prosser: "The result of all this is that the Good Samaritan who tries to help may find himself mulcted in damages, while the priests and the Levites who pass by on the other side go on their cheerful way rejoicing."[8] There is great room here, where intervention can be performed unheroically, for eradicating our legal detriments to action.

This fear of being "caught" by the complicated tentacles of the legal octopus must indeed give the citizen a certain amount of pause. Eighteen years ago, when I was a law student at the University of Chicago, I remember in my course on Torts with Professor Gregory reading a small statement in Prosser, the exact reference to which I forget, but in which Prosser ends his paragraph by saying, "It is things like this that cause the revolutionaries to shout, 'Kill the lawyers first.'" There is in our legal structure, in its great concern for the liberty and privacy of the individual, an enormous concern with preventing the invasion of any small system of interaction by those on the outside. Perhaps some of our legal tenderness toward nonfeasance is the obverse of our very virtuous concern for the privacy of individuals.

Americans are often accused of solving difficult problems of morality by passing laws and then disobeying them. While there is probably a great deal of truth to this characterization, it misses an important point. Laws are statements of public policy and opinion as well as instruments for courts to implement and police to enforce. The very passage of a law is an act of public definition of what is moral or immoral.[9] The suggestions we consider today for revision in the law of nonfeasance may have their most important effect in underlining the moral obligations of the citizen toward his fellow anonymous citizen, rather than in the particular sanctions which they entail.

Law may do a great deal in the cases of indecency, where the accomplished swimmer sits on the boat deck and watches the novice drown when he might easily have saved him. We cannot escape the impression that in the

[8] *Ibid.*, p. 339.

[9] See my *Symbolic Crusade: Status Politics and the American Temperance Movement*, Urbana: University of Illinois Press, 1963, Ch. 7.

kinds of cases which we have been discussing, where a more heroic act is called for, these will not yield easily to legal solutions. The citizen does not act because he is afraid of what may happen to him in the immediate future, because he is afraid of violent reprisals, and because he cannot depend upon the immediacy of police intervention. He does not act because he has no role which will obligate him to act in any specific and definitely expected form, a form that carries its sanctions and rewards to the immediate group around him. The city is a plurality of circles of involvement surrounded by areas of "no-man's land." The urbanite does not venture into new involvements without strong inducements and pressures. Legal sanctions are distant, vague, and uncertain; the danger is here and now.

My remarks have been speculative and rambling and probably hold small comfort for those who would wish heroism to be legalized. There is much that law can, and has, accomplished in reform. Much can probably be done to enforce decent and humane behavior in many areas where nonfeasance is now permissible. Our courts have been moving in such directions. The problems that have generated so much public attention in recent months, however, do not seem to me to be as readily controllable by law. They are likely to remain problems to be solved by policing actions, by institutional Samaritans rather than informal, public ones. These remarks should not seem to be electing the priests and the Levites and rejecting the Good Samaritan. His way is still honored and still effective. Efforts to write his election into law, however, are likely to be as useful or as limited as the New Testament itself.

Citizen Cooperation:
The Perspective of the Police

HERMAN GOLDSTEIN*

Whenever a police official is drawn into the discussion of recent failures on the part of citizens to come to the aid of victims of crime, the discussion invariably comes around to posing a question for the law-enforcement officer. Should a citizen aid the victim or is he better advised to summon the police? The answers provided cover a full range. At one extreme is the police official who vehemently maintains that dealing with attackers is exclusively the function of the police and that the citizen's responsibility is restricted to seeking police assistance. At the other end of the range is, for example, the British police official who recently was quoted as suggesting that the citizen "have a go at it."

The question, unfortunately, does not serve to elicit the kind of response from the police that contributes in a meaningful way to a discussion of the problem. But since the question is so frequently raised, I should like to dispose of it early in my comments.

A police official cannot react intelligently, in my opinion, without taking cognizance of the wide variety of circumstances that may surround any given situation in which a citizen is attacked: the nature of the offense; the number of attackers; the age and physical condition of the attacker and the witness; the location; the time of day; the proximity of other people; and the proximity of police help. Under varying conditions, a decision to act may re-

* Formerly Executive Assistant to the Superintendent of Police of Chicago; now Assistant Professor of Criminal Justice Administration, University of Wisconsin.

flect unusual bravery or downright foolhardiness. Similarly, a failure to act may appear to be a reflection of cowardice or an exercise of good judgment, depending upon the specific circumstances.

So numerous are the combinations of factors likely to be encountered that a police agency itself finds it difficult to formulate any precise criteria to serve as guidelines for its own personnel. This is so, even though the odds are quite different, since an officer, in contrast to a citizen, is armed with both official authority and a weapon. Should a police officer act on his own when faced with an emergency or should he seek assistance? Police agencies respond to this question by establishing very broad criteria and by placing major dependence upon the exercise of good common sense. This is usually accompanied by a standard operating procedure that counsels personnel to resolve all doubts in favor of requesting assistance. Clearly, a police administrator cannot afford to be more precise in advising the layman than he is in advising his own specially trained and equipped force.

Aside from such varied bits of advice as have been elicited from them, the police of this country have been unusually reserved in their comments and in their reactions to the problem of citizens failing to come to the aid of victims of crime. This attitude, in my opinion, reflects a prevalent feeling among law-enforcement personnel that the problem has received attention out of proportion to its magnitude.

The problem is, after all, not a new one. It has been with us for many years. A police officer who has worked in those sections of a large urban area infested by crime will have dealt with many cases in years past in which citizens have been criminally assaulted—on street corners, in bar rooms, and even in the privacy of a home—while others stood idly by. But the very fact that such incidents occurred in crime-infested areas resulted in their going without public attention. As the pattern of behavior has spread to adjoining areas or to buses or subway trains that move in and out of crime-infested areas, it has begun to involve people as victims or witnesses who do not share the same degree of indifference. Their concern and the concern of those who learn of their experience have apparently given rise to our present discussions. But to the police officer, who is caught up in the daily business of dealing with crime, it must be recognized that involvement of different areas and different people does not necessarily result in giving a new definition to what is essentially an old problem.

Whether it be an old or new phenomenon, the greatest significance of the failure of citizens to come to the aid of victims of crime, it seems to me, rests in the fact that it is but a symptom of a much broader, more serious, and constantly growing problem—the lack of citizen support in various aspects of the process by which crime is investigated and criminals apprehended. A patrolman or detective in an urban area daily experiences a variety of frustrations stemming from the failure of citizens to cooperate by not reporting crimes; by not identifying assailants; by not informing on the whereabouts of wanted persons; and by not cooperating in the prosecution of criminal cases. For the officer, it is a natural step to see this apathy extend to those situations in which a citizen is attacked in the presence of others.

It is recognized that in grouping these problems together two quite different issues are involved. One is our commitment to protecting fellow citizens from bodily harm; the other is our commitment to cooperate in the prosecution of those who are alleged to perpetrate criminal acts. It is one thing, for example, when the patrons of a tavern stand by while the bartender is viciously assaulted. It is quite another thing when the patrons fail to apprehend a person who robs the bartender without having caused bodily harm. The obligation felt for preventing injury is apparently thought to be much greater than is the obligation for apprehending the offender. But to the police officer, the responsibility for apprehending the offender is less separable from that of preventing harm. It follows that from his perspective the citizen indifference evident in either situation is an element of the same problem.

This concern by the police with the broader problem of citizen cooperation at least suggests that perhaps our exploration of the narrower issue which is the subject of this conference might be aided by an examination of related situations troubling the police. I should like to describe briefly the two areas of prime concern—and thereby raise the question as to whether these points have any pertinence to the subject under consideration.

I FAILURE TO REPORT CRIMES

The degree to which citizens fail to report crimes is not subject to measurement, but several factors suggest that the number is extremely high.

The failure is often that of the victim. The crime having been committed, he may take the view that no purpose would be served by a report; the harm caused cannot be undone, nor is it likely that any property loss suffered will be recovered. Or the victim may view the reporting of a crime to the police as an acknowledgment of personal weakness. Shamed by being duped, the victim may prefer to have the incident go unnoticed. And among some groups it is common for the victim to respond to a physical attack by seeking personal revenge. To enlist the aid of the police would be considered a sign of weakness by his peers.

The citizen—other than the victim—who fails to report criminal activity that is clearly apparent to him is often the resident who chooses to lose his identity in the anonymous urban complex—strongly committed to minding his own business. His reluctance to report crimes may grow out of a community attitude which defines a person who contacts the police as a "stool pigeon," a "rat," or, most recently and most ignobly, a "fink." Or his attitude may be attributable to a feeling that exists in some communities where police operations are inferior that the police are simply not interested.

All of these attitudes are influenced in large measure by a particular neighborhood's definition of what ought to be considered criminal. A street fight in the upper-class residential section of a large city will result in numerous calls to the police. The same kind of activity in other areas may go unreported unless discovered by police on patrol. The shot of a pistol, the scream of a woman, the tampering with a car, or the carrying of appliances through the streets in the dark hours of the morning—all indications of a possible crime—may bring residents pouring out into the streets in some areas, while not even arousing curiosity in others. These varied reactions, by the way, have important implications for the police administrator. He must make a difficult choice: to allow the indifference to dictate adoption of a lower level of enforcement in those areas in which such indifference exists, or to hold to a uniform city-wide policy of enforcement despite the lack of citizen cooperation in some areas.

II FAILURE TO COOPERATE IN INVESTIGATIONS AND PROSECUTIONS

In the investigation of those crimes that are reported, the cooperation of the victim and witnesses is crucial. This is especially true with regard to the vast majority of so-called street crimes which constitute the major crime problem in our urban areas. Since physical evidence by which the perpetrator might be identified is absent in all but a small handful of cases, almost total reliance is placed upon the cooperation of the victim. He must be depended upon to provide a description of the offender if he was seen, to view photographs of likely suspects, and to identify the alleged offender once he is in police custody.

The frequency with which victims of crime express an unwillingness to cooperate with the police has grown to such proportions that investigating officers today find themselves in the unusual position in many cases of experiencing greater difficulty in eliciting the cooperation of the victim than they do in identifying and locating the offender. Some citizens refuse to talk with the officers after they have filed their initial reports. Others go through the motions of cooperating but clearly give the impression that they have no intention of identifying the offender should they see him. And in some cases the police have reason to believe that the descriptions provided and the information given are fabricated with the specific intent of misleading them.

In part, this reaction is attributable to fear. The victims of street crimes are often citizens who have businesses that are either located or require their presence in crime-infested areas. The nature of the business operation frequently calls for their being alone—a factor which may have resulted in their being selected for attack in the first instance. Cooperation with the police may result in direct reprisal; it may be interpreted as an unusually vindictive act on the part of the victim by the people upon whom the victim depends for his livelihood.

There is also the element of inconvenience. A housewife or a small store operator gradually loses interest as the police request them to view photographs or attend show-ups. Children cannot be left alone nor can a store be left unattended. To meet this problem the police usually offer transportation in all cases and have gone so far in meeting special circumstances as providing a baby-sitter.

If the victim was previously involved in a criminal trial or had heard accounts of those who were involved, the likelihood of cooperation is substantially lessened. The loss of time, endless waiting, and innumerable delays that mark the typical criminal proceeding in a large urban area are a major source of discouragement. Repeated continuances sought on what appear to be questionable grounds are utilized as a defense maneuver designed to wear out the victim or witnesses.

Through a variety of devices, the police endeavor to sustain the interest and attendance of the victim through to the day of trial. If they succeed, the victim is then often subjected to the merciless grilling and browbeating of a defense counsel. Whatever the rationale for this procedure, the common effort to confuse and embarrass is viewed by the victim as an unduly abusive way of getting at the facts. Once having been subjected to what so often is an excruciating experience, the victim and those who learn of his experience, whatever their sense of civic responsibility, will understandably be reluctant to cooperate in future prosecutions.

In some areas of the community, where the prevalence of crime results in frequent contacts with the police of an adversary nature, failure to cooperate is often attributable to the blanket of protection that the citizenry maintains against any form of police intervention. Despite the fact that police interest may be in helping the victim, members of his family may be so conditioned to fear an allegation of criminal involvement as to hide the victim from inquiring police officers in the mistaken belief that he is wanted for a crime. The loss of citizen cooperation because of this attitude is one of the results of the conflicting role which the police are called upon to play as both friend and foe of those who reside in crime-infested areas.

If gaining cooperation of the victim is difficult, obtaining the cooperation of a witness often borders on the impossible. From those who are present at the scene of a traffic accident to those who witness a murder, there is a great reluctance to come forward. The contention on the part of persons present at the scene that they saw and heard nothing is incredible under many of the circumstances that the police confront.

Unwillingness to become involved as a witness is attributable to many of the same factors that dissuade the victim from cooperating. But beyond these considerations the police feel that failure to cooperate reflects the public's view that the task of identifying and apprehending criminals is exclusively that of the police. Indeed, the police sense that onlookers to a crime often view the process of apprehending and identifying a criminal as a sort of game in which both sides—the police and the offender—are given equal odds and from which they, as bystanders, must remain detached so as not to introduce a degree of unfairness by tipping the scales in one direction or another.

Lack of cooperation on the part of witnesses is of special concern to the police at the present time. Recent court decisions pertaining to the admissibility of physical evidence and especially confessions have resulted in creating an even greater need for relying upon the testimony of victims and witnesses in order to achieve successful prosecutions. The police are therefore today placed in the awkward position of requiring greater citizen cooperation at a time when such cooperation appears to be more difficult to come by.

There is a common thread that weaves through all of these problems—the desire on the part of the city dweller not to become involved. It is apparent in the unwillingness of citizens to cooperate in investigations and prosecutions. It is apparent in the failure of citizens to report crimes. It is equally apparent in the problem constituting the major subject of this conference—the failure of citizens to come to the aid of victims of crime.

The frequency with which this factor recurs in our exploration of these problems suggests that we are perhaps overlooking the obvious. Our system for controlling crime and administering criminal justice was, after all, initially designed to meet the needs of a simple, homogeneous, and less urbanized population than we have today. It places very heavy reliance upon the role played by the individual citizen—as victim and as witness. But urbanization has changed things. The prevalent attitude held by the residents of smaller communities, strongly committed to individual action designed to forward the communal good, appears to have been replaced in the large urban areas by an attitude which places a higher value on furthering private ends. Our criminal justice system has not been modified to meet this phenomenon. We continue to place as much dependence upon citizen cooperation in a large complex jurisdiction as we do in a rural community.

But what is more troubling is that we have aggravated the problem through inattention to procedural difficulties that arise in the larger city. By not resolving problems of repeated continuances, gross inefficiency in scheduling, and the air of confusion and mystery created by the wholesale herding of citizens through the process, we have allowed barriers to develop in our criminal justice system that frustrate the efforts of those city dwellers who do sense a responsibility to cooperate.

In searching for immediate solutions to the broad problem of the lack of citizen cooperation, dependence cannot be placed upon long-range efforts to improve the over-all moral tone of society. Rather, we might first turn to the task of facilitating the exercise of whatever degree of responsibility already exists by eliminating some of the barriers that currently frustrate those who do wish to cooperate. For the courts this means the better accommodation of the witness and the victim. For the police this means abandonment of those operating policies that place the burden upon the victim for filing reports and initiating the criminal process.

Secondly, it seems to me that court, prosecution, and police practices ought to be reviewed to determine whether their net effect is to gain community support for law and order, or if they have the adverse effect of antagonizing large segments of the community. The police, for example, should be viewed by the public as an agency functioning in behalf of all law-abiding citizens. Any policy or operating practice that detracts from this image should be subject to careful examination.

We ought also to face more realistically what will undoubtedly continue to be the desire on the part of substantial numbers of citizens in a large urban center not to become involved. Should we attempt to compensate for the loss in citizen participation by devising new methods for meeting some of the problems which the loss creates? Serious consideration, for example, might be given to the need for the state to proceed with prosecutions of serious offenses, given adequate evidence, even if the victim is unwilling to cooperate. In this manner the commitment of the community as a whole to prohibiting such behavior would be reinforced and protected from erosion as the result of indifference.

The task involved in facilitating citizen cooperation, in encouraging proper attitudes toward the police and the courts, and especially in devising means by which to compensate for citizen indifference is not an easy one. It reflects how terribly complex is any effort aimed at modifying our system of criminal justice administration to make it more capable of meeting the peculiar needs of today's large urban areas.

An International Experiment on the Effects of a Good Samaritan Law

HANS ZEISEL*

Should the law insist that we be Good Samaritans and punish us if we are not, or should this remain a matter merely for the individual and social conscience?

Some countries, such as France, Germany, Italy, and the Soviet Union have a Good Samaritan statute. It makes it a misdemeanor, punishable with jail, if someone fails to help avert injury or death to another person, if he could easily have done so without danger to himself. Other countries, such as England, Austria, Czechoslovakia, and the United States, have no such law.

To find out what, if any, difference it makes whether or not a country has such a law, I recently arranged the following experiment:

Identical interviews were conducted in Germany, which has such a law, and in neighboring Austria and the United States, neither of which has such a law. To keep the interviews as comparable as possible and to exclude possible legal experts, the study was limited to university students of any faculty *except law*.

Four different case histories were given to the students, each one constituting a crime against which the German statute is directed. The first case concerns a group of young men who, when asked for assistance, failed to help in bringing water to a burning hamlet. In the second case, an automobile driver, noting a small child on an expressway, drove on instead of stopping and guiding the child off the road. In the third case, a housewife refused entry to her house to a man who had just been attacked on the

* Professor of Law and Sociology, The University of Chicago.

street. She did not even notify the police. In the fourth case, an elderly lady had fallen on the sidewalk and lay there unconscious. A man walking by behaved as if he had not seen her. In all four instances, the respondent was told that serious harm occurred.

Each interviewee was asked three questions—

1 What percentage of people would have acted in the way described?

Germany	37%
Austria	39%
United States	44%

2 Suppose *you* could make our laws, What should the law do about people who behave in this way?

		Germany	Austria	United States
(a)	nothing; this should be left to a person's conscience	42%	62%	75%
(b)	should pay for some of the damage caused	16%	5%	8%
(c)	should be fined	20%	18%	15%
(d)	should receive a jail sentence	22%	15%	2%
	Total Responses	100%	100%	100%

3 In your country, is Good Samaritan behavior directed by law or is such help regarded merely as a moral obligation?

The proportion of interviewees who thought it was a legal duty were:

in Germany	86%
in Austria	26%
in the United States	19%

The data allow the following conclusions:
1 By and large, people know whether or not to help is a legal duty.

2 If one may trust the combined average estimates of these respondents, it makes no difference in personal behavior whether or not such a law exists. The percentages for Germany and Austria are practically identical (37% and 39%).

3 However, where, as in Germany, the law prescribes fines or damages, more people feel that the Bad Samaritan ought to be criminally punished (Germany 44%; Austria, 33%).

But as between Austria and the United States, neither of which has such a criminal statute, the respondents in the United States are far less likely to desire punishment. Only 17% think it proper.

Following is the percentage of respondents who believe assistance should remain only a matter of conscience, without legal consequences:

Austria	42%
Germany	62%
United States	75%

Quite a number of the Americans interviewed volunteered that publication in the newspapers of the behavior of Bad Samaritans would be the proper punishment.

On the whole, the four cases were rated in the same order in each country.

Case No.	Percentage who would behave as the Bad Samaritans described	Percentage who would impose jail sentence
1 Burning hamlet	31%	5%
2 Child on highway	66%	17%
3 Attacked man who asked for help	41%	12%
4 Unconscious lady	31%	24%

Thus people would be least likely to help in the child-highway situation; most likely to help the burning hamlet and the unconscious lady. Not to help her is clearly the worst behavior (24% would punish the failure to help by a jail sentence); not helping to put out the fire is considered the least reprehensible.

Some Moral Aspects of Good Samaritanship

HERBERT FINGARETTE*

Over 2000 years ago the great Chinese philosopher Mencius said: "All men have a capacity for compassion." Mencius said: "My meaning may be illustrated thus: . . . if men see a child about to fall into a well, they will without exception experience a feeling of alarm and distress. This is not because they know the child's parents, nor out of a desire for praise by neighbors and friends, nor out of dislike for the bad reputation that would ensue if they did not go to the rescue. From this we may conclude that without compassion one would not be a human being."

There is no doubt Mencius was right—as far as he went. Yet, as I thought of this text from ancient China, I could not help but think also of the experience two of my colleagues had awhile ago. They were hurrying to a meeting in a relatively strange part of town. Suddenly, from out of a nearby apartment-house window, a woman began crying for help. My friends were of course startled and frightened. They debated for a few moments whether to go their way or rush to the rescue. The screams continued. The impulse to keep on their way was strong; but they finally decided to go into the house. As they rushed up several flights of stairs, they passed a number of apartment dwellers, standing in the hall at their open doors, listening avidly to the increasingly anguished screams. Frightened and breathless, my friends at last arrived and banged on the door. To their utter amazement, the woman herself opened it. It was immediately obvious that the well-meaning

* Professor of Philosophy, University of California, Santa Barbara.

Samaritans had interrupted a glorious family fight. The
woman proceeded to deliver a rapid-fire, full-voice lecture
on a citizen's right to privacy, on the obnoxiousness of
self-appointed Good Samaritans, and on her own good nature which prevented her from reporting the intruders to
the police.

Such are some of the real-life complications faced by
the Samaritan. These practical situations raise three different sorts of critical questions. First, there are the objective
factual questions: What is going on? What can be done?
What is the cost of doing it? The newspaper reader, in the
quiet of his home and well after the fact, thinks he knows
the facts, and it seems obvious to him what should have
been done. But things are often not so simple to the man
on the spot. I must leave the discussion of such important
questions to those who are expert in problems of police
and other rescue tasks.

The second sort of critical question has to do with the
often conflicting impulses and emotions which the potential
Good Samaritan may find in his breast. One might think
of these as factual questions, too, but perhaps as matters
of psychological or subjective fact. They, too, are complex.
We know that the compassionate impulses are not the only
common ones. There is also the impulse to stand and stare
—incidentally disrupting bona fide rescue attempts as often
as not. There are also the latent sadistic impulses—not infrequently the onlookers join in the aggression. There is
commonly fear and repugnance before anyone who is odd,
helpless, suffering, or attacked. Such emotions often evoke
a powerful impulse simply to get away as fast as possible.
What is the inner structure of these emotions and impulses
and what is their strength? What are their causes, their
consequences, their role in the psychic economy and in
the social process? These very critical questions fall most
directly in the field of the psychiatrist and social scientist
rather than the philosopher.

Since we are not merely the victims of our impulses and
beliefs, there is still a third critical set of questions: In
the light of our beliefs and our impulses, what would be

the *best* thing to do, what *ought* I to do? And finally, what do I actually *decide* to do? Such questions are, broadly speaking, the moral and decisional questions.

It may be relevant to note that some psychiatrists or sociologists may deny that this last set of questions is genuinely independent and basic. They may have no place in their theories or equations for moral principles above causality; they may have no place for free choice. For them the question what *ought* I to do may be considered only a symptom of one more psychological force: the impulse to follow some such rule as "help others." They will then conceive of this impulse as having a greater or lesser magnitude, balancing off to some extent the contrary impulses. My action will still be conceived by them, at least in theory, as a mathematically calculable one rather than a free choice.

However, those who must think in terms of law cannot take moral and decisional questions to be a mere subclass of factual questions about causes or forces, whether objective *or* subjective. In law, one must view choice and moral responsibility as fundamental, irreducible categories. What is more, the layman who is the Samaritan in an actual crisis situation *cannot*—I emphasize *cannot*—think of his action as causally necessitated. Imagine the person on the spot saying to himself: "Since my act is the mathematical resultant of the strength of my desires, and since in any case I can't objectively measure my desires, the best thing for *me* to do is to wait to see what I *do* do." Even in this absurd case, the person is *deciding* to wait and see.

These moral and decisional questions then are fundamental, irreducible to factual questions. And so I turn to moral obligation as one basis for decision.

My first proposition is that we do acknowledge that there *is* some obligation to help a person in distress. This has been assumed by speakers today, but it can be briefly shown in the following ways: A person who comes upon a stranger in trouble may be frightened or repelled and inclined to give in to these feelings; but unless he is literally panicked, he will try to justify giving in. He may say to himself—"It's none of my business—I don't know what's behind this; I might even aggravate the injury; there might be trouble later for me or for my family; besides I'm late for my appointment; anyway, why should *I* be the one to stop? Maybe someone else has already gone for help."

Such an inner debate would be pointless if it were not for a *tacit initial assumption* which might be phrased this way: "If a person is in great distress, and if I am the one available to help, then, all else being equal, I *do* have some obligation to help." Only because one tacitly assumes such an obligation does it make sense to run through all the *contrary* obligations and inconveniences in order to justify *not* helping. Sometimes we avoid obvious inner debate by pretending not to notice the person's distress—but this pretense itself reveals our tacit acknowledgment that, if we *do* notice, we *are* under some obligation.

The real problems the Samaritan, then, faces are not such generalities as: "Do I ever have a free choice?"— Or, "Am I in *any* way obligated to help?" Nor do I think the problem is simply a lack of the willingness to carry out the obligation. No doubt we can always do with more good will than exists in this imperfect world. But even the man of good will faces serious problems here. In the practical context, he faces the perplexing questions:

How shall I weigh this obligation-to-help along with *other conflicting* obligations; how shall I weigh it in the light of my conflicting impulses; how shall I weigh it in the light of my objective uncertainty about what is going on here? In short, how can I put specific content into it?

Now one might argue that the obligation to be neighborly is general rather than specific because it is meant as a moral absolute. As such, this obligation would have priority in *every* way over every other consideration. As such, it would be a counsel of perfection, a complete dedication of our existence to this principle. But most of us know we are not, will not, be perfect. We do not live by absolutes. We are only everyday, garden-variety Samaritans.

Suppose we look then to the classical sources in which this obligation-to-help-the-stranger is presented to us; perhaps the context, language, and imagery of the classical sources will provide the clues we need to the specific scope and force of the obligation in practical life.

The first and most obvious classical source for our purposes is clear enough; it is the Gospel story of the Samaritan. It deserves a slightly more detailed attention in my remarks than it has yet been given.

This story in Luke, Chapter 10, is simple enough. Jesus is questioned by a lawyer who asks what is necessary to inherit eternal life. When Jesus asks him what the law on the matter is, it turns out the lawyer can recite the law perfectly, but—the nature of lawyers being apparently everywhere the same—he wants to argue the interpretation of one of the words in it.

The law is this: "Love the Lord thy God with all thy heart and with all thy soul and with all thy strength; and thy neighbor as thyself." The lawyer wants to know: "Who *is* my neighbor?" Whereupon Jesus tells the story of the Samaritan. A man is going along the road from Jerusalem to Jericho when he is set upon by thieves, who strip him and beat him, leaving him for dead. A priest who is going along the road sees him, but passes by on the other side. A Levite, that is to say, a man from one of the quasi-priestly castes, does the same. But a certain Samaritan stops. The Samaritan binds up the poor man's wounds, helps him to a place of refuge at an inn, asks the innkeeper to take good care of the man, gives the innkeeper some money, and assures the innkeeper that if the expenses turn out to be more, the rest will be forthcoming when the Samaritan returns on his way back.

That is the story; and Jesus asks the lawyer: "Which one of the three was the neighbor to the victim?" The lawyer gives the obvious answer—the Samaritan. "Go and do thou likewise," says Jesus.

This story, like many traditional stories at the time, turns upon the differing responses of priest, Levite, and layman. But, typically in such stories, the layman as well as the other two would be Jews. Jesus, however, substitutes a Samaritan, a geographical neighbor but one who was despised and hated by the Jews of the time as being uncouth, unclean, immoral, and heretical. Thus the story as told by Jesus was intended to teach most emphatically that love of neighbor is so universal, so unqualified a principle as to include even the meanest of men being neighbor to the most self-righteous of enemies. The Gospel source also emphasizes *acting* as a neighbor, *decision* rather than legalistic classification. Finally, and of highest importance, the story has to do with eternal life, personal salvation—not with problems of keeping the public order.

When I say that this parable is concerned with the ultimate question of personal salvation through personal decision and unqualified commitment, I have in mind the other side of the coin: whether my soul is saved or not is none of the state's business. Let Caesar regulate his own affairs: keeping the public order and the public well-being. My soul is *my* affair. This was Jesus' teaching; it is also central to our own political tradition.

Let me recall for a moment the main thread of my argument. I have dwelt at some little length upon the parable of the Good Samaritan since it is a classic source par excellence in our own tradition, and as such it might help to put specific content into the obligation of the citizen. However, as we now see, it turns out that the emphasis in the Gospel context is not on practical questions but on the inward and eternal life, commitment and salvation.

If we look to other classical sources for an analogous teaching of neighborly love, we find it indeed. The Old Testament teaches love of neighbor in the Book of Leviticus. The theme of helping one's fellow being is also central in Mahayana Buddhism and in the teaching of Confucius, a remarkable fact in view of the great gaps—philosophical, geographical, and cultural—which otherwise separate these teachings from those of Biblical lands. But here again the teaching is in each case a religious, salvationist one, or a counsel of ultimate human perfection.

The moral of the Good Samaritan parable is not limited to the classical religious sources, however. We can, if we wish, translate it into more general terms, without committing ourselves to supernaturalistic doctrines of the soul, of salvation, or of Heaven or Hell. One such account would consist in seeing that the question, "Shall I help this stranger in his dire need?" is inextricably connected with the question: "What kind of person am I?"—or, more precisely, "What kind of person *shall* I be?"—or, still more precisely yet: "What shall I *make* of myself?" These are truly questions of one's personal salvation or damnation, whether we take these terms in a specific theological sense or not.

It is conceivable that a person might live a terribly rigid and narrow life in which the Samaritan question never comes up in an urgent way; and such a person might be neutral on the issue. *But*—once the occasion does arise, a person cannot be neutral; the issue is forced. Then one must either decide to help the stranger or decide to reject his cry for help. Whichever way one decides, one has been forced to take a stand—and thus to make oneself into a different kind of person from what one was before, perhaps a nobler person, perhaps a meaner person. One's stand toward the Other reflects one's stand toward oneself.

For those who prefer evidence from contemporary sources, I suggest, among a number one might think of, Albert Camus' novel *The Fall*. In this remarkable narrative, Camus shows us the inside story of how the failure to come to a stranger's aid turns out to be only the objective symbol of a life which is an inward mockery of itself. The central figure—incidentally, he is a lawyer—is first called to himself by his failure to save another human being from death; this failure soon reveals itself to him as only the outward expression of a constant but *covert* betrayal of others; and this constant betrayal of *others* he discovers to be only an aspect of an inward *self*-betrayal. Camus presents and justifies his narrative in human terms, but he explicitly connects it with the traditional religious teaching of damnation and salvation: the lawyer's living Hell is presented symbolically as Dante's inner circle of Hell.

Having briefly noted now remarkable a consensus among varied sources can be found, I now only wish to note that the consensus includes the point that this teaching goes to the very heart of one's personal existence, that it is indeed, and in a word, a teaching of salvation, whether secular or religious. Therefore, if I were a Samaritan, as I see it I could take one of two attitudes. One attitude is to look at what I am about to do—or perhaps already have done—as a matter of profoundly personal decision, a matter between me and my conscience or me and my God, as relevant to my own spiritual life or death. There is really nothing more to be *said* here; what is needed is a personal *decision*. And *that*, it seems to me, is the end of that topic. I think it is an error, an obstacle to progress, to base community legal action on this spiritual and personal basis.

There is, however, another attitude I may take. I may put aside the perspective of salvation. I may turn instead to an attempt to understand my obligations in the context of good citizenship, of modest decency rather than ultimate Virtue, of everyday reasonableness rather than "Reason" with a capital "R."

Then the community and its more mundane concerns become relevant. Somewhere, somehow, in the nature of the community we may find the clue to the good citizen's version of the obligation to rescue the stranger. And here, I believe, we do in fact get a clue as to how to produce an answer.

A community is not merely a miscellaneous collection of specific regulations, laws, institutions. Its foundation is in the acknowledgment by its members that there *is* a community, that the members of the community are committed to one another to make some sacrifices of their energies, their wealth, their comfort for the sake of preserving the integrity of the community and enjoying its rewards. In our own case, we are committed to a community which aims to assure to its members a right to life, liberty, and the pursuit of happiness. If we think in these terms, then, it seems to me, there is implied a general acknowledgment of some fundamental and at least minimal obligation to make sacrifices for the sake of public order and the safety of those who belong in the community. This *general* obligation underlies and justifies the specific obligations spelled out in law and custom.

For example, we are generally obligated to respect life and property when we drive a car. But it is not enough to tell drivers that they are obligated to drive safely; we must have *rules* of the road and *customs* of the road. Of course, always in force and underlying these there remains the general obligation to drive safely. The specific rules and customs give guidance as to the meaning of this general obligation in the common driving situations where otherwise legitimate doubt and conflict might reign. Again, we don't merely ask in general that citizens be loyal—we spell out military service laws, laws defining treason, rules for security classification of documents, pledges of allegiance, and so on. We do not merely ask citizens to have a care for the public health—we spell out public health and safety laws. We do not merely ask that all contribute generously to financing government—we have tax laws. Not everything is in law or regulation, of course; a great deal is left to custom—customs of etiquette, of respect for personal privacy, of good faith in various transactions. The general principles of loyalty, health, safety, courtesy, mutual respect remain essential—not only as the justification for custom and rule but also because there are always gray areas and new problems where the custom and rule or law don't quite apply. Even in these borderline areas we often get a useful cue by comparing the doubtful case with the closest parallel cases where law or custom *is* specific. Finally, should one of these gray areas seem sufficiently troublesome, we may spell out new rules or laws, or revise the old, so as to cover the problem explicitly.

In this way, custom and explicit rule provide us with a more or less detailed map of areas which are only broadly delimited by our general communal obligation. This map orients us, even if it does not always directly answer our every question.

If we grant that there is a general communal obligation to help keep the public order and protect the lives and property of the citizenry, what is the case specifically with respect to the person who comes upon a stranger in dire straits? Is our general obligation adequately spelled out in custom or in law?

I am not sure about the current custom. It may be, as our newspapers and police officers suggest, that there really are fewer Good Samaritans today than in earlier generations. Perhaps once there was a custom, and perhaps it is rapidly disappearing. It may be, however, that, as Professor Morris has argued forcefully, there only *seem* to be fewer Good Samaritans because our moral demands have increased. After all, a single killing in the South shocks our moral conscience today, whereas a generation or so ago lynchings were *more* common but *less* noticed. I am not so sure as he that things have not got relatively worse in the recent short run. In any case, this question as to what is really happening to our customs and group values, and why it is happening, is an historical-sociological question of the first importance. As such, it is in the province of the social scientists. But, in any case, I can speak for myself as a potential Samaritan. As far as custom goes, I am not sure what custom is, or was. Is it customary to rush to the aid of the injured or attacked? Or does one customarily run for a policeman or at least a telephone, letting the sufferer manage as best he can? If one has grounds to fear great financial liability, public embarrassment, or even mortal danger, does one intervene at all?— what is the custom here? I frankly don't know what the actual custom is. I suspect it varies with the circumstances and the individuals—in short, I suspect there is no custom but a complete range of all the possible responses.

In any case, whatever used to be the custom, it is evident that nowadays there is concern and confusion in our *minds*. Therefore, *I* cannot look to custom as a guide to my specific obligations in the practical emergency situations I am likely to meet.

In the absence of clear custom, it would seem to me that explicit public policy—as expressed in law and regulation—would be of the essence if we are to have practical guidance about the Samaritan's obligation. But here, I gather, the law provides no guide. Yet this *is* the community's business. This is the way it normally carries on its business. The precise formulation of such law is no doubt a subtle and complex affair. However, I know of no insuperable difficulties in the way of doing it, and we have learned how these difficulties are overcome in Europe. From a moral standpoint—and this is my primary concern here—I think a body of specific law or regulations is essential. It is the only alternative to editorializing platitudes and generalities which substitute the thrill of righteous indignation, and the fascination with scandal, for substantive clarification of genuine confusion.

The law should encourage coming to another's aid by providing legitimate physical, financial, and legal protection; the law should lessen the temptation to avoid bringing aid by providing penalties. Concrete suggestions for such measures have already been forthcoming at this conference. In this way, law, and of course other public regulations, can also define in detail and express the public attitude on these issues. As Professor Tunc has said, the law *can* help shape social attitudes and actions.

I do not mean to claim that this line of action will solve the problem. I have by-passed the sociological, anthropological, psychiatric, and political problems. The *total* problem of the Samaritan involves all these areas. But the *moral* problem of the Samaritan is the one I have been concerned with. It is only one aspect, though an important one.

I have one final, brief qualification to make. Most of what I have said is based on the supposition that the Good Samaritan problem *is* a significant social problem. But it may be that in fact it is not a major social problem except insofar as newspaper sensationalism has made it such. I do not know. If it should be a problem of newspaper sensationalism rather than a problem of increasing public callousness or confusion and fear, then we might do better to let the law alone.

Law, Morals and Rescue

ANTONY M. HONORÉ*

A woman, viciously attacked, lies bleeding in the street.
Fifty people pass by on the other side. A man destroys his
barn to prevent a fire spreading to his neighbor's property. The neighbor refuses to compensate him. A young
potholer foolishly becomes trapped below ground. A more
experienced man, coming to his aid, breaks a leg. When
we contemplate facts such as these, three questions seem
to confront us concerning law, morals, and their interrela-
tion. The first is about the shared morality of our society.
Is there in modern industrial society, which is the only one
most of us know, a shared attitude of praise or condemnation, encouragement, or dissuasion about helping those in
peril? If so, two further points arise. Should the law, with
its mechanisms of inducement, rewards, and compensation,
be used to encourage what the shared morality treats as
laudable and discourage what it reprobates? Should the
law, thirdly, go further and, by the use of threats and
penalties, "enforce" morality, as the saying goes? These,
it seems, are the main issues. In part they concern matters
which, in England at least, have lately stirred up a pas-
sionate debate.[1] Is it justifiable to use the mechanism of

* Fellow, New College, Oxford University.
[1] P. Devlin, *The Enforcement of Morals* (Maccabaean Lecture, 1958), reprinted in *The Enforcement of Morals* (Oxford
U. P., 1965); W. Friedmann in 4 *Natural Law Forum* (1964),
151; H. L. A. Hart, *Law, Liberty and Morality* (Oxford U. P.,
1963); L. Henkin in 63 *Col. L. Rev.* (1963) 393; G. Hughes in
71 *Yale L. J.* (1961) 622; M. Ginsberg in 1964 *British Journal
of Criminology,* 283; A. W. Mewett in 14 *Toronto L. J.* (1962)
213; E. Rostow in 1960 *Cambridge L. J.* 174 reprinted in *The*

criminal law to "enforce" the shared morality, for instance
in matters of sex? Greeks and Trojans have sallied forth
and the clash of arms has rung out. Our concern, however,
is with something wider and different: not sex, not only
"enforcement," not only crime. I shall have a word, later
on, to say in criticism of the use of the word "enforce" in
this context. If we pass it for the moment, it yet remains
true that "enforcement" is only part of what the law can
do in the Good Samaritan situation. Apart from criminal
sanctions, the law can encourage or discourage compliance
with the shared morality by the use of techniques drawn
from tort, contract, and restitution. Even "enforcement" is
not confined to criminal law, because tort law, too, can be
used to impose an obligation to aid others.

Our concern is not only wider but different from that of
the jurists by whose brilliant and elevated jousting we have
been entertained. They have debated whether some parts
of the law which coincide with common morality should
be scrapped. We, on the other hand, wish to know whether
parts of morality, at present outside the law, should be
incorporated in it. (I mean here Anglo-American law and
not those systems in which this has already come about.)
Some people feel that the intrusion of law into the private
sphere of sex is indecent and outrageous. Others feel out-
raged by the failure of the law to intrude in relation to
rescue and rescuers. Is the refusal to "enforce" the moral
obligation to help others itself a moral offense, of which
lawyers and legislators have been guilty in the English-
speaking world this hundred years? Does the affront of this
refusal bring the law and lawyers into disrepute? Should
the law encourage or even insist on Do-Goodery? Or
would this be an intrusion into yet another private sphere,
not of sex, but of conscience?

Clearly we have a moral issue on our hands, and one

Sovereign Prerogative (Yale U. P., 1962); N. St. John-Stevas,
Life, Death and the Law (1961); R. S. Summers in 38 *New
York U. L. Rev.* (1963), 1201; B. Wootton, *Crime and the
Criminal Law* (Stevens, 1963), 41.

which is concerned not with the "enforcement" of morals but with its non-enforcement. A number of writers, following Bentham[2] and Mill,[3] have advocated a legal obligation to rescue. Ames[4] and Bohlen[5] put forward an earnest plea to the same effect. But, though they mentioned, they did not closely analyze the moral issues. It is with these that I shall be principally concerned.

I THE SHARED MORALITY IN MATTERS OF RESCUE

An essential preliminary to the survey of the larger vistas of law and morals is to clear our minds about our moral views in the matter of aid to those in peril. By "our moral views" I mean the shared or common morality. Obviously this is not the same as the statement of what people actually do in a given society—the common practice of mankind. Their actions may fall short of their moral ideals and pretensions. Nor is it the same as that which an individual may accept for himself as morally obligatory. There is a distinction between that which the individual accepts for himself and that which he regards as being of general application. A man may think he has higher ideals, a stricter sense of obligation or duty, than the ordinary run of men could well be expected to entertain. This cherished personal morality, it seems to me, is no part or ingredient of the shared morality, though it may come, in time, to spread to others and so to influence the shared morality.

The shared morality consists, rather, of those moral ideals and duties or obligations which the bulk of the com-

[2] J. Bentham, *Principles of Morals and Legislation*, 323 ("Who is there that in any of these cases would think punishment misapplied?").

[3] J. S. Mill, *On Liberty*, Introduction ("There are also many positive acts for the benefit of others, which he may rightfully be compelled to perform . . . such as saving a fellow-creature's life").

[4] J. B. Ames, *Law and Morals, supra*, pp. 1–21.

[5] F. Bohlen, *The Moral Duty to Aid Others As a Basis of Liability*, 56 U. Pa. L. Rev. (1908) 215, 316.

munity regard as applying to persons generally. But is the notion, defined, anything more than a figment? Ought we to refrain from speculating about its content until social surveys have determined whether it really exists? I think one must frankly concede that the results of properly conducted surveys would be far more authoritative than the guesses of moralists or lawyers. The survey which Messrs. Cohen, Robson, and Bates sought to ascertain the moral sense of the Nebraska community on parent-child relations[6] is, no doubt, a forerunner of what will, in time, become common practice. The shared morality of which I am speaking is not, however, quite what the Nebraska inquiry was attempting to ascertain. In that inquiry "community values" were defined as the "choices, expressed verbally, which members of the community feel the law-making authorities ought to make if confronted with alternative courses of action in specified circumstances."[7] These choices surely represent opinion as to legislation on moral issues rather than the shared morality itself. They tell us what people think legislators should do, not what they think ordinary citizens should do. No doubt there is a close, even a very close, connection between the two. Our view of what the law should be will be powerfully shaped by our notions of right and wrong, of what is desirable and what objectionable, but surely the two cannot without more be identified? It must *a priori* be an open question whether people who share moral ideas also think that these should be mirrored in the law. If they do, that is also a fact susceptible of and demanding confirmation by a properly conducted survey.

It remains doubtful, therefore, whether a suitable technique has yet been evolved for testing the existence and content of the shared morality of a community. Certainly the results are not yet to hand in a usable form. In the meantime, life does not stand still. Decisions must be

[6] J. Cohen, R. A. H. Robson, and A. Bates, *Ascertaining the Moral Sense of the Community*, 8 *Journal of Legal Education* (1955–56) 137.

[7] *Ibid.*

reached with the aid of such information and intuition as we may possess. We cannot shirk the question of what our shared morality says about rescues and rescuers on the excuse that one day, we hope, a truly reliable answer will be available.

It is unwise in thinking about the shared morality to treat morality as an undifferentiated mass. For instance, there is a distinction between moral ideals and moral duties.[8] This is not the same as the previous distinction between a man's personal morality and the morality which he regards as of general application. Of course, a connection exists. A person may accept as an obligation for himself what he thinks of merely as an ideal for others. Broadly speaking, moral ideals concern patterns of conduct which are admired but not required. To live up to them is praiseworthy but not exigible. Moral duties, on the other hand, concern conduct which is required but not admired. With an important exception, to which I shall come, merely to do one's duty evokes no comment. Moral duties are pitched at a point where the conformity of the ordinary man can reasonably be expected. As a corollary, while it is tolerable, if deplorable, to fall short of the highest ideals, it is not permissible to neglect one's duties.

Certain virtues, notably altruism and generosity, depend on absence of obligation. It is not altruistic to pay one's debts, or generous to support one's parents (in the latter case the duty may in Anglo-American law be merely moral, but this makes no difference). Other virtues seem to hover between the status of ideals and duties. Is this, perhaps, true of the "neighborliness" which the parable of the Good Samaritan is meant both to illustrate and to inculcate? According to Matthew[9] and Mark,[10] the precept "love your neighbor as yourself" expresses a "commandment" and presumably imposes an obligation. Luke,[11] in

8 E. Cahn, *The Moral Decision* (1956), 39.
9 Matthew 22:34.
10 Mark 12:28.
11 Luke 10:25.

contrast, treats it as pointing the way to perfection or
"eternal life," a moral ideal. It may be that giving aid to
those in peril is sometimes an ideal, sometimes a duty. At
least three situations demand separate treatment:

1   The first is the rescue undertaken by one who has a
professional or quasi-professional duty to undertake rescues. A fireman or life-saver is a professional rescuer. Doctors, nurses, and other members of the medical profession
have a duty to save life, which, at times, demands that they
should give help in an emergency. A priest must comfort
the dying, a policeman must stop acts of violence. Besides
these true professionals, there are what one may call devoted amateurs; for instance, experienced mountaineers or
potholers, who hold themselves out as ready to effect rescues and, I am told, often welcome the chance to display
their skills. Strictly speaking, none of these are "volunteers." They are only doing what they are bound by their
calling or public profession to do. A doctor is not praised
for coming promptly to the scene of an accident; that is
only what we expect. He would be blamed if he delayed
or refused to come. But this morally neutral reaction is
appropriate only when the rescuer acts without risk or serious inconvenience to himself. If the fireman, policeman,
or life-saver risks life or limb to help the imperiled, he deserves and receives praise, because there is an element of
self-sacrifice or even heroism in his conduct, though what
he does is clearly his duty. Heroism and self-sacrifice, unlike altruism, can be evinced both by those who do their
duty and those who have no duty to do.

2   The second is the rescue undertaken by one who has
special ties with the person imperiled. Family links, employment, and other associative ties may generate a duty
to come to the help of a class of persons more limited than
those whom the professional or professed rescuer is bound
to assist. It is a parent's duty to snatch his child from the
path of an oncoming automobile, an employer's to rescue
the workman who has been trapped in the factory machine. It may well be their duty to risk their own safety
should that prove necessary. Like the professional rescuer,

they can expect no encomium merely for helping, but if they risk themselves they merit commendation.

3   The third situation is that of a person not bound by his profession or by special links with the person imperiled to come to his aid. Even in this case, common opinion would, perhaps, see a limited duty to assist when this is possible without risk or grave inconvenience to the rescuer. "It is undoubtedly the moral duty," an American judge has said, "of every person to extend to others assistance when in danger, to throw, for instance, a plank or rope to the drowning man or make other efforts for his rescue, and if such efforts should be omitted by anyone when they could be made without imperilling his own life, he would, by his conduct, draw upon himself the censure and reproach of good men."[12] Common humanity, then, forges between us a link, but a weak one. The duty stops short at the brink of danger. Samaritans, it is held, must be good, but need not be moral athletes.

It is in this third situation alone, when the rescuer, bound by no professional duty or special tie to the person imperiled, exposes himself to danger, that we really call him a "volunteer." I appreciate that in Anglo-American law the notion of the "volunteer" has been at times twisted beyond recall. In order to deny the rescuer a remedy, the doctrine of voluntary assumption of risk has sometimes been extended to bar those who were merely doing their duty or responding to an appeal for help.[13] Conversely, in order to afford the rescuer a remedy, courts have at other times treated the altruist as if he were simply doing his plain duty and concluded that his action was a necessary consequence of the hazard and so of the fault of the person who created it.[14] But this is just legal fiction.

If this moral morphology is reasonably accurate, we

---

[12] U.S. v. Knowles (1864) 26 Fed. Cas. 801.

[13] Cutler v. United Dairies (1933) 2 K.B. 297.

[14] Pollock, *Torts* (15th ed.), 370; Haynes v. Harwood (1953) 1 K.B. at 163; Morgan v. Aylen (1942) 1 All E.R. 489; Baker v. Hopkins (1959) 1 W.L.R. 966.

have four types of rescuer and non-rescuer to contend
with. The first is the priest or Levite who passes by on the
other side. The second, in ascending order of excellence,
is the man who does no more than he is bound to do,
whether his duty arises from his profession, from some
special link with the person imperiled, or from common
humanity. The third is he who, in doing his duty, exposes
himself to risk: possibly a hero. The fourth is the true volunteer altruistically exposing himself to danger to help
those to whom he is bound by no special tie: perhaps a
hero, too.

What should the law have to say to them?

II   THE MYTH OF NON-INTERVENTION

First, should the law encourage or discourage the rescuer,
or should it remain neutral? Members of my generation
remember non-intervention as the name of a policy which,
during the Spanish Civil War, ensured the victory of the
side which cheated most. It was called by Talleyrand a
metaphysical conception, which means very much the same
thing as intervention. So with the intervention of law in the
sphere of morals. There is no neutrality. If the law does not
encourage rescue, it is sure to discourage it. If it does not
compensate, it will indirectly penalize. If the rescuer who
suffers injury or incurs expense or simply expends his skill
goes without compensation, the law, so far as it influences
conduct at all, is discouraging rescue.

Perhaps one day sociology will devise means of discov-
ering whether people are really influenced in what they do
by the thought of legal remedies. In the meantime, it would
be altogether too facile to assume that they are not. A
doctor living near a dangerous crossroads is continually
called to minister to the victims of the road. The injured
are unconscious or, if conscious, are in no mood to contract or to fill in National Health cards. Will the doctor
come more readily and care for them more thoroughly if
he knows he will be paid? If so, he is a man, not an angel.
A mountain guide with a hungry family is called to rescue

a foolish climber trapped on the north face of the Eiger. Does anyone imagine him to be indifferent to the question how his family will be kept if he is killed?

The law cannot stay out of the fight and, if it cannot, there is surely a strong case for compensating the rescuer. To do so will be in the interests of those who might be saved. The community applauds the Good Samaritan. So the law, if it encourages rescue, is helping to satisfy the interests of individuals and the wants of the community. If we think of law as being, among other things, a social service designed to maximize welfare and happiness, this is exactly what the law ought to do. One department of the law's service to society will be its moral service, which it performs by encouraging with the appropriate technical remedies whatever is morally approved and discouraging what is condemned.

Unquestionably there are limits to this function of the law. I will deal with only three. The most obvious is the limit set by oppression. If the encouragement of the shared morality and the discouragement of its breach would be a hardship to some without sufficient corresponding benefit to them or to others, the law should not endorse it. The fact that racial prejudice is approved in a given community does not mean that the courts must hold leases to Negroes in white residential areas void. But the encouragement of rescue will oppress neither rescuer nor rescued. The rescued benefits from being saved, and even if he is compelled to compensate the rescuer he will be, by and large, better off. It is true that compensation may be burdensome and I should not care to argue that civil remedies are necessarily less harsh than punishment. If an uninsured person has to pay heavy damages, he is worse off than if he were fined, for the fine, unlike the damages, is geared to his means. But this fact depends on the rules about assessment of damages in Anglo-American law, and these might be changed. It would be no hardship to suggest that the rescuer should receive compensation, if necessary, from the person imperiled, in accordance with the latter's means: *in id quod facere potest,* as the Roman formula ran.

Another limit or supposed limit may be set by the principle that virtue should be its own reward. Strictly speaking, I doubt if this applies to proposals for compensation as opposed to rewards. Still, the doctor's claim to be paid for his ministrations to the unconscious victim of a road accident may be called a claim for reward. Would it be an inroad on his virtue that he was entitled to be paid? Surely the argument is obtuse. No one is compelled to claim a reward he does not want. The doctor, like the finder of lost property, can preserve immaculate his moral idealism if he wishes. No one can be compelled to be compensated.

A third limit concerns the border line between altruism and meddling. Of course we do not want our next-door neighbor to rescue the baby every time he screams or to interrupt our family quarrels. But this merely shows that the received morality draws the line at officiousness. The test of what is officious will usually be whether the intending rescuer would reasonably suppose that his help will be welcome. If the victim objects or would be expected to object, the rescuer should abstain. But this can hardly apply to those victims who are too young or too deranged to know their own interests, and one might justify the rescue of a person attempting suicide (in a jurisdiction in which suicide is not a crime) on the ground that those who attempt it often lack a settled determination in the matter.

The line will be difficult to draw exactly, but lawyers are professional line-drawers. The relevant factors are easy enough to list: the gravity of the peril, the chances of successful intervention, the attitude of the victim, and the likelihood that another better-qualified rescuer will act.

None of the three limits mentioned seems to alter the proposition that the law would be a poor thing if it did not in general encourage rescue. The means available to do this are essentially the compensation of the rescuer for expenses and injury and the rewarding of his services. It is convenient to take these separately.

1 *Injury.* No immediate difficulty is felt if the rescuer

is covered by a personal accident policy or an insurance scheme connected with his employment, as would usually be true of firemen and other professional rescuers. There will still remain the question whether the insurer should be entitled to shift the loss to the person responsible for the peril. Certainly it makes for simplicity if he cannot.

When there is no insurance cover the problem is: where should the compensation come from? Most people would be inclined to place it in the first instance on the person through whose fault the peril arose, whether the person imperiled or another. In order to justify making the person imperiled liable when he had been at fault, Bohlen argued that the basis of liability was the tendency of the defendant's conduct to cause the rescuer to take the risk involved in the attempted rescue.[15] If "cause" is to be taken seriously, this suggests that the rescuer who acts under a sense of obligation would recover for his injury, while the pure altruist would not, because the latter's act is a fresh cause. Yet altruism is not less but more worthy of the law's encouragement than the conscientious performance of one's duty. If in *Carnea v. Buyea*[16] the plaintiff who snatched the defendant from the path of the runaway automobile had been unrelated to the defendant, could that reasonably have been a ground for denying him a recovery? Surely the remedy should not be confined to cases where the peril "causes" the rescue, but should extend to those in which it merely prompts the rescuer.

Other writers and courts rely on foreseeability as the ground of liability. This, too, is open to objection. Suppose an intrepid but foolhardy explorer is stranded in an area where rescue is atrociously difficult and rescuers scarce. By the heroism of a James Bond he is saved. Surely the fact that rescue could not be foreseen makes no difference to Bond's claim for compensation? Is not the real basis of liability the twofold fact that the person imperiled has created a risk from which he wishes to be saved (whether he

[15] F. Bohlen, *Studies in the Law of Tort*, 569 n. 33.
[16] 271 App. Div. 338. 65 N.Y.S. 2d 902 (1946).

thinks rescue likely or not) and that his peril has prompted
another to come to his aid (whether it has "caused" him
to do so or not).

I have been dealing with the rationale of the imperiled
person's duty to compensate the rescuer when the former
is at fault. Legally speaking, this is the case that has evoked
discussion, because it said that the person in peril owes
himself no duty. When the peril is created by a third person, the objection is inapplicable. If the third person is at
fault, he should be liable to compensate the rescuer for
the reasons already given. If no one is at fault, it still remains a question whether compensation should be payable
by either the person imperiled or the state. A remedy
against the innocent person in peril can be justified either,
if he is saved, on the ground that he has benefited at the
rescuer's expense and should not take the benefit without
paying the cost of its procurement or (whether he is saved
or not) on the ground of unauthorized agency. The guiding notion of this (the Roman *negotiorum gestio* and the
French *gestion d'affaire*) is that the agent, acting without
the principal's authority, nevertheless does what the principal might be presumed to want done, when it is impracticable to obtain his consent. (If there is actual consent, for
instance, if the person in peril calls for help, so much the
easier, legally speaking, to justify giving a remedy.)[17]

Anglo-American law, in contrast with civil systems, is
impregnated with the maxim, "Mind your own business,"
though recently there have been signs of a change. If we
outflank the maxim by asserting that, to a limited extent,
the peril of one is the business of all, it seems fair to make
the person imperiled, though free from fault, indemnify
the rescuer albeit only so far as his means reasonably
permit.

None of the headings so far mentioned may afford an
adequate remedy to the rescuer. In that case a state compensation scheme might well fill the gap. If the state is to
compensate the victims of crimes of violence, as is now

[17] Brugh v. Bigelow (1944) 16 N.Y.S. 2d 902 (1946).

done in England,[18] why not compensate the equal heroism of those who suffer injury in effecting rescues?

2 *Expenses.* In principle the same rules should apply to expenses incurred by the rescuer as to injuries received by him. Two points may be noted. One is that the expense of organizing a rescue may nowadays be enormous. Suppose the Air Force presents the lost mariner with a bill for gasoline, maintenance of aircraft, wages of crew, and so on, perhaps incurred over several days of search. The crushing liability must be mitigated by having regard for the mariner's probably slender means. The other point is that in Anglo-American law there is a traditional reluctance to grant tort actions for negligence when the loss suffered is merely pecuniary. The rescuer who incurs expense but suffers no physical injury may thus find the way barred. It seems that courts will have to extend the bounds of the tort of negligence and the law of restitution if adequate remedies are to be supplied without legislative intervention. There are already some signs that this is happening.[19]

3 *Rewards.* The moral objections to rewarding altruism, we saw, are misconceived. But is there a positive case to be made in favor of rewarding rescuers? In practice, outstanding acts of courage in effecting rescue are marked by the award of medals and decorations. Many persons saved from danger would think themselves morally bound to offer something to their rescuers. But a legal claim to be paid is usually voiced only by the professional rescuer, especially the self-employed, who may spend much time and energy in this way. Take our friend the doctor who lives near an accident black spot. It is mere fiction to say that the unconscious victim impliedly contracts to pay for treatment.[20] Two other theories are possible: one, that

[18] Assessed by the Criminal Injuries Compensation Board (1964).

[19] Hadley Byrne v. Heller (1964) A.C. 465.

[20] Cotnam v. Wisdom 83 Ark. 601, 104 S.W. 164. 119 Am. St. R. 157 (1907); Greenspan v. Slate 12 N.J. 426, 97 Atl. 2d 390 (1953).

payment is less a true reward than compensation for loss of profitable time; the other, that the person in peril, if he could have been consulted, would have agreed to pay for the treatment because medical services are normally paid for. The second theory, unlike the first, has a narrow range, because it does not extend to a rescuer whose services are normally given free.

III A LEGAL DUTY TO AID THOSE IN PERIL?

My third question raises an issue concerning what is usually called the "enforcement" of morals. The use of this word is, I think, apt to mislead. Literally speaking, the law cannot force citizens to do anything, but only to submit to deprivation of freedom, or to having their money taken from them. Even if "enforcement" is taken, as it normally is, in an extended sense, the notion that morality is enforced by law carries with it the false implication that it is not enforced apart from law. Yet the chief agent for enforcing morality is public opinion. If the approval or disapproval of family and friends is not visited on those who conform or rebel, the conduct in question is not part of the shared morality. Few people, I imagine, would rather incur the censure of family and friends than pay a sum of damages or a fine. This should lead us to suspect that the law, when it imposes a duty to do what the shared morality already requires, is not enforcing but *reflecting, reinforcing,* and *specifying* morality.

There are strong reasons, I think, why the law should reflect, reinforce, and specify, at least that segment of the shared morality which consists in moral duties owed to others. The first is the advantage to those who stand to benefit. It is true that legal incentives probably influence no more than a tiny minority, but they certainly influence some. A driver sees the victim of a highway accident bleeding by the roadside. He knows he ought to stop, but is tempted to drive on in order to keep an assignment. The thought that there is a law requiring him to stop may pull him up short.

Even if the impact of the law is confined to a few, there is a special reason for reinforcing the duty to aid persons in peril. Peril means danger of death or serious injury or, at the least, of grave damage to property. The more serious the harm to be averted, the more worth-while it is to save even a handful of those who would otherwise suffer irretrievable injury or death.

Secondly, there are some reasons for holding that the law ought in general to mirror moral obligations. In doing so, it ministers to an expectation entertained by the majority of citizens. The lawyer is, perhaps, so used to rules which permit men to flout their moral duties that he is at times benumbed. Promises made without consideration are not binding. A promisor can normally not be compelled to perform his promise but only to pay damage. Children need not support their parents. Samaritans need not be good. When we first learned these rules in law school, I daresay we were a little shocked, but the shock has worn off. It has not worn off the layman.

There are several elements in the sense of shock which laymen feel at the permissive state of the law in regard to moral duties. First, there is the "sense of injustice" of which Edmund Cahn has spoken.[21] If the law permits others to do with impunity that which I am tempted to do, but resist, what is the point of my resistance to temptation? The moral-breaker, like the unpunished lawbreaker, secures an unjust advantage at my expense.

A second element in the layman's sense of shock is the feeling that the law, like an overpermissive father, has set its standard too low. Just as a child loses respect for a father who allows him to back out of his promises, so the community will fail to respect the law which does likewise. It is, I imagine, another of those indubitable and unprovable commonplaces which are the very meat of jurisprudence that people's attitudes to particular laws often depend on their reverence for the law as a whole. If so,

[21] E. Cahn, *The Sense of Injustice* (1949); *The Moral Decision* (1956).

the failure of the law to reflect and reinforce moral duties undermines other, quite distinct laws. It may not be sensible for people to think of law in this way as a single, personified whole, but apparently they do.

A third element in the layman's sense of shock is the feeling that the guiding hand has failed. People to some degree expect a lead from the law, not merely threats and incentives. Rules of law which mirror moral duties have, among other things, an educative function. They formulate, in a way which, though not infallible, is yet in a sense authoritative, the content of the shared morality. They specify morality by marking, with more precision than the diffused sense of the people can manage, the minimum that can be tolerated.

The law cannot make men good, but it can, in the sphere of duty at least, encourage and help them to do good. It not only can but should reinforce the sanctions of public opinion, for the reasons given, unless it would be oppressive or impracticable to do so. I need say little of the practicability of imposing a duty to aid those in peril. France, Germany, and other countries have tried it out and found that it works reasonably well. But would it be oppressive? The mere fact that the majority is shocked at certain conduct does not, in my view, justify them in imposing civil or criminal liability unless there is also a balance of advantage in doing so. Difficult as it may be to strike a balance, we have in the case of rescue to add to the evils of injustice, disrespect, and want of guidance (should the law impose no duty to act) the possible benefit to those in peril if such duty is imposed. Then we must subtract the hardship of making people conform to accepted standards of neighborliness or suffer penalties. If the balance is positive, the law not merely may, but should, intervene. It has been urged that there is something peculiarly irksome in requiring people to take positive action as opposed to subjecting them to mere prohibitions. Why this should be so is a mystery. Perhaps we have a picture of Joe lounging in an armchair. It is more effort for him to get up than to stay where he is. But this is not how the law operates. Prohibitions are usually imposed because there is a strong urge or temptation to disregard them. To control the violent impulses of our nature is surely more arduous than to overcome the temptation selfishly to leave others in the lurch. Certainly there are important spheres, for instance, taxation and military service, where the law does not shrink from demanding positive action. Why should it do so in the law of rescue?

If it is argued that to require aid to be given to those in peril saps the roots of altruism by diminishing the opportunities for its exercise, the reply would be that the proposal is merely to impose a legal duty in situations where morality already sees one. Those who go beyond their moral duty will also be going beyond their legal duty. They lose no occasion for displaying altruism, merely because the law reflects a situation which *de facto* already exists.

The apparent objections to the introduction of a legal duty to rescue hardly withstand scrutiny. Perhaps the most substantial of them, in Anglo-American law, is simply tradition. Self-reliance, the outlook epitomized in the words, "Thank you, Jack, I'm all right," an irrational conviction that because law and morals do not always coincide there is some virtue in their being different,[22] all combine to frustrate the promptings of moral sensibility. One cannot but sense in some judicial utterances a certain pride in the irrational, incalculable depravity of the law, as if this demonstrated its status as an esoteric science, inaccessible to the common run of mankind. As the Russians said of Stalin: a monster, but ours. I will quote one or two.

"The only duty arising under such circumstance [i.e., when one's employee catches her hand and wrist in a mangle] is one of humanity and for a breach thereof the law does not, so far as we are informed, impose any liabil-

---

[22] Historicus (Sir W. Harcourt), *Some Questions of International Law* (1863), 76, cited in R. Pound, *Law and Morals* (1924), 40. The argument that there is value in moral experiments does not apply to experiments in leaving others in the lurch.

ity."[23] Hence, there is no need to help her to free her hand. "With purely moral obligations the law does not deal. For example, the priest and the Levite who passed by on the other side were not, it is supposed, liable at law for the continued suffering of the man who fell among thieves, which they might and morally ought to have prevented or relieved."[24] In the case from which the quotation is taken, it was held to be no legal wrong for a mill owner to allow a boy of eight to meddle with dangerous machinery, in which his hand was crushed. Indeed, the boy was guilty of committing a trespass when he touched the machinery.

Two thousand years ago a Jewish lawyer demanded a definition of the term "neighbor." This makes him, I suppose, an analytical jurist. Whether the tale of the Samaritan answered his perplexities we cannot say. But he would surely have been astonished had he been informed that there were two answers to his question, one if he was asking as a lawyer, another if he was asking as a layman. To him, neighbor was neighbor and duty, duty. Perhaps this ancient lawyer's tale has a moral for law and lawyers today.

[23] Allen v. Hixson 36 S.E. 810 (1900).
[24] Buch v. Amory Manufacturing Co. 69 N.H. 247; 44 Atl. 809 (1897).

The Duty to Act: A Proposed Rule

WALLACE M. RUDOLPH*

[In the original version of Professor Rudolph's paper, the opening pages were devoted to a brief survey of the current Anglo-American law with respect to the Good Samaritan problem. Since Professor Gregory's paper, which appears earlier in this collection, covers this problem in detail, that material has been omitted, and Professor Rudolph's article here begins with his proposed rule.]

With the assurance from the European experience that an obligatory duty to act is workable, we have attempted to formulate a duty-to-act rule which would fit within the present common law pattern. After a statement of the rule, we will discuss its application to the major problems of compensation, indemnification, diffuse responsibility, and officious intermeddlers.

The rule:

A person has a duty to act whenever:

1 The harm or loss is imminent and there is apparently no other practical alternative to avoid the threatened harm or loss except his own action;

2 Failure to act would result in substantial harm or damage to another person or his property and the effort, risk, or cost of acting is disproportionately less than the harm or damage avoided; and

3 The circumstances placing the person in a position to act are purely fortuitous.

* Professor of Law, University of Nebraska.

In developing this rule, no attempt has been made or, in our opinion, should be made to alter the existing scheme of social distribution. Such changes in distributive justice, the proper share each person should have in society, as opposed to retributive justice, the re-establishment of shares to persons who have been deprived of them by a wrongful act, are, as Aristotle pointed out in his *Ethics,* for the legislature and not for the courts.[1]

The proposed rule does not require a rich man to give money simply because a poor man is without funds. Nor does it apply to the classic hypothetical of the starving beggar who asks the millionaire for money in order to avoid starvation. If the rich man had food with him, he might be required to share it, for the presence of food would be purely fortuitous and within condition three of our rule. But he is not required to share his money, because a man's wealth is not a fortuity. Since his situation does not satisfy condition three of the rule, to impose a duty to act upon him would render him subject at all times to sharing his wealth with his less fortunate brethren. This would involve distributive and not retributive justice and would not be consistent with the policy behind the rule. But this does not mean that money could not at times be required. If money alone could solve the problem and were it purely fortuitous that a particular person was chosen to give, then money could be required. Thus though condition three protects the classic rich from being obligated to the classic poor, it does allow, under limited circumstances, a person of means who is temporarily without funds to require someone else to lend him money, if the resources to be saved by lending the money exceed substantially the risk of losing the money.

It has been suggested that the law today is inconsistent, unfair, and at odds with the best moral thinking of the community. On the one hand, the citizen has been taught consideration for others and love of his fellow man. Yet if

[1] Aristotle, Nicomachean Ethics—Book V, in Morris, *The Great Legal Philosophers* 16 (1959). Here Aristotle distinguishes between retributive and distributive justice.

he acts according to these teachings, he may be punished by the very society which propagates them. Of all persons, the volunteer is the least protected by the law. He seems always to be treated as an officious intermeddler. He is treated thus because the courts fear that to alter the present law would be to open a Pandora's box of new legal problems.[2] For example, would the party who benefited by an act performed under duty be required to pay for its performance? If so, what should be the rate? the value to

[2] "Because of this reluctance to countenance 'nonfeasance' as a basis of liability, the law has persistently refused to recognize the moral obligation of common decency and common humanity, to come to the aid of another human being who is in danger, even though the outcome is to cost him his life. Some of the decisions have been shocking in the extreme. The expert swimmer, with a boat and a rope at hand, who sees another drowning before his eyes, is not required to do anything at all about it, but may sit on the dock, smoke his cigarette, and watch the man drown. A physician is under no duty to answer the call of one who is dying and might be saved, nor is anyone required to play the part of Florence Nightingale and bind up the wounds of a stranger who is bleeding to death, or to prevent a neighbor's child from hammering on a dangerous explosive, or to remove a stone from the highway where it is a menace to traffic, or a train from a place where it blocks a fire engine on its way to save a house, or even to cry a warning to one who is walking into the jaws of a dangerous machine. The remedy in such cases is left to the 'higher law' and the 'voice of conscience,' which, in a wicked world, would seem to be singularly ineffective either to prevent the harm or to compensate the victim.

"Such decisions are revolting to any moral sense. They have been denounced with vigor by legal writers. Thus far the difficulties of setting any standards of unselfish service to fellow men, and of making any workable rule to cover possible situations where fifty people might fail to rescue one, has limited any tendency to depart from the rule to cases where some special relation between the parties has afforded a justification for the creation of a duty, without any question of setting up a rule of universal application." Prosser, *Torts* § 54, at 336–37 (3d ed. 1964).

him? the cost to the person acting? If the latter, what happens when the result of the action is detrimental even though the action was not negligently performed? In addition, what happens when in performance of this duty the person acting is injured? Is he indemnified? fully? partially? only when the person helped has been negligent? not at all? Suppose further that the first person with a duty to act fails to act and a second person acts in his stead and is injured. Who should pay for the loss? the person benefited by the act of the injured party or the person who previously refused to act? and what of the problem of diffuse responsibility? This problem may be illustrated by the drowning man at a crowded beach. In all the crowd, who is responsible for saving him? Notwithstanding the difficult problems that a change in the rule of conduct concerning the duty to act would entail, we believe that these problems can be solved and that the solutions lie in orthodox common law rules.

Admittedly, this rule does reverse the common law rule concerning the duty to act, but it in no way changes any other rules of law. For example, where the law of damages does not allow recovery for economic losses, emotional injury and the like, a person who failed to act would not be responsible for such damages. As a rule, such a person would not be liable for more damages for failure to act under the proposed rule than he would be for acting voluntarily and negligently under the present rules.

In addition, we recognize certain other exceptions to the general rule. Such exceptions relate to bodily security and personal rights. Ordinarily a person who is opposed to the transfusion of blood should not be held liable for failure to give blood, even though his failure resulted in a loss of life. In a society where the belief in the sanctity of bodily security was less strongly entrenched, the duty to give blood might be imposed. But even in our society, the professional donor or any other person who has already begun to give blood could logically be required to continue to do so. In both these cases, the parties have indicated (by giving blood) that their bodily security was subordinate to some other interest. This other interest would have to be judged by determining whether it involved something disproportionately less important than the interest to be served by giving blood.

Personal rights, such as the right against self-incrimination, are also not changed by the rule. Although a witness may be required to testify under the rule, he may still claim the fifth amendment even though his testimony could clear a person of a charge of murder. Thus, too, a man present at a gambling establishment or a house of prostitution could still claim the fifth amendment (assuming gambling and fornication are illegal) when asked to testify concerning a murder which had taken place on the premises.

Thus the claim to bodily security and personal rights would ordinarily excuse the individual from his duty to act. Religious beliefs, on the other hand, would not be considered absolute excuses. Thus the orthodox Jew may have to exert effort on Saturday and the Christian Scientist may have to bring medical help. This is so for several reasons. In most cases, the religions themselves have provided for excuses in emergency situations. Then, too, subjective standards are difficult to apply. Only where a belief, such as that involving bodily security or monogamy in marriage, has been accepted by the entire society is it accorded the status of an absolute excuse. These excuses are treated separately from the three conditions of the rule because they are absolute. Under the rule, all other excuses are relative, and the cost or effort of the person required to act is judged only in relationship to the harm or damage to be avoided: the greater the harm or damage possible, the greater the duty to act. Thus we can say only that there can occur no harm or damage great enough to force the abdication of personal rights or bodily security or that such rights are absolute and outside the scope of the rule. Religious beliefs can make no such claim.

The exceptions which we have been discussing, if they are exceptions, would affect the application of the rule in very few cases. Because the rule changes legal relationships, however, problems will arise concerning the legal consequences which should attend breach. These problems concern the awarding of damages against the person required to act and the relationships of third parties to the persons directly affected by the rule. The problems of relationship, which include questions of compensation, indemnification, subrogation, proximate cause, and damages, can best be discussed through examples. The major distinctions arise in the respective applications of the rule to professionals and amateurs. Because under the rule they would be treated differently, the application of the rule to each group will be discussed separately.

DUTY OF PROFESSIONAL TO ACT

The term "professional" is easily defined for our purposes. He is a person who holds himself out to the general public as willing and able to do a certain kind of work for a fee. Thus a doctor, a lawyer, a carpenter, a plumber, or a tree surgeon is a professional when the work or act he is asked to do relates to the normal work he does for a fee. Conversely a doctor is not a professional if he is required to repair the plumbing nor is a carpenter a professional if he is asked to mend a leg. Let us now proceed to the easiest hypothetical case—that involving a doctor.

Suppose D, a doctor (whose name appears, by chance, as the first one in the yellow pages), receives a call from P, a patient, at 1:00 o'clock in the morning. P complains of pains on the right side, says that he is unable to move, and insists that the doctor come to see him. P also states that his house has been quarantined by the health authorities because of measles, which P's son has contracted, and that he is heavily in debt and has no funds with which to pay D. D answers that he does not make house calls, but that he will come if P agrees to pay him five times his usual fee in cash when he arrives and to indemnify him against the risk of catching measles. D insists on this indemnity because he has not been inoculated against measles. P says that he cannot raise the money nor can he grant the indemnity. In reply, D tells him to call another doctor.

After considerable delay, P contacts another doctor, S. By the time S arrives, P's appendix has burst and he dies insolvent. The second doctor, S, catches measles and his eyesight is affected. P's administrator and S both sue D in a jurisdiction that has adopted the proposed rule.

In defense of the complaints, D moves to dismiss, stating that:

1 P had no money to pay him and therefore he had no duty to act.

2 P had refused to pay him a fee five times greater than his usual fee because of P's need of D's services.

3 D was an employee of an organization, such as a prepay medical group or a governmental organization, which forbade him from treating persons not in the eligible group, which P was not.

4 P was a member of a race that was personally repulsive to him, a Caucasian, and as a member of the secret Black Muslim Society he had sworn not to have any dealing with members of the white race.

5 D was being called upon in emergency cases more than other doctors because his was the first name in the alphabetical list of doctors.

6 Treating P involved too great a risk of catching measles, a disease for which D had neglected to be immunized.

7 D had retired from practice three months earlier and the only reason that he was listed in the classified section was that the new phone books had not yet been published.

8 D had told P that he had arranged to have R, a young doctor, take his emergency calls and had given R's number to P.

9 D owes no legal duty to the second doctor.

What is the ruling on the first defense? Normally one does not have to do business with a person who may not be able to pay for the service required. Even public utilities are not required to give services away and the thirteenth amendment forbids involuntary servitude. Yet in applying the rule to this defense, we find that the doctor is required to act. P met every requirement of the rule: harm was imminent (a burst appendix), failure to act could cause death, and no facts show that D was receiving a disproportionate share of the emergency business. The risks to D were that he might contract measles and that he might not be able to collect his fee. But the possible loss of a fee or the contracting of a disease cannot compare with the loss of life itself. In addition, it is clear that the moral sense of the community, even under the present rules, would move most men to act in this situation.

If the first defense fails, so must the second defense. Hence, the only issue is whether in an emergency situation one person may with impunity take advantage of another. The answer, of course, is no. The law of duress would allow the party agreeing to the extortionate charge to refuse to pay the agreed price or to recover such payment.[3] In all other ways, the same problems concerning

---

[3] See Post v. Jones, 60 U.S. 150 (1856). In this case "salvors" would not give assistance to a stranded whaling vessel, unless the vessel were sold to them at a very profitable price. The original owner was entitled to libel the vessel to set aside the sale. In discussing the case Mr. Justice Grier stated: "The crew were glad to escape with their lives. The ship and cargo, though not actually derelict, must necessarily have been abandoned. The contrivance of an auction sale, under such circumstances, where the master of the *Richmond* was hopeless, helpless, and passive—where there was no market, no money, no competition—where one party had absolute power, and the other no choice but submission—where the vendor must take what is offered or get nothing—is a transaction which has no characteristic of a valid contract. . . . The general interests of commerce will be much better promoted by requiring the salvor to trust for compensation to the liberal recompense usually awarded by courts for such services. We are of opinion, therefore, that the claimants have not obtained a valid title to the property in dispute, but must be treated as salvors." *Id.* at 159–60.

For a comparable emergency in the business field, see King Constr. Co. v. W. M. Smith Elec. Co., 350 S.W.2d 940 (Tex. Civ. App. 1961).

duty to act which surrounded the first defense arise here as well.

The third defense, that D had contracted with either a prepay group or a governmental group to treat only eligible persons, could not in any way affect D's duty to act. Individual contract rights, as in the case of inpecuniosity, cannot excuse a person from acting in an emergency situation. The only possible question raised by this contract is whether the prepay group or the government is entitled to the fee for treating the sick individual.[4]

The fourth defense, that of personal prejudice, is not difficult to handle. Although one of our basic freedoms seems to be the freedom to dislike whom we choose to dislike, statutes in the public utility field have made nondiscrimination a primary duty because of the partial monopoly position of such utilities.[5] Furthermore, the common law has required nondiscrimination of inns, restaurants, and other establishments affected with a public interest. Certainly in a more obviously monopolistic situation—*e.g.,* an emergency—where no alternate source of supply exists for the services required, a rule of nondiscrimination ought to be applied. This rule should apply whether the animosity were individual or directed at a group of persons such as that mentioned in the fourth defense. Again the only possible argument that can be made for this defense is that it relates to inviolable religious beliefs or bodily security. In a country devoted to the notion of equal citizenship, this viewpoint is, of course, inadmissible. In an orthodox Hindu country such as pre-independence India, however, where the cost or damage caused by contact with

---

[4] See United States v. Drumm, 329 F.2d 109 (1st Cir. 1964). In this case a government inspector was required to account to the government for the salary he received for part-time work with a company he was required to inspect. See also Bennett—Pacaud Co. v. Dunlop, [1933] Ont. 246, [1933] 2 D.L.R. 237, where one working for another unknown to his principal was required to account.

[5] See 41 Stat. 474 (1920), 49 U.S.C. §§ 1(4), 2, 3 (1958).

an untouchable might be greater than the loss or damage to the untouchable if the higher-caste person did not act, this same viewpoint might be acceptable.[6]

The fifth defense, that D was being called more often than other doctors, is more difficult to handle. D might argue that the fortuity requirement has not been met when he is repeatedly called because his name appears at the beginning of a list of doctors. The spelling of his name is itself a fortuity, however, and D must accept the disadvantages of being the first doctor listed in the phone book along with the advantages which have undoubtedly accrued to him by reason of occupying that position.

The sixth defense, that the risk placed upon D is too great, raises problems even within the rule. First, in applying the rule, we can see that no person has a duty to act if such action imposes upon him risks comparable in nature to the risk to be avoided. Indeed since the risk to D was considerably greater because he had not been inoculated than the risk to inoculated persons would be, D would not be required to go unless no inoculated persons were available. This latter instance does no more than restate the rule involving emergencies, for except in cases of diffuse responsibility, no emergency exists when other help is available. In a diffuse responsibility case, however, if the same call were made to a clinic where one doctor was inoculated and the other doctor was not, then only the doctor who was inoculated would be required to go. But this latter circumstance is not really an exception to the rule, since under requirement two the inoculated doctor would be more eligible because no harm would befall him. If, on the other hand, the clinic contained either two inoculated or

---

[6] This relates to the efficacies of religious beliefs. Thus if helping an untouchable would pollute a high-caste Indian, the cost of the depollution would have to be considered in judging whether what was to be saved was worth the cost under section two of the rule. If a life were at stake, the high-caste Indian would be required to act, but he might not be required to act if other untouchables were available to help.

two uninoculated doctors, the doctor receiving the call would be obliged to go. A further discussion of the problem of diffuse responsibility will follow.

The sixth defense must ultimately fail because the conditions are such that the danger to D which comes of exposure to measles is disproportionately less than the danger to P of a burst appendix. The rule clearly states that the danger to the person required to act must be disproportionately less than the danger or the damage to be avoided by the required act. But the question arises as to whether a different standard of judgment should apply in the case of a professional than in the case of the nonprofessional. For the rule applies equally to professionals and nonprofessionals, but the standards of measuring danger differ depending upon the actor's ability to handle the danger. Thus a professional would be required to act even in the presence of considerable danger, whereas the nonprofessional would not be required to act. This circumstance may be explained in two ways. First, some risks are normal for the professional. The rule may require a test pilot to fly an experimental plane in an emergency, whereas the rule would not require an amateur pilot to fly under similar circumstances. Second, the risk to the professional is actually less due to his superior skill, training, or preparation. Surely the test pilot would be more capable of coping with an emergency than an amateur pilot. And certainly a doctor would know better than the layman how best to minimize the danger of contagion and how best to cure himself if he were taken ill. Thus what on the surface would seem to be a variable standard of duty would actually be the same standard applied to persons of different skills. In the final analysis, then, a standard which requires a slightly greater actual risk could be imposed upon the professional if the risk related directly to and were characteristic of his profession. In the situation described above, for example, one must admit that for a doctor the risk of contagion is normal and that by becoming a doctor one consents to expose himself to such risks.

The seventh defense, that D had retired from practice,

raises a question basic to the right of freedom of occupation. Certainly the rule concerning the duty to act involves involuntary servitude; but because the rule applies only to emergencies, one may disregard the modest limits imposed on freedom of occupation. Thus in the present case, the doctor is called simply because he is a doctor. That he is retired is purely fortuitous. But the fundamental right of a person to choose his own work is at stake. To impose a higher duty on a retired doctor than on a layman would seem to be an insupportable infringement of freedom. What then of the case of a doctor who has perfected a particularly difficult operation which only he can perform? Perhaps he has now become an artist and has decided to give up medicine and devote his life to painting. Ought a patient who requires such an operation be left to die because the doctor has become an artist?

From the point of view of the patient, the rule should apply. The loss of his life is imminent, and he has no other alternative. The failure of the doctor to act would accordingly create a loss disproportionate to the cost to the doctor of completing the operation. Moreover, that the patient has contracted the disease is purely fortuitous. From the point of view of the doctor, however, the requirement of his services is not fortuitous. He carries his skills with him and thus he would be continually subject to call. Indeed, the case of the doctor is like that of the rich man in the earlier example. Instead of having to distribute money to the poor, however, the doctor would be required to distribute his time (a good more valuable than money)[7] among those needing his services. Thus according to part three of the rule, he is not required to act, for the duty to act arises only when the circumstances on both sides are fortuitous. In the hypothetical case, the choice of the doctor is not fortuitous and would interfere with his chosen occupation. He is required to act only if the circumstances

---

[7] We must realize that each person has a finite period of time to live and, although money is not infinite, some very rich people might find it impossible to spend their fortunes.

are truly fortuitous. Why then do we make professionals respond to emergency calls? Because by choice they have held themselves out to the public as willing to supply the service. Furthermore, in some cases (*e.g.,* doctors, lawyers, architects, and plumbers), the professional has even asked the state to limit the number of persons able to supply the service.[8] Certainly, then, members of such professions and trades ought to be required to act in emergency situations. Presumably carrying out their profession is what they wish to do. There is no special loss of freedom, but only a possible rearrangement of time.

To recapitulate, then, we see that under certain circumstances a professional has a duty to act, but that he may desist from any particular employment. The problem that remains, however, is whether the "monopolist" professional (*i.e.,* the professional who has mastered a particular skill) has a duty to act. The answer is that he may refuse to act if the call upon him is not fortuitous; otherwise he would be continuously subject to the demands of others. For, unlike the general run of professionals, he could not substitute emergency work for planned work. But, like every other citizen, he would be subject to emergency calls that were fortuitous. In the usual course of practice, however, he could not be called upon to treat everyone who needed his particular skill, since the need for such treatment is not an emergency but a general condition of the community. As we stated earlier, such economic problems are beyond the scope of tort law. Our rule applies only to emergency situations.

The eighth defense, that D had supplied an adequate substitute, is a valid defense if D in fact believed that the substitute were adequate and could be contacted as easily as D. In most situations, however, no substitute will be

---

[8] Most states have statutes requiring licensing and specialized education. Under such circumstances the number of persons entering the professions have been limited. The American Medical Association has been accused of attempting to limit entrance into the field of medicine.

available, for due to the nature of an emergency, time will prevent it. Undoubtedly normal emergency facilities will take care of most cases.[9] And if these are available, no duty to act exists.

The eighth defense arises from the second doctor's suit against D. For coming to P's aid and for losing time because he was ill with measles, S, the second doctor, is suing for fees. As to the first claim, D could not be primarily liable. P, not D, called for the services. Nevertheless, D had a duty to attend, for he could not establish either defense 5 (*i.e.*, too great a risk) or 6 (*i.e.*, retirement). If D had this duty, he could not forsake it without having to compensate the person who did discharge the duty. To test this proposition, let us assume the additional fact that P was a prepaid contract patient of D. Would not S have a right to look to D if P could not pay him? S could at least force P to assign to him P's chose in action against D.[10] Under the new rule, D's duty to act is the same as though he had a contracted duty to act, and S, therefore, should be able to look to D as a guarantor of P's obligation to pay S. What then of S's injury, *i.e.*, the measles contracted while attempting to treat P? In this case, S, like D, is a professional. S, therefore, could be reimbursed for his injuries only if all professionals received compensation for injuries sustained while carrying on their professions. Normally professionals are not indemnified or reimbursed for injuries characteristic of their professions on the theory that their fee covers the amount necessary to compensate them for the risk. This principle is, of course, the opposite of that applicable to employees, unskilled workers, or amateurs. Whether the rule is based upon recognition of the professional's skill, knowledge, control, or the fact that

[9] Most cities have emergency service through either fire or police departments or public hospitals. Thus certain persons are in the business of answering emergency calls. Whenever they were available, such persons would have a greater duty to act than would a bystander.

[10] *Restatement, Contracts* § 151 (1932).

his fee includes an insurance factor, the application of the rule that no compensation will be allowed for injuries incurred by a professional while discharging his duty to act seems clearly indicated. Hence, under proper application of the rule, S may recover only the amount of his fee from D, and he may do so only if P is unable to make the payment.

DUTY OF AMATEUR TO ACT

Thus far we have considered only the case of the professional. From that discussion, we discerned that for nonprofessionals different rules apply in regard to compensation for services, indemnification for injuries, and the conditions under which the duty is imposed. Most other considerations apply equally to amateurs and professionals, including the problem of diffuse responsibility discussed below. Since the operation of the rule can best be understood through illustration, we turn again to a hypothetical case.

An illustration of the duty of an amateur to act might involve the question of what a traveler would be obligated to do if he discovered a dangerous condition on a road. If, for example, such a traveler discovered that a large tree had fallen across the road on a blind curve, what would be his duty were it probable that the next traveler on the road would run into the obstacle? Obviously the duty to remove the tree does not belong to the first traveler. The removal would be the duty of the owner of the highway— *i.e.*, the state, if it is a public highway, or the owner of the land, if it is a private road. The duty might also fall upon the abutting owner, if the tree were formerly on private land adjacent to the highway or road. In any case, the ultimate responsibility is not that of the first traveler. What then are his duties under the rule? First, if upon reaching the obstruction he sees another traveler proceeding in such a manner as to indicate that he will hit the obstruction, the first traveler has a duty to warn the second traveler of the danger. Under the present rule, it seems that one person does not have a duty to warn another of impending danger even when it is clear that the second person is unaware of that danger. A simple "look out" is all that the proposed rule requires. And in most cases people do give this warning. Indeed, giving such a warning is almost a reflex action. Under the rule, of course, such a warning is required. An emergency exists; there is no practical alternative for avoiding the danger; failure to warn would result in substantially more harm than the cost of warning the endangered person; and the person who is in position to warn is there by chance.

To agree that there is a duty to warn is the beginning of the problem. How long and how far does this duty extend? Suppose that an automobile does not approach immediately. Must the traveler wait? Clearly, if in some way he can inform the highway department or the owner of the road that the danger exists, he has done his duty, except when the danger is imminent. Then he may not leave immediately. He may leave only after the highway department or the owner of the road has had time to see to the safety of the traveling public. Suppose, however, that he cannot contact anyone who has the basic responsibility for the highway. Perhaps, after waiting ten minutes, another car approaches. He signals the driver and tells him of the danger. The man thanks him profusely and is about to drive on. Our traveler immediately says that he is leaving, and he tells the new traveler that the latter now has the duty to warn. The new traveler refuses and drives off.

What then is the first traveler's responsibility? May he be kept there indefinitely? The answer must, of course, be no. Yet if he may not be detained indefinitely, how long may he be detained? The law's answer is a reasonable time. Accordingly, in applying the rule, we see that, when the cost to the person required to act becomes too great, he is no longer required to act. In this hypothetical case, then, if the first traveler were unable to stop anyone, he would only be required to put up the best warning possible—*i.e.,* a light, a flare, or a smaller obstruction that would tend to slow down an oncoming driver. He should also stop at the nearest police station to tell the authorities of the danger. Certainly, if a policeman were to arrive while the traveler was still at the scene of the danger, then to inform the policeman of the danger would be sufficient to carry out the traveler's duty.

In any case, after notifying the person in control that danger exists, the duty may not then extend to removing the danger but only to warning the possible victims. If on the other hand it is impossible thus to ameliorate the danger, then a duty to remove the danger may exist. Assume that in the hypothetical situation the best course is to remove the tree and that the first traveler does remove it. What rights has he? Is he paid for his labor? If so, by whom? If he is injured while removing the tree, is he indemnified? If so, by whom? If, instead of removing the tree, he orders a tree company to do so, is he responsible for payment? And if he is responsible, can he recover such payment from another person?

For the sake of clarity, let us assume that the road is private and that the owner is known but not available. It is the duty of the owner, when he knows of a dangerous condition, to take appropriate action either by removing the danger or by warning licensees and invitees of such danger.[11] Hence, our traveler would be entitled to pay-

---

[11] "As in the case of trespassers, the occupier's duties to licensees are most curtailed where a mere condition of the premises is the source of harm. 'An owner of land,' it has been said, 'ordinarily owes no duty to a licensee, any more than he does to a trespasser, to keep his premises in a safe condition, because the licensee or trespasser must take the premises as he finds them and assumes the risk of any danger arising out of their condition.' Thus the occupier need not inspect the premises to discover defects or other dangerous conditions. If, however, he learns of such a condition and should realize that it is unreasonably dangerous to a licensee, and if the occupier 'cannot reasonably assume that the licensee knows [of the condition], or by a reasonable use of his faculties would observe' it, then the occupier is under the duty to use due care to avoid the injury, either by removing the danger or by giving reasonable

ment for the reasonable cost of doing such work or for having it done. Moreover, if the night were harsh and cold, then he would be entitled to receive compensation for the cost of doing the work under extreme conditions. If the job required professional skill and the work done by the traveler only partially accomplished the purpose, then he is entitled merely to the reasonable value of a day laborer's work. Injury to the traveler while he does the work raises the question of indemnification. If he were a professional and had been hired by the owner to do this work, he would not normally be entitled to indemnification, for he would be subject to the defense of assumption of risk. If, on the other hand, the owner had hired a young boy who had not understood the risks, the owner might well be responsible for the injury. In our case, the traveler is an amateur who is required by the rule to do some act. Clearly no argument exists concerning assumption of risk by such a person. The amount of compensation to which an amateur is entitled, however, would be lower than that which a professional would receive for the execution of the task, for the fee charged by the professional for his services includes an amount necessary to cover the risk.

But what of the person who refused to stop to help our traveler? Is he responsible? If under the rule our traveler had a right to turn over his duty to the second traveler, such a traveler is mediately responsible. Still, however, the person who has the ultimate responsibility for the road would also be responsible to the second traveler.

Suppose in the fallen-tree situation that a person had already been injured because of the obstacle and that the traveler finds him pinned under a car. Assume further that the most reasonable step to be taken were to extricate the victim from under the car and that in doing so our traveler were injured. Who is responsible? The victim or the owner of the land?

---

warning of its presence." James, *Tort Liability of Occupiers of Land: Duties Owed to Licensees and Invitees,* 63 *Yale L.J.* 605, 606 (1954).

First, it is clear that the injured person is or would have been benefited by the acts of the traveler. The injured person could have and, if asked by the traveler, would have contracted to have the traveler help him. We realize that except when medical help is the help furnished, some courts have refused to recognize either an implied or expressed contract for the care of an injured person.[12] Under our rule, however, since one person is required to act for the benefit of another who is in danger, a legal arrangement with rights and duties arises. What are the terms of this arrangement? If the services required are the services of a professional and if a professional supplies them, then the price would be the customary charge for the service. And if the professional is injured, there is no need to indemnify him, since the cost relating to the risk of injury is included in the professional's charge.

An entirely different problem arises when the person who has a duty to act has no special skills. How do we compensate him if he is injured? We cannot treat him as the law now treats the volunteer because, unlike the volunteer, he has a duty to act. This duty would negate any assumption of risk simply because the actor has no choice. Quite clearly then, a person who acts non-negligently in accordance with the rule and who is injured thereby must be indemnified for the injury. If such is the rule, then who must indemnify him? Obviously the persons whom the actor hoped to or did benefit. Thus in our hypothetical situation, the person pinned under a tree is the person whom the actor hopes to benefit. The victim is, therefore, at least

---

[12] Falcke v. Scottish Imperial Ins. Co., 34 Ch. D. 234, 248 (1886), where Lord Bowen said, "The general principle is, beyond all question, that work and labor done or money expended by one man to preserve or benefit the property of another do not according to English law create any lien upon the property saved or benefited, nor, even if standing alone, create any obligation to repay the expenditure. Liabilities are not to be forced upon people behind their backs any more than you can confer a benefit upon a man against his will."

mediately responsible. If, however, some other person caused the injury to the victim, then that person is ultimately responsible to the actor who is injured in his attempt to help the victim. For, even under the present law, such a person is responsible to mitigate or alleviate damage or injuries caused by him to another.[13]

But all attempts to aid a victim may not be helpful to the

[13] *Restatement, Torts* § 322 (1934) provides: "If the actor by his tortious conduct has caused such bodily harm to another as to make him helpless, the actor is under a duty to use reasonable care to prevent any further harm which the actor then realizes or should realize as threatening the other."

"The words 'further harm' include not only an entirely new harm due to the dangerous position in which the other has been placed by the actor's tortious act . . . but also any increase in the original harm caused by the failure to give assistance . . . and any protraction of the harm which prompt attention would have prevented . . . ." *Restatement, Torts* § 322, comment *b* (1934).

This rule is well illustrated by the following hypothetical: "A and B are both driving carelessly along a lonely ill-lighted road. In consequence, a collision occurs by which B is thrown out of the car into the middle of the road, bleeding profusely and unconscious. A drives on without giving B any attention. A could easily have checked the flow of blood by applying a tourniquet. His failure to do so results in B's death. A is liable under a death statute." *Restatement, Torts* § 322, illustration 4 (1934). "The rule stated in this Section expresses a duty of affirmative action imposed upon the actor because his tortious conduct has rendered the other helpless. The rule is not an extension of the principle of 'legal cause' nor an extension of the doctrine of 'last clear chance.'" *Restatement, Torts* § 322, comment *e* (1934). See also Annot., 80 A.L.R.2d 299 (1961).

Some states have statutes making it the duty of the non-negligent driver to aid his negligent counterpart in an auto accident. Once this duty is established, all the considerations raised by our proposed rule apply to such a legally imposed duty to act. These statutes are an important first step in imposing a general duty to act, because no valid distinction can be drawn between an innocent participant in an accident and a bystander in their duty to an accident victim.

person ultimately responsible. For example, in a state with a limitation on recovery for wrongful death, the saving of the victim's life by a third party might result in a higher instead of a lower verdict against the person ultimately responsible.[14] To state this proposition is to show its fallaciousness, for if the tort-feasor himself refused aid in such circumstances, he would be responsible in most jurisdictions both in tort and criminally. We can conclude, therefore, that he who is responsible for indemnifying a person who is injured in performance of a duty to act is the same person who must compensate him for acting. In other words, the person who would have been benefited if the actor had accomplished his purpose must also indemnify the actor if he is injured while fulfilling his duty to act.

INTERMEDDLERS

Whether the rule extends to compensating intermeddlers or to indemnifying them for their injuries is a question of major significance, since damages in a situation where in-

---

[14] "The result was that it was more profitable for the defendant to kill the plaintiff than to scratch him, and that the most grievous of all injuries left the bereaved family of the victim, who frequently were destitute, without a remedy. Since this was intolerable, it was changed in England by the passage of the Fatal Accidents Act of 1846, otherwise known as Lord Campbell's Act, which has become a generic name for similar statutes. Every American state now has a statutory remedy for wrongful death. Most of the statutes were modeled upon Lord Campbell's Act, which is a 'death act,' and creates a new cause of action for the death in favor of the decedent's personal representative for the benefit of certain designated persons." Prosser, *op. cit. supra* note 25, § 121, at 924.

"*Under rather less than one-third of the death acts, the discretion of the jury is at least partly controlled by a maximum limit of recovery on behalf of all beneficiaries for a single death. These amounts, however, vary considerably under the different statutes.*" Prosser, *op. cit. supra* note 25, § 121, at 932. (Emphasis added.)

demnification is required could far exceed the benefit to
the person whom the actor attempts to help. Because the
question of the officious intermeddler is involved in the
operation and extent of the rule, it can best be discussed
through illustrations of the operation of the rule. In each
case the question will arise as to whether it is reasonable
for a person to act under the given circumstances. Obviously it is unreasonable for a person to attempt to save
another person's fifty-dollar watch at the risk of his life,
nor does our rule require that he do so. The rule requires
a person to act only if the cost or loss to him is disproportionately less than the loss or harm he could prevent
by acting. Under this rule, one would not be required to
act at the risk of his life in order to save a fifty-dollar
watch. A concomitant rule would be that no one would be
required to indemnify him if he were injured while so acting. The actor would be treated (as under the law he is
now treated) either as a mere volunteer or as an officious
intermeddler.

The problem then is not that of officious intermeddlers
but of the reasonableness of the person who acts. Undoubtedly man's motives are neither completely selfish nor
completely unselfish, but the application of this rule does
require an investigation of motives. Hence a judgment
could be made on the basis of the facts known to the actor
at the time he decided either to act or not to act. Because
of the emergency nature of the circumstances, however, he
must be given the benefit of the doubt, and he must not be
judged by hindsight. Such judgment is difficult, but judgment of this sort is rendered presently in every area where
persons are now required to act (*e.g.,* under laws relating
to public officials, servants of public utilities, and simple
negligence).[15] Certainly decisions in this area will be no

[15] "The courts have been compelled to recognize that an actor who is confronted with an emergency is not to be held to
the standard of conduct normally applied to one who is in no
such situation. An emergency has been defined as a sudden or
unexpected event or combination of circumstances which calls

more difficult than in any other area of law.

But what happens when the result of the act is not beneficial but in fact makes matters worse either by further injuring the victim or by injuring the actor? First, we can safely say that the ordinary rules of negligence would apply in the same way that they do under the present rule. If the person required to act negligently injures the victim he is attempting to save, then he is liable for the consequences. But the standard of care required is only what is reasonable under the circumstances. If, on the other hand, the actor negligently injures himself, the victim would not (as he was required to do for a non-negligent injury) be required to indemnify the victim. These rules do not solve the problem, however, when there has been no benefit to the victim. In admiralty law, persons salvaging are paid only if they benefit the owners.[16] Even in the normal quantum meruit case,

---

for immediate action; and although there are courts which have laid stress upon the 'instinctive action' which usually accompanies such a situation, it seems clear that the basis of the special rule is merely that the actor is left no time for thought, or is reasonably so disturbed or excited, that he cannot weigh alternative courses of action, and must make a speedy decision, based very largely upon impulse or guess. Under such conditions, the actor cannot reasonably be held to the same conduct as one who has had full opportunity to reflect, even though it later appears that he made the wrong decision, which no reasonable man could possibly have made after due deliberation. His choice 'may be mistaken and yet prudent.'" Prosser, *op. cit. supra* note 25, § 33, at 171–72.

[16] "First, there must be a service to maritime property which is in real or impending danger. Secondly, the service must be voluntary in nature. Thirdly, there must be at least partial success in saving property, or a proximate contribution to the ultimate success. . . .

"The antiquity of salvage is the antiquity of maritime trade itself. Since the seas were the primary highways of commerce when maritime customs were developing, merchants and traders influenced the evolution of maritime law. The earliest maritime codes speak of salvage awards as proportions of property saved, and give no consideration to any award for saving lives. The

payment is only for a benefit.[17] But such rules do not seem appropriate in a situation where a person is required to act. In such a case, the pay should be the same whether the actor is successful or unsuccessful.

Although the example of the traveler sets out the main principles of the rule, it does not exemplify all aspects of the rule. One still must ask: What happens when the action benefits the actor more than the person allegedly benefited? What rights does a person have to allow his property to decay? And, in the alternative case, does the right to abate a nuisance involve a duty to do so? In order to explore more fully the application of this rule and its ramifications, we must consider the following hypothetical cases.

Hypothetical Case I: A person, either the contiguous owner or a stranger, sees a broken section of fence which previously enclosed a herd of cattle. What are his duties?

Hypothetical Case II: Perishables, say twelve crates of lettuce, are delivered to the wrong business address. What action must be taken by the person who discovers the perishables?

Hypothetical Case III: A passing stranger discovers a diseased elm tree in a neighborhood where there are many elm trees that are free of disease. What action must such a person take?

Hypothetical Case IV: A garage mechanic who is hired

---

law of salvage was intended to motivate the saving of property for the benefit of owner and salvor alike, and experience quickly proved a material reward to be the most efficacious method of achieving that end. Consequently, the salvor has a lien of highest priority upon the property saved, whether ship or cargo. This lien accrues immediately upon the performance of the service, and gives the salvor a right to proceed *in rem* against the property itself. If necessary, the property may be sold, and the salvor may have his claim satisfied from the proceeds of the sale." Jarett, *The Life Salvor Problem in Admiralty*, 63 *Yale L.J.* 779, 780–81 (1954).

[17] See Annot., 59 A.L.R. 604 (1929); 58 Am. Jur. *Work and Labor* § 35 (1948).

for a motor tune-up notices that the brakes are badly worn. What action must be taken?

Hypothetical Case V: A passing stranger sees a person who is obviously drunk attempt to start his car in a busy part of town. What action must be taken?

Hypothetical Case VI: A customer in a restaurant notices a puddle of salad oil on the floor. What duty does he have?

In the first hypothetical, what is the rule when a person sees a fence broken and valuable cattle escaping? Clearly he has a duty to notify the owner. But what if he does so and the warning is ineffective, or what if he cannot contact the owner? Is he required to hire a crew either to round up the cattle or to fix the fence? First, let us consider the contiguous owner. In such a case, the duty to act coincides with the duty of the contiguous owner to protect his own property. The cost of fixing the fence or herding the cattle is, of course, chargeable to the original owner if the original owner had a duty to keep his animals on his own land. If instead of a contiguous owner a third party were to see the animals escaping, he would probably have a duty both to the original owner and to the contiguous owner. The contiguous owner, however, would only be mediately responsible. The original owner would be ultimately responsible. Assume that the third person could contact neither the owner nor the contiguous owner and that he attempted to hire a fence repairman who either refused to act or asked for a guarantee for his fee. What remains for the stranger to do? Applying the rule to such a situation, the stranger must act unless the cost of repairs is disproportionately more than the savings to be made. Since his duty arose fortuitously, he would be responsible to the repairman who finally did act, but he would be able to charge either the owner, who is ultimately responsible, or the contiguous owner, who is mediately responsible, for the cost of the repairs. This answer assumes that a proper judgment was made and that the cost of saving the cattle and fixing the fence was considerably less than the value of the cattle.

What to do about the perishable lettuce raises a similar question. In this case, it can be assumed that the owner does not want the goods to spoil. The major difference between this case and that of the cattle is that the rotting of the lettuce would not cause damage to other property. In the cattle case, on the other hand, the owner has a duty to stop such damage, and in certain cases he could probably be enjoined from allowing his cattle to run. In the case of the perishable lettuce, again the most obvious action is to notify the owner. And if the owner or the person who is responsible for delivering the goods can be notified, the duty to act is complete. Then either the owner or the person who misdelivered the goods would be responsible for the lettuce, and if they wished that the lettuce rot, it would be their business. But what happens if no one is available to give directions? The goods must be sold for the best price reasonably available, and the proceeds, less expenses, must be turned over to the owner.[18]

The third hypothetical, which involves the spread of

---

[18] The procedure required under the proposed rule is the same procedure required by *Neb. Rev. Stat.,* U.C.C. § 2-603 (1964): "Merchant buyer's duties as to rightfully rejected goods.

"1 Subject to any security interest in the buyer (subsection (3) of section 2-711), when the seller has no agent or place of business at the market of rejection a merchant buyer is under a duty after rejection of goods in his possession or control to follow any reasonable instructions received from the seller with respect to the goods and in the absence of such instructions to make reasonable efforts to sell them for the seller's account if they are perishable or threaten to decline in value speedily. Instructions are not reasonable if on demand indemnity for expenses is not forthcoming.

"2 When the buyer sells goods under subsection (1), he is entitled to reimbursement from the seller or out of the proceeds for reasonable expenses of caring for and selling them, and if the expenses include no selling commission then to such commission as is usual in the trade or if there is none to a reasonable sum not exceeding ten per cent on the gross proceeds.

"3 In complying with this section the buyer is held only to good faith and good faith conduct hereunder is neither acceptance nor conversion nor the basis of an action for damages."

Dutch elm disease, raises the issue of officious intermeddling. If the disease were not contagious and if it would not spread to another's property, the only duty would be to contact the owner of the diseased tree. Once the owner is informed, no further action would be necessary, because the law recognizes the right of a person to destroy his own property. If the owner could not be found, then other action would be required, providing that the cost of such action would be disproportionately less than the loss to be averted by acting. Such action would probably include calling a tree surgeon. The persons benefited (*i.e.*, the actual owner and the contiguous owners) would be ultimately responsible, and the actor would be mediately responsible to the person called to help. Assume, however, that the first tree surgeon contacted by the actor refused to come, that a second tree surgeon was called, and that neither the contiguous owners nor the actual owner had funds to pay the bill. The first tree surgeon would then have to indemnify the second tree surgeon for the cost of destroying the diseased tree. This is, of course, the same case as that of the doctor described above who must indemnify a second doctor for the cost of treating a patient whom the first doctor refused to treat.

Since in the present case more than the actual owner's interest is involved, the duty of a third party to act does not run exclusively to the owner. The actor can, therefore, satisfy his duty by informing a contiguous owner or, in most jurisdictions, a public official. The power of interested individuals and public officials to abate a nuisance is indisputable.[19] Hence, if the actor is a stranger, he would only be required to inform a proper party. The cost distribution of averting the danger would follow the method now provided for abating nuisances. If the owner refuses or is unable to act, the public official or a person who is injured by the nuisance may act and may then charge the cost to the owner.[20]

[19] *Restatement, Torts* §§ 201–3 (1934).
[20] City of San Antonio v. Mackey's Estate, 22 Tex. Civ. App. 145, 54 S.W. 33 (1899).

The fourth hypothetical (that of the garage mechanic who discovers faulty brakes) involves the same principles. Thus the owner of a car may not wish to repair it, but that he should have the right to drive a car with improper brakes is absurd. Indeed, such action is considered criminal in most jurisdictions. Hence, when the mechanic discovers the faulty brakes, he must either inform the owner of the defect or he must repair the brakes. Furthermore, the mechanic may have a duty to inform the police if, after advising the owner of the defect, the owner refused to repair the brakes and intended to drive with improper brakes.[21]

[21] See Broeder, *Silence and Perjury Before Police Officers,* 40 *Neb. L. Rev.* 63, 64–65 (1960), where he states:

"The conventional answer, however, is misleading. While the part about misdemeanors is true—the law has never, except perhaps in the case of law enforcement officers, imposed any affirmative duty to report misdemeanors, regardless of the circumstances—the matter as to treason and felonies is not nearly so clear cut. As a matter of fact, nothing about the subject seems ever to have been altogether clear, and modern American authority at least would seem to compel the drawing of various distinctions. Much may depend, for example, on whether we are speaking about a simple failure to disclose felonies to the authorities with no intention on defendant's part of aiding the felon or of profiting from his silence or of impeding a police investigation or on whether such factors are present. Other distinctions may also occasionally be important. There is some reason to believe, for instance, that failing to disclose information concerning another person's felonies when requested to do so by law enforcement officers may be quite different from simply failing to volunteer information, that law enforcement officers are perhaps dealt with differently in this area from other people and that various groups of persons who might otherwise be subject to criminal liability for failing to speak out may be protected because of their businesses or professions or because of the way in which information concerning the felonies comes to their attention. . . .

"Probably it is best to begin with the history and the English law on the question. Such distinguished common law commentators as Coke, Hale, Hawkins, East, and Blackstone unqualifiedly

The fifth hypothetical case (that of the drunken driver) presents a problem similar to that of the garage mechanic. The only difference is that, because of voluntary drunkenness, the driver cannot be made aware of the danger. If the person who sees the drunk is a member of his family or either a tavern keeper or a social host who has contributed to his drunkenness,[22] such a person would have a duty to act even though his presence is not fortuitous. Our rule applies only when the person who sees the drunk is a stranger. Undoubtedly a warning will not be heeded by the drunk. Hence, since the public as well as the drunk are involved, a warning to the police would be the appropriate action. A problem arises only when the police are unavailable. Then the only appropriate action would

---

asserted that a simple failure without any ulterior purpose to disclose another's felony to the authorities was punishable as a common law misdemeanor—known as misprision of felony—and that it was a misdemeanor even to stand by and watch a felony without at least attempting to prevent it and this latter apparently without regard to the bystander's ability effectively to intervene. And such statements, particularly as regards the criminality of failing to disclose felonies to the authorities, have many times been repeated by later English and American commentators so as to give them almost the force and effect of law."

[22] The duty in such cases may be inferred from the liability imposed upon such persons by Dram Shop Laws. See, *e.g., Ill. Stat. Ann.* ch. 43, § 135 (Smith-Hurd Supp. 1964):

"Every person, who shall be injured, in person or property by any intoxicated person, shall have a right of action in his or her own name, severally or jointly, against any person or persons who shall, by selling or giving alcoholic liquor, have caused the intoxication, in whole or in part, of such person; and any person owning, renting, leasing or permitting the occupation of any building or premises, and having knowledge that alcoholic liquors are to be sold therein, or who having leased the same for other purposes, shall knowingly permit therein the sale of any alcoholic liquors that have caused, in whole or in part, the intoxication of any person, shall be liable, severally or jointly, with the person or persons selling or giving liquors aforesaid . . . ."

be an attempt to stop the drunk by force. Part two of the rule would here be applicable. In accordance with part two, if the possibility existed of substantial physical danger to the actor, he would have no duty to act.

Hypothetical case number six illustrates the fact that in most cases the duty to act is merely a duty to warn. If a customer notices a dangerous condition, *i.e.*, a puddle of salad oil on the floor of a restaurant, what must he do? He must warn the owners of the store or, if someone were about to walk near the oil, he must warn such a person.

In view of the preceding illustrations, it is clear that the application of this rule is no more difficult than the application of any other rule. But, in questions of diffuse responsibility, application of this rule is somewhat more complex.

DIFFUSE RESPONSIBILITY

In the emergency setting, diffuse responsibility is exemplified by the hypothetical case of the drowning man at the crowded beach. The presence of all the people at the beach is fortuitous, and the danger, at least to persons with swimming ability, is substantially less than the danger to the drowning man if nothing is done. Clearly the persons with the most ability to swim have a greater duty because to such persons the risk is less than to non-swimmers. If a professional life-guard were present, he alone would have the duty. But if no life-guard were present, then all able swimmers would have a duty to save the drowning man. Yet what would happen if everyone refused to act? Before discussing this problem, we must decide what happens to one who does act in the emergency.

If such a person saves the drowning swimmer, he is entitled to compensation. His claim would be against the person benefited. Our prior analysis has shown that the person primarily liable is the drowning man. But if he had been put into the dangerous position by the negligent action of another person, then that other person would be liable.

Thus, if either the person saved or the person who caused the danger can pay the fee, no further problem exists.

The same answer applies to indemnification in the event that the rescuer is injured or drowned. If such is the case, he or his estate must be indemnified by the person benefited. If, however, the drowning man is not saved and dies penniless and if no other person contributed to the drowning, who is to pay the would-be rescuer for his injuries and trouble? To answer this question, we may return to the example of the doctor. In that case, if the first doctor refused to act, the second doctor could look to the first in the event that he was unable to collect from the person benefited. This procedure must also apply to questions of diffuse responsibility, though no one person in a group of equally qualified persons would seem to have a greater duty to act than the others (as would be the circumstance in our example of the clinic doctors). For in such cases it would seem that all would be equally liable. Thus if the swimmer who attempted to save the drowning man were drowned in the attempt, the remaining swimmers could be held responsible to the estate of the rescuer. If no one acted, however, the entire group of swimmers would be liable to the estate of the deceased victim on the same basis. This rule could and should be applied in all cases of diffuse responsibility, whether they come under the duty to act in emergencies or not. For the emergency rule merely establishes the duty to act, whereas the duty to contribute should apply whenever the law finds that all members of a group are equally responsible for a certain duty. Thus contribution should be required for the upkeep of a common stairway just as contributions should be required from all children in a support-of-parents case.[23]

Clearly, then, diffuse responsibility can be difficult only if the law refuses to recognize contribution. We realize that in some situations it will be difficult to know all of the persons who might have the duty, but in such cases the group will be large, and the hardship of contributing will

---

[23] *Neb. Rev. Stat.* §§ 68-101, -102 (Reissue 1958).

be small. That there should be no contribution by persons equally liable is unjust, and the mere fact that the conventional tort rule does not permit contribution should not govern the apportionment of damages under the proposed rule. Courts should not be required to apply undesirable old rules to new situations. Here they would have the opportunity to limit a rule which is generally considered unfair.

RELATED PROBLEMS

The preceding discussion relates strictly to the proposed rule. In that discussion, we have claimed that the suggested change of the common law rule of no duty to act was not an attempt to alter the present economic distribution of goods in society, and we believe that an examination of the changes to be wrought by the adoption of this rule will bear us out. Nevertheless, an adoption of this rule will cause at least some reconsideration of certain other rules of law. Basically the areas of law that are most closely related to the problems of the duty to act are the last clear chance rule, the duty of the sovereign to compensate for the use of personal goods or services, and the application of the proximate cause rule to this new duty to act.

First, let us look at the rule concerning the last clear chance. As stated above, the application of this rule has led to a mass of incoherent, illogical decisions.[24] Fortunately, however, the problem posed by the last clear chance

---

[24] Prosser, *Torts* § 65, at 443 (3d ed. 1964) summarizes the criticism as follows:

"This variety of irreconcilable rules, all purporting to be the same, and the lack of any rational fundamental theory to support them, suggest that the 'last clear chance' doctrine is more a matter of dissatisfaction with the defense of contributory negligence than anything else. In its application, it is not infrequent that the greater the defendant's negligence, the less his liability will be. The driver who looks carefully and discovers the danger, and is then slow in applying his brakes, may be liable, while the one who does not look at all, or who has no effective brakes to apply, may not. Recognition of the absurdity of such distinctions has played a considerable part in the extension of

rule may be easily solved by the adoption of the present rule. By definition, the facts in a last clear chance situation always indicate an emergency, for the person required to act is the only person who can avoid the accident. What happens then when our rule is applied to a last clear chance situation? Suppose that a bus full of passengers is approaching a child who is playing in the street. Assume that the child is negligently attended and that the bus is proceeding non-negligently. Thus only action by the bus driver can save the child. Must the driver act? Yes, if by so acting the danger to himself, his passengers, and his cargo is disproportionately less than the harm to be avoided. Assume then that the driver acts to save the child, and that because of his action, five passengers receive whiplash injuries and some valuable glass carried by the bus is broken. Under the rule, the child or the person who negligently let the child wander into the street is ultimately responsible for all of the damages. But in the event that such persons are impecunious, who is mediately responsible? It must be assumed that the bus company is mediately responsible. Under the normal carriage contract for hire, the carrier is an insurer against loss except for acts of the sovereign, acts of God, and acts of the public enemy. The carrier would be responsible for the damage resulting from acts required under the rule. The same criterion would apply in the case of personal injury. For the rule that the highest degree of care is required of common carriers would probably result in liability of the carrier. In the latter circumstance, a caveat must, however, be issued if the danger to the passengers were of a certain magnitude. For the driver would not then have a duty to act since the danger to the driver, to his cargo, and to his

the doctrine to new situations. Nor is it easy to defend a rule which absolves the plaintiff entirely from his own negligence, and places the loss upon the defendant, whose fault may be the lesser of the two. It is probable that the future development of the law of contributory negligence will lie along the lines of statutory or common law apportionment of the damages, rather than the last clear chance."

passengers would not be disproportionately less than the danger to be avoided. In the preceding case, mediate responsibility would shift to the passengers if, for example, they were guests instead of paid passengers. The guests in such a case would have to bear the loss if the loss to them was substantially less than the harm avoided. Thus it appears that the proposed rule works consistently within the present legal rules and that, unlike the present last clear chance rule, it is applicable to problems related to damage to third parties and to the defendant actor.

Another related problem is the duty of citizens to act on the command of the sovereign. This is another exception to the present rule of no duty to act. Under the present law, a citizen must give both his time and property to the state when in an emergency the sovereign calls upon him to do so. Thus a policeman may order a citizen to help chase a fleeing felon even at the risk of loss of property and life to the person required to act.[25] Again, in time of war, the state may requisition goods and services as easily as it may draft men into the armed forces. The same rule applies in cases of natural disasters such as fires or floods. In such cases, the state may call upon all citizens to act and, under certain circumstances, may even destroy private property. Because this exception to the no duty to act rule has not been thought out either as a rule of law or as a constitutional matter, no compensation is normally paid to persons who lose property, life, or health. There have been a few cases, however, in which workmen's com-

---

[25] See, *e.g.*, *Neb. Rev. Stat.* § 28-728 (Reissue 1964): "Whoever, having been called upon by the sheriff or other ministerial officer, in any county in this state, to assist such officer or other officer in apprehending any person charged with or convicted of any offense against any of the laws of this state, or in securing such offender when apprehended . . . neglects or refuses to render such assistance, shall be fined in any sum not exceeding fifty dollars." See also *Ala. Code* tit. 14, § 404 (1940); *Ariz. Rev. Stat. Ann.* § 13-542 (1956); *Cal. Pen. Code* § 150; *Okla. Stat.* tit. 21, § 537 (1951); *Wyo. Stat.* § 6-181 (1957). See generally Note, *The Private Person's Duty to Assist the Police in Arrest*, 13 *Wyo. L.J.* 72 (1958).

pensation has been paid to a person required by the police to aid them in pursuance of their duty.[26] If properly analyzed, all action required by the state of its citizens (either in giving services or property) should be compensable under the fifth amendment. Under that amendment, the state has no right to require property or service without the payment of compensation.[27] This rule of compensation could, and probably should, apply to situations not involving emergencies, such as wrongful imprisonment and interrogation of either alleged criminals or insane persons.

Under the proposed rule, every citizen in a disaster area would have a duty to act. At the same time, such a person would be entitled to compensation for his services and indemnification for any losses or damages suffered while acting for the public good. Thus, in an epidemic, doctors could be mobilized and drugs requisitioned. In a flood situation, individuals could be drafted to man dikes, and property could be destroyed in order to save lives and other property. This power to save the community at the expense of the individual exists under the present law, but the existing law makes little or no provision for compensating those who are engaged in the work of saving the community. Moreover, in most cases relief is given only through private legislation or administrative claims provisions. Under the rule, however, the cost of this service

[26] See, *e.g.*, Riker v. City of New York, 204 Misc. 878, 126 N.Y.S.2d 229 (Sup. Ct. 1953); Industrial Comm'n of Ohio v. Turek, 129 Ohio St. 545, 196 N.E. 382 (1935); Blackman v. City of Cincinnati, 66 Ohio App. 495, 35 N.E.2d 164 (1941).

[27] "Most courts have held these provisions [forbidding the taking of property without just compensation] to be self-executing, so that even where the legislature fails to provide a procedure for prosecuting such claims against the state, an action may be maintained in the courts to recover compensation . . . ." James, *Tort Liability of Governmental Units and Their Officers*, 22 *U. Chi. L. Rev.* 610, 618 (1955). For a modern application of this principle, see the action of Judge William East's order to the United States to pay a lawyer ordered to defend an indigent. *Time* Magazine, July 10, 1964, p. 46.

would be assessed against the person helped. In the case of disasters such as floods and fires, the cost would be assessed against the governmental unit charged with the duty of protecting the area affected by the natural disaster. In the event that an agency other than God negligently causes a disaster, the rule would require that the cost be assessed against that agency.

A duty to act rule already partially applies in the public disaster field. The proposed rule would rationalize its application. Moreover, the proposed rule would provide for a fair distribution of losses sustained in such a disaster. And, under the proposed rule, no changes would be made in determining how losses from a disaster are to be borne, but the full costs of combating the disaster would be shifted to the state or to the agency of the state which was authorized to act in the emergency situation. Adoption of the rule is thus consistent with the general trend of the law of torts toward the socialization of costs and away from arbitrating allocation of losses.

SUMMARY

Adoption of the proposed rule will do little to change the behavior of the individual, except insofar as it might create an environment in which he could be a better citizen. But the rule will protect and compensate the few Good Samaritans who are sometimes penalized for their virtues. Moreover, the rule will not turn anyone into a busybody, for the consideration of reasonableness of action will not allow more protection to the really officious intermeddler than he now has under the law. Nor will such a rule cause persons to fear for their property because of an act they inadvertently failed to do, since in most cases our marvelously complex economy has provided specialists who perform such acts. And since the circumstances of a real emergency will always be clear and the action required will be performed instinctively, in practically all such situations the rule will simply protect the man who acts as society expects him to act.

The Good Samaritan Act of 1966: A Proposal

WARREN P. MILLER AND MICHAEL A. ZIMMERMAN*

ARTICLE I

Section 1 : [Short Title.]
This Act shall be known and may be cited as Good Samaritan Act of 1966.

Section 2 : [Legislative declaration of public purpose; Power of state to compensate individuals: Power of state to limit liability of individuals.]
[Direct action by persons intended to prevent the commission of certain crimes, to assist peace officers in the apprehension of criminals, or to aid or rescue individuals in distress benefits the entire public. Therefore, the State shall compensate persons in appropriate instances for the death, injury, or property damage they sustain as a result of their meritorious actions and shall encourage similar meritorious actions by limiting the liability of these persons in carrying out the established public purpose, and by placing the burden of loss on other individuals.]**

or

[Direct action by persons to prevent the commission of certain crimes and to assist peace officers in the apprehension of criminals benefits the entire public. Moreover, direct action by persons to aid or rescue individuals in dis-

---

* Messrs. Miller and Zimmerman were third-year students at The University of Chicago Law School at the time this suggested model statute was drafted.
** *Editor's Note: Where alternate sections or parts of sections have been drafted, the alternatives are indicated:* [. . .] *or* [. . .].

tress benefits as a group those in need of aid or rescue. Therefore, the State shall compensate individuals or provide them with a remedy for compensation in appropriate instances for the death, personal injury, or property damage they sustain as a result of their meritorious actions and shall encourage similar meritorious actions by limiting the liability of these persons in carrying out the established public purpose and by placing the burden of loss on other individuals.]

Comment on Section 2
This section would be required in any state where the legislature is constitutionally forbidden to enact any law which authorizes the expenditure of state funds to individuals unless there is a stated public policy favoring the payments. Two public policy clauses have been included, covering two different schemes of compensation. Although both schemes permit full realization of this Act's purpose, the first alternative provides for direct state compensation in all cases, while the second placed the burden of compensating the Good Samaritan on the benefited party, which may be the state or one of its political subdivisions, or, where negligence is a factor, on the negligent party.

In both alternatives the constitutional prohibition against authorizing direct state compensation to individuals is met by stating that the acts of individual Good Samaritans benefit, as a group, individuals in distress; since the group may at some time include any person in the state, the state is therefore indirectly benefited by any single act of aid.

Both public policy clauses point out that the Act encourages Good Samaritanism in two ways. The first is by compensating Good Samaritans for any pecuniary loss they sustain because of their actions; the second is by limiting their liability for their actions while rendering aid. It is commonly believed that one important reason why people are reluctant to act as Good Samaritans is that they fear they will be held liable for injuries to the persons whom they aid. Many members of the medical profession in particular refuse to volunteer their services to treat injured persons, even when they know that their assistance would be beneficial, because they fear that no matter how capably they act, they may still be sued for malpractice.

Finally, the Act rejects the imposition of a legal duty to give aid as an alternative to encouraging acts of aid. The drafters feel that the obligation to be a Good Samaritan is a moral one, and that moral obligations should be encouraged, not required. Moreover, legislatures in the past have been reluctant to enact laws requiring affirmative action by a person having no previous relationship to a situation.

Section 3 : [*Right of self-defense.*]
Nothing in this Act modifies or enlarges whatever rights of self-defense any person has under the statutes or common law of this State.

ARTICLE II

Section 4 : [*Definitions : Good faith.*]
(a)   As used in this Article
1   *"person"* means any natural person who is not a peace officer
2   *"gross negligence"* means lacking that standard of care which even careless or reckless men are accustomed to exercise
3   *"commit"* includes try to commit
4   *"protect"* includes try to protect
5   *"prevent"* includes try to prevent
6   *"apprehend"* includes try to apprehend
7   *"assist"* includes try to assist.
(b)   *"Good faith"* refers to a belief that
1   the immediacy of the situation requires that action be taken to protect from death or additional serious injury during the discharge of his duties a peace officer who has been injured while discharging his duties; or
2   no peace officer is present and the immediacy of the situation requires that action be taken
(aa)   to prevent the commission of a crime involving ac-

tual or impending death or serious injury to the
victim, or a forceful taking of property from the
victim; or
(bb)   to apprehend an individual who has committed a
crime involving actual or impending death or serious injury to the victim, or a forceful taking of
property from the victim, and who is fleeing from
the scene of that crime, where he who holds the
belief has witnessed the crime; and that
he who holds the belief may provide the protection, prevention, or apprehension required; provided that the facts
that he believes to exist in subsections b(2aa) and b(2bb)
above actually constitute a crime under the statutes or
common law of this State; or
3   a peace officer requested assistance and that he who
holds the belief is following or trying to follow the
peace officer's instructions.

Comment on Section 4b

The Act confers the benefits of Sections 6, 7, and 8 on the
Good Samaritan if he intervenes in good faith in the
enumerated situations; that is, if he honestly believes that
facts which permit intervention actually exist, he may recover for his own injuries and be excused from liability
for injuries to others even though his belief was erroneous.

Subsections b(2aa) and b(2bb), however, provide that
the Good Samaritan, although permitted to make mistakes
of fact, is not excused from mistakes of law. The facts
as he believes them to be must constitute a crime, even
though they need not represent what actually took place.
Thus, he comes under the terms of this Article if he aids a
young boy who he honestly believes is being assaulted by
an older man, even though the older man is in fact a plain-
clothes policeman arresting the boy. But if, for some reason, assaulting a boy is not a crime under the laws of the
state, the Good Samaritan is not protected.

Section 5 : [No requirement of criminal intent.]

For the purposes of this Article, an individual commits a

crime under the statutes or common law of this State, even though he is legally incapable of forming a criminal intent because of age, insanity, intoxication, or otherwise.

Comment on Section 5

Many of the situations in which this Article seeks to encourage Good Samaritanism involve acts of actual or possible violence to the victim. Not uncommonly, the people who commit such acts are "not in their right minds" and as a result may be even more dangerous to their intended victim or to the Good Samaritan who intervenes, even though their actions, because of their age or mental state, are not criminal. The drafters feel that it would be illogical to make the Good Samaritan's right to recover or liability for his acts hinge on the presence of a criminal intent when the presence of such an intent is often vaguely or arbitrarily determined and the absence of such an intent does not decrease the risk of harm to the victim or the Good Samaritan. The Good Samaritan is expected to know what acts violate the laws of the state, but he should not be expected to know the intricacies of the law of *mens rea.*

Section 6: [*Acts to prevent certain crimes, apprehend criminals, and assist peace officers: Compensation.*]
If any person in good faith

(a)   voluntarily protects from death or additional serious injury during the discharge of his duties a peace officer who has been injured while discharging his duties; or

(b)   if no peace officer is present,

1   prevents the commission of a crime involving actual or impending death or serious injury to the victim, or a forceful taking of property from the victim, or

2   apprehends an individual who has committed a crime which the person witnessed and which involved actual or impending death or serious injury to the victim, or the forceful taking of property from the victim, and who is fleeing from the scene of that crime; or

(c)   assists a peace officer in the discharge of his duties when he or another peace officer requests the assistance;

and as a result of his actions in protecting, preventing, apprehending, or assisting sustains death, personal injury, property damage, or any combination of these, he shall be paid the compensation provided in Section 14 of this Act by the ____. (Insert [State agency] or [governmental body whose peace officer he was protecting or assisting or whose laws he was trying to enforce]).

Comment on Section 6

This Section provides for compensation in four well-defined situations. In the first, protecting an injured peace officer, the Section permits the Good Samaritan to balance the immediacy of the situation and the possibility that his actions will be beneficial against the possibility that he will interfere with the duties of peace officers, who are generally better qualified to act in the situations likely to be encountered here.

In the second and third situations, concerning the prevention of crime and the apprehension of criminals, the Section encourages intervention by compensating any injured Good Samaritan who believed a serious crime existed, even though his aid was ineffective or his belief erroneous. It rejects the view that unnecessary intervention should go uncompensated by failing to require material assistance or success as a condition for recovery.

In the fourth situation, where a peace officer requests assistance, there is a common law or statutory duty to act. Under this Section, the Good Samaritan is entitled to compensation for injuries whenever he acts in good faith in following the instructions of the peace officer.

Compensation authorized by this Section may be provided in alternate ways, depending on whether or not direct state compensation is allowed. In the first alternative, the Good Samaritan recovers directly from the state through an agency. The second alternative attacks the doctrine of governmental immunity by allowing recovery from municipal, county, or state governments on the theory that the Good Samaritan should recover from the benefited party. If the Good Samaritan acted to prevent a crime or apprehend a criminal, the benefited party would be the governmental unit whose laws were being violated; if the Good Samaritan assisted or protected a peace officer, the benefited party would be the peace officer's employer.

Section 7: [*Acts to prevent certain crimes, apprehend criminals, and assist peace officer: Limitation of liability.*]

(a) If any person by his acts or omissions in protecting a peace officer under the provisions of Subsection 6a of this Act causes death, personal injury, or property damage to the individual from whom the peace officer requires protection, he is not liable for that death, personal injury, or property damage unless his acts or omissions which cause that death, personal injury, or property damage constitute the use of more force than the peace officer is authorized to use to protect himself.

(b) If any person by his acts or omissions in preventing the commission of a crime under the provisions of Subsection 6b(1) of this Act causes death, personal injury, or property damage to the individual who is committing the crime, he is not liable for that death, personal injury, or property damage unless

1 he is grossly negligent in believing that the acts or omissions which cause that death, personal injury, or property damage are necessary to prevent commission of the crime, or

2 he causes that death, personal injury, or property damage by his use of a deadly weapon where the crime involves only the forceful taking of property from a victim, and the person is grossly negligent in believing that the victim is in danger of death or serious injury.

(c) If any person by his acts or omissions in apprehending an individual who has committed a crime which the person witnessed and which involved actual or impending death or serious injury to the victim or the forceful taking of property from the victim, and who is fleeing from the scene of that crime, under the provisions of Subsection 6b(2) of this Act causes death, personal injury, or property damage to the individual whom he apprehends, he is not liable for that death, personal injury, or property damage unless

1 he is grossly negligent in believing that the acts or omissions which cause that death, personal injury, or property damage are necessary to apprehend the individual, or

2 he causes that death, personal injury, or property damage by use of a deadly weapon.

(d) If any person by his acts or omissions in assisting a peace officer under the provisions of Subsection 6c of this Act causes death, personal injury, or property damage to the individual, if any, for whose apprehension the peace officer requests assistance, he is not liable for that death, personal injury, or property damage unless

1 his acts or omissions which cause that death, personal injury, or property damage constitute the use of more force than the peace officer is authorized to use to apprehend the individual, or

2 he causes that death, personal injury, or property damage by his use of a deadly weapon, and the peace officer who requests assistance did not authorize use of a deadly weapon.

Comment on Section 7

A Good Samaritan was excused from tort liability under the common law where he used force to prevent the commission of any felony as long as he reasonably believed that a felony was being committed and used no more force than a reasonable man would deem necessary. He could even use deadly force if the felony was one which ordinarily imperiled human life and he had reason to believe that it could be prevented in no other way, or that if he used less force, he might endanger his own life.

The rule which governs prevention of crime in this Section changes the common law requirement of a felony and emphasizes that the section applies to situations where violence is likely—crimes involving death, serious injury, or a forceful taking of property. In addition, the rule encourages Good Samaritanism by two provisions. It permits privileged intervention wherever the Good Samaritan honestly believes such a crime is occurring, and it allows him to act with a lower standard of care than the common law allowed in determining how much force would be necessary; he may use as much force as a grossly negligent person would use. Thus, the Section provides the trier of fact with an objective standard of care, gross negligence; but, at the same time, it takes into account the fact that circumstances may cause the Good Samaritan to act recklessly or carelessly.

The Section also alters the common law rules dealing with arrest by a private citizen without a warrant to the extent that these rules apply to the acts of apprehension which the Article encourages. At common law, if a person arrested another for a felony without a warrant, he escaped tort liability if the felony for which the arrest was made actually had been committed and the Good Samaritan had reasonable grounds to suspect that the arrested individual was the guilty party. In addition, the Good Samaritan could arrest another for a misdemeanor committed in his presence as long as he acted without hesitation. This rule applied, however, only if the misdemeanor constituted a breach of the peace or an attempt to commit a felony and the arrested person actually was the guilty party.

On the other hand, the Section does not require for a privileged apprehension that a crime actually have been committed. It is enough if the facts as the Good Samaritan believes them to exist constitute an actual crime. Nevertheless, before the Good Samaritan may act under the Section, he must have witnessed the acts supposed to be criminal and must honestly believe that the fleeing individual has committed them. Moreover, he is not protected if he causes harm by using a deadly weapon. With the imposition of these restrictions, the drafters believe that the benefit to society as a whole by increased acts of Good Samaritanism outweighs the possible inconvenience to the few who might be mistakenly apprehended.

Finally, the Section extends the area of permissible in-

tervention by encouraging the giving of aid to a peace officer who is seriously injured.

*Section 8 : [Injuries to third parties : Limitations of liabil-
ity : Recovery from State.]*

(a)   If any person by his acts or omissions in protecting, preventing, apprehending, or assisting under the provisions of Section 6 of this Act causes death, personal injury, or property damage to an individual other than one
whose death, personal injury, or property damage is the
subject matter of Section 7 of this Act, he is not liable for
that

1   death, personal injury, or property damage if caused
    unintentionally, unless

(aa)   he is grossly negligent in believing that the acts or
       omissions which cause that death, personal injury,
       or property damage would facilitate the protection,
       prevention, apprehension, or assistance required, or

(bb)   he causes that death, personal injury, or property
       damage by his use of a deadly weapon when that
       use creates a risk of unintentional harm to any in-
       dividual which even a grossly negligent person
       would not take; or

2   personal injury or property damage if caused inten-
    tionally, unless

(aa)   he is grossly negligent in believing that the acts or
       omissions which cause that personal injury or prop-
       erty damage would facilitate the protection, pre-
       vention, apprehension, or assistance required, or

(bb)   he causes that personal injury or property damage
       by his use of a deadly weapon.

(b)   Any individual other than one whose death, personal
injury, or property damage is the subject matter of Section
7 of this Act who is specifically denied a remedy for death,
personal injury, or property damage under Subsections
a(1) or a(2) above shall be paid the compensation provided in Section 14 of the Act by the ____. (insert [State
agency] or [governmental body whose peace officer he was

protecting or assisting or whose laws he was trying to en-
force]).

(c) No individual may recover under the provisions of
this Section if his own negligence contributed to his death,
personal injury, or property damage.

Comment on Section 8

At common law, the Good Samaritan was not held liable
for unintentional harm caused to innocent bystanders while
making a privileged arrest, unless he realized or should
have realized that his actions created an unreasonable risk
of causing such harm.

This Section uses a different test for determining liability
and increases the number of situations to which it applies.
If the Good Samaritan does not use a deadly weapon, it
looks to the relationship between the act which caused the
injury and the purpose which motivated the act: where a
reckless or careless man could believe that the act would
facilitate protection, prevention, apprehension, or assistance, the Good Samaritan is not liable. Nevertheless, innocent bystanders who are injured are not without a remedy.
They may recover a limited amount for their injuries from
the state, even in situations where, because the Good Samaritan acted reasonably, the common law denied them
any recovery. The rationale for this policy is that, as any
imposition of liability on the Good Samaritan deters Good
Samaritanism, the law should remove the deterrent, and as
society as a whole is benefited by increased acts of Good
Samaritanism, it should bear the loss to innocent third
parties. Finally, if the Good Samaritan does use a deadly
weapon, this Section, although it lowers the standard of
care, otherwise applies the common law test.

If the harm to innocent bystanders was intentionally
caused while the Good Samaritan was making a privileged
arrest, the common law severely restricted his immunity.
He could make offensive bodily contacts or materially
harmless invasions of the bystander's rights without liability; he was liable however for any actual bodily harm or
pecuniary loss he caused.

Under this Section the Good Samaritan is not usually held liable for intentionally caused harm, and the scope of privileged activities includes protection, prevention, and assistance in addition to apprehension. Nevertheless, when the innocent third party is denied recovery from the Good Samaritan, he may recover from the state. Moreover, the Good Samaritan is not totally immune from liability. He is liable for his own gross negligence in providing aid, and he is neither excused from liability for intentionally caused death nor authorized to use a deadly weapon.

ARTICLE III

Section 9: [Scope of Article: Election of remedies denied: Applicability to peace officer.]

(a) No person or individual may recover compensation for death, personal injury, or property damage under the provisions of this Article if that death, personal injury, or property damage was caused by any act or omission in protecting, preventing, apprehending, or assisting under the provisions of Article II of this Act.

(b) This Article applies to a peace officer unless he is seriously injured while discharging his duties and is voluntarily protected by a person other than a peace officer from death or additional serious injury during the discharge of his duties.

Comment on Subsection 9a

This Subsection prevents a plaintiff from claiming damages under Article III when his proper remedy is under Article II. For example, one who prevents the commission of a crime under Subsection 6b(1) may attempt to recover for his injuries by suing the victim of the crime under Section 11 (second alternative). But this Subsection establishes that if Article II is applicable, there can be no recovery under Article III, even though for some reason the claimant should fail to recover under Article II.

Comment on Subsection 9b

The drafters affirm in this Subsection that a person is not denied the benefits and protections of Article III merely because he is a peace officer. If the conditions of Subsection 6(a) are not met, then Article III may apply. Thus a Good Samaritan who aids or rescues an injured peace officer may receive the benefits and protections of this Article as long as the immediate danger of injury in the discharge of the peace officer's duties has ceased. Similarly, when a peace officer is not discharging his duties, he is, for the purposes of this Article, a private citizen; he may be an aided or rescued individual or an innocent third party with all of the consequent rights and duties thereof. It must be pointed out, however, that a peace officer cannot be an aiding or rescuing person under Article III if he is fulfilling his legal obligations as a peace officer.

Section 10: [Definitions: Good faith: Limitation of applicability.]

(a)   As used in this Article

1   *"person"* means any natural person

2   *"gross negligence"* means lacking that standard of care which even careless or reckless men are accustomed to exercise

3   *"aid"* includes try to aid

4   *"rescue"* includes try to rescue

(b)   *Good faith* refers to a belief that an individual requires aid because of his serious injuries or rescue from impending death or serious injury and that he who holds the belief may provide the aid or rescue required.

(c)   The term *person* as used in this Article does not include

1   one who aids or rescues an individual to whom he owes an affirmative duty to aid or rescue under the statutes or common law of this state, or

2   one who desires to establish a relationship to his actual or potential economic advantage between himself and the aided or rescued party.

Comment on Section 10

LIMITATION OF APPLICABILITY The common law establishes a duty of affirmative action in certain relationships such as parent and child or nurse and patient; and where the beneficiaries of this duty also come under this Act, the obligors would not get the benefit of its widened immunity or remedies for injury. Moreover, under this Section, the courts and the legislature may enlarge the group of people having affirmative duties without affecting the operation of the Act on those remaining.

Subsection 10c(2) refers to ambulance and wrecker drivers and similar persons who make their living attending to the victims of situations covered by the operation of this Act at the scene of the injury or accident.

Section 11 : [Compensation for injuries : Recovery by aiding or rescuing person.]
[If any person gratuitously and in good faith either aids a seriously injured individual or rescues an individual from impending death or serious injury and sustains death, personal injury, property damage, or any combination of these as a result of his actions in aiding or rescuing or in arranging for additional aid or rescue, he shall be paid compensation by the State agency, as provided in Sections 14 and 15 of this Act.

A person who receives compensation from the State agency under this Section is not barred from recovering additional damages for his death, personal injury, property damage, or any combination of these under other statutes or the common law of this State. However, if he settles an action for damages or obtains a judgment, the State agency may recover from him all or part of the amount he receives from the settlement or judgment, up to the full amount of the compensation paid by the State agency under this Section.]

or

[If any person gratuitously and in good faith either aids a seriously injured individual or rescues an individual from impending death or serious injury and sustains death, personal injury, property damage, or any combination of these as a result of his actions in aiding or rescuing or in providing for further aid or rescue, he has a civil cause of action for

(a) all his damages against any individual or individuals whose negligent acts or omissions caused the situation which prompted the aid or rescue; or

(b) the compensation provided in Section 14 of this Act against the individual whom he aided or rescued if the negligent acts or omissions which permit recovery under Subsection 11a above did not occur and if his actions left the aided or rescued individual better off than he would have been had there been no aid or rescue.]

Comment on Section 11

Since few men voluntarily risk serious injury, even if compensation is available, this Section may not greatly encourage Good Samaritanship. Nevertheless, it does justice by shifting the heavy burden placed on Good Samaritans when their well-meaning acts lead to their own injury or property damage.

Basically, the Act offers two alternative theories of recovery. Subsection A is based on the notion that society as a whole should provide an immediate and certain administrative remedy without detracting from the Samaritan's existing rights. Subsection B assumes that the burden should be placed on those involved in the rescue. An antecedent tort-feasor must compensate the Good Samaritan for his entire injury; and a non-negligent, but benefited, recipient of aid must provide a limited amount of compensation. (The drafters realize that it is difficult to allocate an expense where there is no negligence and the device of a limited remedy is their solution.) All the Samaritan need do to recover is to believe that aid was necessary and that his acts could provide it. In one situation, under Subsection B, however, the Samaritan cannot recover; this is where the recipient of aid was neither negligent nor benefited. The drafters felt that this innocent individual already had

the burden of his own injuries and could not be required
to contribute to the Samaritan's compensation. One theory
considered and rejected on this problem was that if the
non-negligent and non-benefited recipient of aid had requested or accepted the aid, then he should indemnify the
Samaritan for his injury. The view was rejected because
the situation calling for aid is often one of emergency
where people are more or less forced to call for help and
cannot therefore be said to imply a promise of indemnity.

In addition, the remedy in this Section, whether administrative or judicial, cuts through the obstacles erected by
the common law. Under the common law, a Good Samaritan could recover compensation for his injuries only
under limited circumstances. He could not take reckless
risks, or, in some jurisdictions, ignore a safer method of
rescue. More important, he could not recover unless someone's negligence was responsible for the situation prompting
aid. The Act adopts this latter rule, but goes beyond it.

*Section 12 : [Injuries to aided or rescued individual: Limi-
tation of aiding or rescuing person's liability.]*
If any person gratuitously and in good faith either aids
a seriously injured individual or rescues an individual from
impending death or serious injury and who causes death,
personal injury, or property damage to the aided or rescued
individual by his acts or omissions in aiding or rescuing or
in arranging for additional aid or rescue, he is not liable for
that death, personal injury, or property damage unless
caused by the person's grossly negligent acts or omissions
which place the aided or rescued individual in a worse
position than he would have been if aid or rescue had not
been given, or by acts or omissions intended to harm him.

Comment on Section 12
One of the purposes of this Act is to encourage Good
Samaritanism, and this Section assumes that encouragement is best accomplished by limiting the Good Samaritan's
liability to the rescued party. The underlying policy judgment is that although a few individuals injured by Samari-

tans will lose their remedy, persons, on the whole, in need of rescue will benefit by increased Good Samaritanism. A reasonable assumption of fact here is that in situations involving serious injury or threatened death, some aid is better than none.

The policy decision to limit liability was accomplished by changing the common law standard of care. That standard required Good Samaritans to act reasonably in giving aid. Under the Act, Good Samaritans, if they do not intentionally harm, are held to the standard of care of a careless person. In addition, to incur liability, they must leave the rescued party in a worse position than he would have been without rescue. Thus, a victim cannot complain solely because he did not get the best of care. Finally, if the standard of care seems too generous, it can be pointed out that it is limited to situations involving serious bodily injury or threatened death; in these situations Good Samaritanism is very much needed, but the possible liability could be costly.

Under Section 12, doctors are held to the same standard of care as laymen. Several state legislatures have dealt with the problem of doctors' immunity and have arrived at different conclusions as to standard of care. Unlike laymen, doctors fear suit more than liability. Because of the difficulties of proof, they hardly ever lose malpractice suits; but such suits can injure their reputations. If the Act had held doctors to the standard of care of careless doctors rather than careless laymen, many lawyers might believe they could make out a case and sue, even under the lower standard of care. Few doctors, however, will ever be as careless as careless laymen; thus, under the Act, doctors can practice Good Samaritanism with substantial guarantees of immunity from suit. Moreover, the lower standard for doctors is justified in that they are the most valuable of all Good Samaritans and should be commensurately encouraged. For the same reason, the exemption from liability does not end if the doctor takes the injured person to his office or a hospital and treats him there. To revert to the old standard of reasonableness might be to discourage the kind of activity that should be encouraged. Note, however, that aid, wherever given, must still be rendered gratuitously for this Act to apply.

Section 13: [*Injuries to third parties: Limitations of aiding or rescuing person's liability: Recovery from other individuals.*]

(a) If any person gratuitously and in good faith either aids a seriously injured individual or rescues an individual from impending death or serious injury and by his acts or omissions in aiding or rescuing or in arranging for additional aid or rescue causes death, personal injury, or property damage to an individual, not the aided or rescued individual, he is not liable for that

1 death, personal injury, or property damage if caused unintentionally; or

2 personal injury or property damage if caused intentionally

unless the person is grossly negligent in believing that the acts or omissions which cause that death, personal injury, or property damage would facilitate the aid or rescue or the arranging for further aid or rescue.

(b) Any individual who is not the aided or rescued individual and who is specifically denied a remedy for death, personal injury, or property damage under Subsection 13a above has a civil cause of action for

1 all his damages against any individual or individuals whose negligent acts or omissions caused the situation which prompted the aid or rescue; or

2 the compensation provided in Section 14 of this Act against the individual who was aided or rescued if the negligent acts or omissions which permit recovery under Subsection 13b(1) above did not occur.

(c) However, no individual may recover under Subsections 13a or 13b above if his own negligence contributed to his death, personal injury, or property damage.

Comment on Section 13
At common law, a person could intentionally injure the

property of another in order to protect the public from harm; this is the doctrine of necessity and the injuring party is not liable for damages. But the doctrine does not apply where the Good Samaritan acts to save an individual from harm, for he is then protecting a private rather than a public interest.

On the other hand, the Act immunizes the Good Samaritan from liability where he intentionally injures the person or property of another in the course of a private rescue and also discards the common law requirement that he act reasonably in determining what action would alleviate the danger. Under the Act, the Samaritan must act in good faith and according to a plan of rescue, exercising as much care as a careless or reckless person in choosing acts to facilitate the rescue.

The drafters believe that statutory immunity is necessary both to encourage Good Samaritanism and to alleviate the burden placed on the well-meaning Samaritan where, in the course of rescue, he causes loss to an outside party. The Act accomplishes these worth-while goals without shifting the burden wholly to the Good Samaritan's innocent victim. Finally, the Good Samaritan is not excused from common law liability for death which he intentionally causes.

ARTICLE IV

Section 14 : [Compensation : Limitations.]
Compensation provided in this Section for death, personal injury, or property damage is limited to the following amounts:
(a) *For death*
An amount equal to the deceased's earnings for the twelve months preceding his death or the average of his annual earnings for the five years preceding his death, whichever is higher, but not to exceed a total compensation of $5000.

The compensation for death may be recovered only by an individual or individuals whom the deceased was actually supporting at the time of his death. If compensation for death is recovered in an administrative proceeding or a civil action, any individual whom the deceased was actually supporting at the time of his death who does not join in the original proceeding or action is barred from seeking recovery in a later proceeding or action against the State agency or the party from whom compensation is sought; but if compensation is awarded, it must be divided equally among all individuals who have a right to a share of the compensation;

(b) *For personal injury*
1 All reasonable and necessary medical expenses.
2 If because of his injuries an individual cannot be gainfully employed or is employed in a position for which his earnings are less than they would have been if he had not been injured, he is entitled to recover the loss or diminution of his earnings until he regains his previous earning capacity; however, he may not be compensated for loss or diminution of earnings sustained more than sixty days after the day of the injury;

(c) *For property damage*
The expense necessary to restore physically damaged property to its condition before the damage occurred or, if the property was destroyed or damaged beyond repair, its fair market value at the time it was destroyed or damaged beyond repair.

Comment on Section 14
Section 14 establishes limits on the compensation which can be obtained in certain situations. The remedy against the agency is limited in order to prevent a large drain on the state's financial resources. The remedy in some civil suits is limited as a means of allocating the cost of injury between the injured party and the aided or rescued individual, where no negligent party exists to bear the expense. It is believed that such an allocation is a fair way to encourage Good Samaritanism. Finally, the Section's method for limiting recovery is to place dollar maximums on some categories of damage and to eliminate recovery for others, such as pain and suffering, entirely.

Section 15: [*Claims for compensation by the state; Agency: Director: Hearing examiners: Hearings: Evidence: Witnesses: Determination of claims: Awards: Judicial review.*]

[* * * * * * * * * * * * *]

Comment on Section 15

If the legislature decides to provide direct state compensation, a separate administrative agency should be established. Although it would be desirable to discuss in detail many of the agency's specific requirements, this comment provides only an outline of what those requirements are.

It is suggested that the agency might be patterned after the state's tort claims agency; in any case, the provisions of the state's administrative procedure act must be applied. Additionally, in providing for the administration of the provisions of this Act, the legislature must take into consideration that one of the agency's most important duties is to provide speedy settlement of all claims made against it. The agency's director should be authorized to provide as many tribunals for awarding claims as are necessary to prevent a backlog of claims. The agency should also establish hearing procedures that would facilitate prompt disposal of claims. It should require claimants to file complete, documented accountings of all losses and expenses for which they seek compensation and should disallow any claim that has not been documented to the satisfaction of the hearing examiner.

The hearings should be held as soon as possible after the claims are filed, perhaps no more than thirty days after filing; but there should be a requirement that notice of the hearing be sent to all interested parties, including the beneficiary of the Good Samaritan's aid, a reasonable time before it is held.

All interested parties, including the agency, should be allowed to call witnesses and present evidence at the hearing in order to facilitate a proper disposition of the claim. The agency should establish its own rules of evidence, although they need not conform to those used in a court of law. All testimony should be given under oath, and there should be provisions for prosecuting witnesses for perjury.

If the Act is to have full effect, the agency should be allowed to draw on state funds to whatever extent is necessary to provide compensation. It would be self-defeating if the agency were allowed to determine what compensation should be paid but had no authority to make or order payment without approval from some other body.

Finally, there should be a right of judicial review of the agency's determinations to satisfy the due-process requirement.

ANCHOR BOOKS

SOCIOLOGY